Great

MW01222508

Edited by
Christopher R. Gabel, Ph.D.
James H. Willbanks, Ph.D.

Combat Studies Institute Press
US Army Combined Arms Center
Fort Leavenworth, Kansas

Library of Congress Cataloging-in-Publication Data

Great Commanders / Edited by Christopher R. Gabel, Ph.D. and
James H. Willbanks, Ph.D.
p. cm.
Includes bibliographical references
ISBN 978-0-9855879-7-0 (alk. Paper)

1. Generals – Biography. 2. Leadership – History. 3. Military
Biography.
I. Gabel, Christopher R. (Christopher Richard), 1954- II. Wilbanks,
James H., 1947 –

UB 200.G74 2012
355.0092'2—dc23

2012034997

Contents

Figures

Maps

Foreword

With the publication of Great Commanders, the Combat Studies Institute continues its mission of publishing CGSC Faculty scholarship and adding to the body of historical literature the thoughts and research of these distinguished Professors. These analyses are both interesting and useful in their discussion of what attributes and circumstances yield an extraordinary commander of martial forces. As the editors point out, this volume is not a study of the "greatest" commanders; rather, it is an examination of commanders who should be considered great. The seven leaders examined, in the various domains of ground, sea, and air, each in their own way successfully addressed the challenges of military endeavor in their time and changed the world in which they lived. Not only should students of history find this volume interesting, but practitioners of warfare, who may be given the solemn duty and responsibility of command, may garner insights into the qualities and abilities possessed by those commanders deemed to be "great."

CSI – The Past is Prologue!

Roderick M. Cox
Colonel, US Army
Director, Combat Studies Institute

Acknowledgments

We would like to thank Mr. Crosby Kemper and the Kansas City Public Library, Mr. Bob Ulin and the CGSC Foundation, and the National World War I Museum at Liberty Memorial for sponsoring the lecture series from which these essays were drawn. We are also grateful to the staff of the Combined Arms Research Library at Fort Leavenworth. And, of course, we are indebted to the Combat Studies Institute for agreeing to publish this collection.

Preface

In the fall of 2010, members of the faculty of the Department of Military at the U.S. Army Command and General Staff College met with Mr. Crosby Kemper, CEO of the Kansas City Public Library. The Library has a very aggressive public outreach program that includes a number of lectures series covering a wide range of areas and topics, but Mr. Kemper was interested in adding a new program on military history. Accordingly, he reached out to the Department of Military History at the Command and General Staff College, which has one of the largest groupings of military historians in the United States. The result of the discussions that followed was a seven-part monthly lecture series co-sponsored with the Kansas City Public Library by the CGSC Foundation and the National World War I Museum at Liberty Memorial. The lecture series began in November of 2010 and involved monthly presentations on great military commanders in history. The lectures were given by subject matter experts from the CGSC military history faculty. The essays in this collection are drawn from those lectures.

We will begin with an introduction that discusses what makes a great commander. The introduction will be followed by seven biographical essays and a selected bibliography.

August 2012

Christopher R. Gabel, PhD
James H. Willbanks, PhD
Fort Leavenworth, Kansas

Introduction
by Christopher R. Gabel, Ph.D.

The command of military forces in combat is unlike any other field of human endeavor. If war is the ultimate form of human competition, then the commander is the ultimate competitor. The commander operates in an environment of chance, uncertainty, and chaos, in which the stakes are, quite literally, life and death. He or she contends against an adversary who is using every means, fair or foul, to foil his plans and bring about his defeat. The commander is ultimately responsible for every variable that factors into military success or failure—training, logistics, morale, equipment, planning, and execution. The commander reaps the lion's share of plaudits in victory, but also must accept the blame in defeat, warranted or not. Very often the line that separates fame and ignominy is slender indeed.

It is not difficult to identify "great" commanders, though the overwhelming majority of generals who win battles are never considered "great." Something more than a favorable ratio of wins to losses is needed to establish greatness. From the perspective of history, the greatness of a commander also hinges upon the context within which he operated. Victories won against inept opponents, or victories which fail to lead to the attainment of greater objectives, seldom elicit much admiration. Victories won through the simple application of overwhelming superiority in numbers or materiel are often similarly discounted. The truly great commander is generally considered to be one who attains the unexpected or the unprecedented; one who stands above his contemporaries through his skill on the battlefield, or through the sheer magnitude of his accomplishments.

In selecting the seven great commanders presented in this volume, the contributors sought to cover a wide spectrum of military endeavor, encompassing a very broad time-frame, different nationalities and cultures, and representatives from ground, sea, and air warfare. The commanders selected were masters of warfare in their particular time and environment. Each capitalized upon the social, political, economic, and technological conditions of his day to forge successful military forces and win significant and noteworthy victories that profoundly altered the world in which he lived.

In regards to social context, the societies from which these seven leaders sprang varied tremendously, ranging from the nomadic tribal cultures of Asia to American industrial-age egalitarianism. Each commander faced particular challenges in operating within the social norms of his day and age. These norms govern how leaders are selected, who serves in the military, and to what purpose military operations are conducted. The great commander recognizes these norms, and extracts the maximum possible military effectiveness from them.

Similarly, this study embraces a wide variety of political contexts. Each of the seven commanders herein proved adept at operating within the political milieu of his era, understanding if not manipulating the political systems of his country to best advantage. Ascension to a position of high command is as much a political as a military process, and the waging of a successful military campaign relies first and foremost upon a clear grasp of the political purpose underlying military operations. Three of the seven were not only great commanders but also sovereign rulers. It is probably axiomatic that any great commander is also politically astute, at least within the military institution that produced him.

Warfare is also closely shaped by its economic context, and the commanders in this study were both enabled and restrained by the economic world in which they lived. Ultimately, economics determines how many men, how much materiel, and how much treasure can be expended in waging any given war, and the successful commander makes the most of the resources his economy affords him.

Technology is commonly thought to be one of the key determinants in victory or defeat, but wars won chiefly through technological superiority are actually rather rare in history. Of the seven commanders represented here, only one—Curtis LeMay—employed technology that was essentially unavailable to his adversary. Even LeMay found that technology alone does not automatically deliver victory. One mark of the great commander is the ability to exploit commonly-available technology with a skill and effectiveness that his opponent cannot match.

Finally, each of the commanders in this study demonstrated extraordinary qualities of leadership in the cauldron of combat. Moral courage, force of will, and a capacity for critical reasoning under stress are all required for a commander to succeed in the chaos, fog, and friction of war. All of the commanders represented in this volume possessed these traits to a remarkable degree.

In a sense, the selected commanders are intended to be representative rather than exhaustive. Many other generals could have been included— some familiar names will be conspicuous by their absence. Since the circumstances and context of every war differ, there is no intent to prove that these are the "greatest" seven commanders ever—any attempt to apply a "scorecard" mentality to war as practiced in different places and times is essentially futile.

This volume begins with Alexander the Great, who wielded perhaps the finest army ever to wage war prior to the advent of gunpowder, and whose tactical and operational prowess bordered on genius. Born the heir to the throne of a kingdom on the periphery of the Greek world, Alexander used the military instrument forged by his father to overthrow the Persian empire and carry his banners to the Indus River. Alexander's battle were tactical masterpieces, which is all the more remarkable considering that he exercised personal leadership at the decisive place and time on the battlefield.

Next is Genghis Khan, who forged an effective political and military entity from the fractious horse-tribes of Asia and established through conquest one of the great empires in history. A remarkably enlightened and charismatic leader, Genghis Khan was also a superb strategist who set the conditions for victory long before the first arrow was fired. His Mongols were neither the first nor the last of the nomadic peoples to explode out of the great steppes of Asia and overthrow dynasties from China to the Middle East, but his conquests and those of his successors had a profound and lasting impact upon the destiny of the entire Eurasian landmass.

Napoleon Bonaparte, like Alexander and Genghis Khan, was possessed by a seemingly insatiable appetite for conquest. Napoleon also was born on the periphery of the world he came to dominate, rising from the minor nobility, ultimately to crown himself emperor. He harnessed the forces unleashed by the French Revolution, creating a military instrument that overthrew the status quo in Europe, and whose name has become synonymous with aggressive maneuver warfare and battles of annihilation. At its apogee, the Napoleonic empire encompassed virtually all of Europe—with the exception of the British Isles. The fact that Napoleon's empire terminated at the English Channel is due largely to the efforts of Horatio Nelson.

Nelson epitomized the art of naval warfare in the age of sail, and through audacity, tactical prowess, and personal leadership shaped the destiny of Europe. Something of a maverick within the venerable Royal Navy, Nelson belies the stereotype of naval commanders as cold and calculating technocrats rather than true leaders. His courage, both physical and moral, was at its greatest when the stakes were highest.

John J. Pershing represents a new breed of commander for the industrial age. He inaugurated the "American Century" by forging and leading the United States' first great expeditionary army—a hastily-raised army of amateurs led by a handful of professionals, flung headlong into the greatest war the world had ever seen. The product of a sleepy constabulary army, Pershing created a mass industrial-age army capable of holding its own among the great armies of Europe. Pershing himself sat at the highest seats of power as one of the arbiters in the fate of Europe.

Erwin Rommel, the consummate troop leader, practiced the tactical level of war in that conflict. With the advent of World War II, Rommel made the transition from infantry to armor, winning fame as one of the great practitioners of "blitzkrieg." Given an independent command, in a remote theater at the end of a tenuous supply line, Rommel cemented his reputation as a master of mechanized combined arms warfare.

Finally, Curtis LeMay represents air power for this collection of essays. A pioneer of military aviation, LeMay brought pre-nuclear strategic bombing to its apogee in an aerial campaign that epitomized "total" war in the 20th Century. He carried two burdens—the task of winning a war, and the challenge of establishing the credibility of strategic, independent air power. In what is perhaps the most technologically-oriented arena of warfare, LeMay demonstrated personal courage, shrewd decision-making, and inspirational leadership.

This project originated as a lecture series presented at the Kansas City Public Library in 2010-2011. Both the lecture series and this book are intended to encourage the audience to delve further into the study of military history. No work of this sort can ever be the last word on the subject, but hopefully this volume will serve as an illustrative introduction to the topic of command in war, and will entice the reader to learn more about the individual commanders, the eras in which they lived, and the broader topic of military history.

Chapter 1

Alexander the Enigma

by Edward Bowie

The individual military achievements of Alexander of Macedon, styled "The Great," are singular. No other figure in military history accomplished so much, at such a young age, in so short a period of time. He launched his career as a commander at the tender age of 16 when, while acting as the King's temporary regent, he decisively subdued a rebellion by wild Balkan hill tribes using only such residual troops as were available to him while the Macedonian Army campaigned elsewhere. At 18, he proved a stalwart and surpassingly brave deputy commander during the pivotal battle at Chaeronea against the last coalition of independent Hellenic states and personally led the assault that destroyed the cream of Greece's fighting men; the fearsome Theban Sacred Band. Supreme Macedonian Commander at 20, he ruthlessly obliterated the remnants of Theban resistance, forced the majority of Greek states including proud, once mighty, Athens into an unequal alliance, and even intimidated the diminished, but still formidable, Spartans into quiescent neutrality.

At 21, he led an Army of fewer than 50,000 Macedonians and allied Greeks across the Hellespont into "Asia." In three years he established firm control of Asia Minor, the ancient lands of the Levant, and Egypt. A year later, he led his forces into the heart of the vast Persian Empire, systematically destroyed its best armies, and made himself the head of a superpower. Over the following five years he extended his reach to subjugate the ferocious tribal states of the Hindu-Kush, the warrior kingdoms of the Indus Valley, and the untamed peoples of the Hormuz. He was dead at 33, having conquered an immense empire and actively planning additional campaigns of subjugation in Arabia and the central Mediterranean. Alexander's is an unequalled record of military accomplishment for sixteen years of effort. Still, the question presents itself; is conquest alone sufficient to be designated a "Great Commander?"

Alexander the Great is perhaps the single most famous name in world history. It is a name synonymous with military glory. Most school children can assert with innocent exaggeration his alleged accomplishment - he "conquered the world." In fact he did no such thing. He did not even conquer all of the Greco-centric world that his tutor Aristotle taught him existed. In modern geographic perspective, Alexander's conquests would not fill all of northern Africa. From an ancient geo-political perspective, however, his accomplishment should not be underestimated.

Figure 1. Alexander the Great bust in the British Museum (artist unknown) from 2d-1st Century BC. Photo by Andrew Dunn (3 December 2004)

In a sustained campaign lasting almost ten years (perhaps the longest contiguous military operation in history) he gained control of an area stretching further from West to East than the continental United States. He subjugated or usurped sovereignty over almost every significant civilization known to the classical Greeks. He spent virtually his entire adulthood from age sixteen to thirty-two at war. He fought (literally "fought," as his habit was to exercise command by example in the front rank) hundreds of engagements great and small against scores of diverse enemies expert in widely different military practice - and he won them all. His was by far the largest empire ever created up to his own time and he extended the influence of Western Civilization beyond the Indus River and north of the Himalayas. So, despite his singular fame and achievements, it is surprising to discover just how much of an enigma the historical Alexander and his empire actually are and how little can be known about him or his accomplishments with certainty. No contemporaneous histories or chronicles concerning Alexander survive. Modern scholarship knows Alexander from no more than four ancient sources, the earliest reliable of which was written more than 300 years after his death.[1]

First are the so called "Romances," also known as the "Pseudo Callisthenes," after Alexander's Athenian court historian killed by Alexander under suspicion of treason (suggesting the possibility of bias), and purporting to be based on his original writings. This work includes some of the most famous and popular stories about Alexander, such as his encounter with the philosopher Diogenes and the Gordian knot. Most serious scholars, however, dismiss these as a series of mostly-fanciful tales that began accruing in the 1st century BC and expanded through the medieval period, perhaps as late as the 14th century. So it is sad to learn that the many popular vignettes from Alexander's life and many of his most famous and often repeated quotations are under deep suspicion of being apocryphal. Second was the work of Diodorus, a Greek historian writing between 60 and 30 BC, but who fails (in his surviving works) to cite his sources and whose status as a Sicilian-Greek scholar, a people long oppressed by Macedonian overlords, may have given him an axe to grind. Third was Plutarch, another Greek, albeit this time living in the rapidly-Romanizing world of the early 1st Century AD. Plutarch purportedly based his work on original contemporary sources consulted in the Great Library of Alexandria, but his biographical sketch was part of a comparative study in leadership, contrasting Alexander with Julius Caesar and therefore subject to all the narrow focus and bias such a study implies. Finally there was another Roman-Greek, Arrian, whose late 1st century AD work has the great virtue, as Arrian claimed, of being based upon then existing original sources, including the memoirs of Alexander's intimate colleague and subordinate commander, Ptolemy. Arrian himself was a highly accomplished soldier and imperial administrator and was therefore better positioned than most commentators to evaluate Alexander from a military perspective. Given this paucity of reliable sources, attempting an objective evaluation of Alexander is a daunting and precarious task.

Confusion extends even to his many titles. The appellation "Great" was not current in his time. Indeed, during his reign and for a long time after his death, Alexander was widely reviled in the Greek world and by the many subjects of his Eastern Empire. The several Macedonian successors to his fragmented empire had little incentive to venerate him lest their own considerable accomplishments seem diminished by comparison. It was the Romans of the 1st Century AD, a people historically inclined to celebrate empire builders, who anointed Alexander "Great." It is, however, a superlative the Romans used remarkably sparingly and was a sign of their extraordinary esteem, having granted such title to no more than five individuals in history as they knew it.[2]

Properly he was "King Alexander III of Macedon," born a royal prince of the quasi-Greek aristocracy that dominated the large and geographically diverse area above the Greek peninsula that, at Alexander's birth, defined the porous cultural and geographical northern boundary of the Greek world. The thin patina of classical Greek culture adopted for generations by the Macedonian elite did not extend to the practice of monogamy and Alexander's father Phillip had at least two wives. Nor was simple primogeniture a necessary guarantor of sovereign succession, so Alexander's rise to power was not inevitable. Alexander was one of several royal princes and other contenders whom he managed to outmaneuver – by means honorable or otherwise – to ascend the Macedonian throne. Alexander also could and did claim the title "Hegemon" in as much as he seized leadership of the coalition of notionally independent Greek states forged by Phillip through war and intimidation into the League of Corinth.

"The Invincible" was an honorific Alexander also enjoyed in his lifetime. Possibly, depending on the ancient source, this was a title suggested to Phillip by the royal augurs during the celebration of Alexander's birth. Possibly it was a portent revealed, as she claimed, to his mother Olympias during a mystical communion with the Gods. Certainly it was a prediction made for him by the Oracle at Delphi during a visit Alexander made while engaged in his brief war to be "elected," or at least accepted, as Hegemon of the Corinthian League. But since he was holding that unfortunate young woman literally at sword point at the time, and as she knew Alexander was seeking anything that would enhance his growing reputation and legitimacy, she may well have been telling him something she thought expedient. The prophecy of invincibility was repeated for him a few years later by the Egyptian high priests of Amon at Siwa, but by then the Delphic prediction had no doubt made its rounds and they too can be forgiven if they were simply repeating something they knew Alexander wanted to hear and that would help speed him on his way elsewhere. Whatever its origin, Alexander's public reputation as "invincible" probably became his most controlling private motivation.

He came to be regarded by many in that pagan world as the personification of the amalgamated Greek/Egyptian deity "Zeus-Amon." His mother Olympias, violently estranged from Philip early in Alexander's childhood, told him that it was Zeus, whom she alleged came to her in the guise of a serpent and impregnated her with a lightning bolt, and not Phillip, who was his real father. The Siwa priests also reinforced this divine paternity, but they may again have simply been repeating a flattering and prudent gossip. No doubt, given Alexander's tremendous ambitions and the odds arrayed against him in his attack on the Persian Empire, he found this to be a useful, even if fictional, report. To be thought a demigod was equally, no doubt, very pleasing to his oversized ego. Finally, Alexander could with justice claim the Persian imperial title "Great King," won by right of his conquest and usurpation of the Persian Archemenid dynasty. Indeed, in the last years of his life, this seems to have been the title and role with which Alexander most closely identified –to the consternation and disgruntlement of his Macedonian companions.

Given all of the ambiguity, what can be said about the private Alexander with confidence? The combined sources suggest a man of out-sized talents and abilities. He became king in 336 BC following the assassination of Phillip by a disaffected courtier and the merciless elimination of other contenders - a conspiracy in which Alexander may or may not have been personally involved. At his ascension he was only 20 years old, but already an impressive, even intimidating, figure despite his youth (although this is something of a modern misperception for, by the standards of the ancient world, he was not in fact extraordinarily young – Philip had been only 22 when he became king). Alexander had a complex and contradictory character, the product of a chaotic and difficult childhood. From his mother, a royal princess from the neighboring "barbarian" kingdom of Epirus, he developed a multifarious cultural identity and a penchant for the mystical rites and practices of the exotic nature cults to which she was an initiate. From Phillip he received a practical tutorial in both power politics and generalship from a man who was a master at both. Alexander's conspicuous paranoia was probably a product of his parents' open mutual hostility, the chronic and vicious intrigue of the Macedonian court, and young Alexander's own tenuous and shifting status as the royal heir apparent. Besides which, as a Macedonian king, he was always a target – even paranoids have real enemies. At his mother's encouragement, he found role models in the heroes of ancient myth, especially Achilles, whose legendary martial prowess and courage he consciously sought to emulate. Alexander acquired his Greek philosophical worldview from his tutor Aristotle, brought by Philip from Athens to his capital at Pella to give the prominent sons of Macedon some cultural polish and legitimacy. From all of these sources and from his own eminence and precocious abilities he developed his formidable and temperamental ego.[3]

For the analyst the problem of choosing among the many competing ancient and modern interpretations of Alexander and his accomplishments immediately presents itself. Do we embrace Alexander the builder who founded great cities such as Alexandria and Kandahar, or Alexander the demolisher who destroyed great cities such as Tyre and Persepolis? Do we celebrate the pious intellectually enlightened protégé of Aristotle or the megalomaniacal semi-barbarian whom often met any criticism or affront with fatal violence? Do we accept biographer Mary Renaud's version of Alexander as the best and most visionary of princes - the great unifier of people who bridged cultures, or historian Victor Davis Hanson's description of a supremely talented, but self-indulgent, dissipated, alcoholic thug – a man who brought death and displacement to millions and enslavement to thousands more? Even Alexander's role in ushering in the so-called Hellenistic Age when Western and Eastern cultural influences deeply penetrated and profoundly influenced each other is a hotly debated subject of historiography.[4] Was Alexander's legacy a golden age of cultural rapprochement, or murder, "ethnic cleansing," and genocide? It is an often remarked phenomenon that historical interpretations tend to say more about the historian's own time, bias, and personal temperament than about the actual historical subject. In the limited historical records the scholar and analyst can see in Alexander almost anything they are predisposed to see and so there are as many Alexanders as there are commentators who have interpreted him. Alexander's personal contradictions and the conflicting narratives ensure he will remain an enigma.[5]

Fortunately, within the theme of this book, the task is more manageable as it need concern itself with only one aspect of Alexander's identity – that is, as a "Great Commander." The introduction established the broad criteria for the historical figures included in this book: "The commanders selected were masters of warfare in their particular time and environment. Each capitalized upon the social, political, economic, and technological conditions of his day to forge successful military forces and win significant and noteworthy victories that profoundly altered the world in which he lived."[6] By that standard, emphatically and unambiguously, Alexander was a Great Commander. He was a charismatic, bold, and inspiring leader. He successfully managed the complex internal politics of a fractious and touchy officer corps that reached precariously across several cultures. He designed, executed, and sustained large military campaigns across enormous distances without over-stressing his state's demographic base or bankrupting the economies upon which those operations depended. He possessed a penetrating intellect and strategic sagacity. A gifted tactician, he fought four major battles against competent and often numerically superior forces on ground of their own choosing and not only defeated, but utterly routed them. He was a master of military engineering, having conducted six sieges of major cities and dozens – perhaps scores – of smaller towns and fortresses. While never a focus of his action, he proved adept and creative in naval and amphibious operations which were an important adjunct to his campaigns in the Eastern Mediterranean and in India. A brilliant logistician, he routinely supplied his forces in very difficult circumstances that ranged over the entire spectrum of topographical and climatic conditions in Eurasia. When confronted by every military method or tactic that existed in his time, including terrorism and guerilla warfare, Alexander adapted rapidly to dominate each. In sixteen years of near constant military activity encompassing hundreds of separate engagements he never lost a fight. In terms of purely tactical success, he was arguably the greatest commander in history.

Alexander was also fortunate. Luck, as both Napoleon and Clausewitz remind us, is a very significant factor in the achievements of any great commander and Alexander was extraordinarily lucky on many levels. Not least among these was his spectacular good fortune in inheriting the finest army in the world as a legacy from his father. Phillip, who himself had considerable claim to greatness, managed, in the space of little more than a generation, to transform a nation composed primarily of sheep herds (albeit, sheep herds inhabiting a region uniquely abundant in mineral and agricultural resources) into the best equipped, best organized, and most innovative fighting force in the hyper- militarized world of the 4th Century, BC.[7] In a series of impressive campaigns, Phillip used his forces to first secure control of the Northern Balkans and then to extend his hegemony south. He eventually united all of the chronically fractious independent city-states of classical Greece (excluding the rump state of Sparta) into the nominally cooperative – if fragile and resentful – League of Corinth.

Phillip was himself fortunate to be operating in the comparatively permissive environment of a Hellenic world destabilized by 150 years of major warfare that began with the First Persian Invasion about 492.

The Persian threat forced sweeping economic and political change on the deeply conservative Greeks. Before they could adjust fully to the new social realities, internecine Greek warfare reached apotheosis in twenty-seven years of titanic and suicidal struggle for domination between Sparta and Athens known as the Peloponnesian War. These conflicts left the former great powers of Greece diminished and vulnerable. Weakened classical Greek power, however, modifies, but does not entirely explain Phillip's accomplishments. He still had to subdue numerous Hellenic states for whom war had become a near constant occupation and who could avail themselves of the impressive military innovations and refinements which desperate conflict had driven. To accomplish that, Phillip imaginatively combined, refined, and improved on the best military practices of his age.

In forging the Macedonian military machine Phillip created the first truly professional army in the Western world and established the template upon which all current conventional armies are based. He standardized equipment within formations organized according to their intended tactical function. The rank and file (volunteers as well as conscripts) were issued their kit gratis from government-operated armories and manufactories. Pay and remuneration were standardized according to military rank and duty without excessive regard to private status. Command and administrative structures were rationalized and made permanent with reasonable opportunity for advancement and recognition based (in part) on merit and demonstrated ability. Institutionalized provision was made for the full range of support functions from commissary through medical services to disability and veterans' pensions. Indirect command and control was exercised through a regular and consistent chain of command from army down to squad with orders relayed by an elaborate system of voice commands, visual signals, and music. In contrast to the rather xenophobic and ad hoc tendency of the Southern Greeks, Phillip adopted and institutionalized the best innovations from both Greek and barbarian military practice, recombining these elements into a singularly effective and synergistic whole.

The Macedonian tactical system was based on four fundamental elements: Heavy Infantry, Light Infantry, Light Cavalry and Heavy Cavalry, but it also made indispensible use of traditionally armed troops, artillery and engineers, naval forces and the specialized skills of local troops as they were available. Phillip modeled his Heavy Infantry after the concepts of the mercenary general, Iphicrates, who had extended the traditional hoplite seven-foot stabbing spear into an eighteen- to twenty-foot pike. In order to effectively manage this heavy and awkward weapon with two hands, individual body armor was greatly reduced or eliminated and the large hoplon shield, from which Greek infantrymen ("hoplites") derived their name, shrunk to a light buckler that could be suspended from the neck. The members of these modified phalanxes gained protection from the standoff provided by the deep hedge of iron-tipped pikes. Groups of heavy infantrymen were organized into disciplined "syntagma" or companies composed of 256 pikemen arrayed in ranks and files of 16 men each. The heavy Macedonian phalanx had relatively little tactical flexibility and was slow moving, but it could generate enormous momentum in the attack and could establish a formidably intractable defensive base.

Also following the ideas of Iphicrates, The Macedonians fielded large formations of Light Infantry – primarily missile troops called "peltasts" – who rapidly deployed in amorphous, but regulated formations to shower enemy troops with barrages of arrows, javelins, and lead sling bullets, relying on their own agility and mobility for protection. Light Cavalry also relied primarily on missiles as their primary weapons; either short javelins or arrows launched from composite bows. They performed the same range of critical tasks – scouting, flank security, envelopment, and pursuit - that modern armies rely upon mechanized cavalry to perform. Under the right tactical circumstances they could even join a general assault against disorganized or badly positioned infantry.

Heavy Cavalry, although perhaps inspired by the eccentric practice of some wealthy steppe warriors, was Phillip's unique military innovation and was a key to the Macedonian approach to set-piece battle. These were relatively heavily armored horseman armed with a 12-foot lance and a heavy slashing saber. They were mounted on large powerful horses selected for their aggressive spirit and conditioned through patient training to be steady in the confusion of close-quarters combat. Phillip used his heavy horse in the then-non-traditional role of mounted shock troops. He is even credited with developing the remarkable mounted wedge formation designed to penetrate and disrupt enemy infantry and cavalry lines. Although these heavy horsemen were originally drawn from the sons of the aristocratic elite (hence their famous status as "Companions"), they were eventually expanded to include formations comprising the "able" from more modest backgrounds and designated "hetairoi." The same regularity and consistent command and control Phillip had imposed on his infantry was extended to his cavalry, which were organized into squadrons of 200-300 riders each divided into troops of 50-60. These innovations gave Macedonian cavalry a high degree of flexibility in deployment. They were capable of rapid changes in direction of maneuver and attack with minimal disruption to their formation. In addition to his role as overall commander, Alexander generally led the senior squadron of heavy cavalry as "Hipparch" and placed himself at the very tip of the lead assault formation.

As well as these basic tactical elements, the Macedonian system also comprised significant formations of medium infantry equipped similarly to the traditional Greek hoplite, but under more uniform organization and training. These medium phalanxes provided greater flexibility and mobility than the heavy pikemen and provided the essential connective link to the cavalry formations. They were also indispensible for specialist tasks such as leading a breach assault or escalading a wall in a siege, serving as marines in a naval fight, or providing a rapid infantry reaction to an unexpected threat or opportunity. Phillip also created the first regularly organized corps of engineers whose technical prowess and creativity transformed the ancient practice of siege craft. Under assault from the formidable Macedonian machines directed by highly skilled specialists, Phillip and Alexander successfully concluded their sieges not in months or years, as had been the traditional norm, but often in weeks – sometimes days. The equipment and techniques they developed continued to define siege warfare for millennia until they were eclipsed by the introduction of gunpowder weapons in 13th Century AD. The engineers were also critical in sustaining mobility over difficult terrain and bridging obstacles, an essential element in Alexander's scheme of relentless, all-season warfare.

While less frequently mentioned by historians, naval forces also represented a vitally important capability for power projection and sustainment. Although generally inferior to the largely Phoenician fleet which served the Persian Empire, the Macedonian and allied Greek fleet was nevertheless critical in securing Alexander's supply lines and protecting the transport ships which were the most efficient and practical means of transporting the hundreds of tons of food and material required daily by the army in the field.

Under Phillip, the Macedonian nobility was, for all practical purposes, transformed into a professional officer corps. Alexander could and did rely on a large group of capable subordinate commanders and staff officers. As complement to his own remarkable skills, Alexander was well served by a group of highly competent subordinate generals - many, such as Parmenion and Ptolemy, justly famous in their own right - and some of whom went on to rule powerful successor empires themselves.

Together, these elements made a military machine of unprecedented agility, flexibility, and sustainability capable of adapting itself to dominate virtually any tactical situation, project power across enormous distances and maintain a high operational tempo in difficult, poorly resourced environments far from its strategic base. So sophisticated was the Macedonian system that it even had what approached an institutionalized tactical doctrine in which light forces deployed to create or to deny the enemy tactical opportunities, the heavy infantry formed a solid base of maneuver, and the heavy cavalry was used as a "hammer" to smash through the enemy line then wheel and crush the enemy force against the heavy infantry "anvil." The medium infantry formed the flexible continuity connecting the different formations ready to provide immediate support to the cavalry and missile troops or act as a reserve. Alexander appreciated the utility of this doctrine, but never allowed himself to be rigidly bound by it. He always found his army able to adjust itself rapidly to his sudden creative insights or unconventional inspirations.

In addition to these impressive capabilities, the Macedonian Army possessed one final attribute that was equally important in explaining Alexander's unprecedented record of achievement. The Macedonian Army was a fighting force of exceptional and terrifying ferocity. The average Macedonian soldier was, even by the standard of his time, ruthless, relentless, and remorseless. Collectively the Macedonians displayed a singular bloody-mindedness seldom exceeded by any military force in history. Terror and intimidation were primary weapons in their arsenal and they used them with unapologetic vigor. Perhaps the only fundamentally original innovation of Alexander was his technique of aggressively and relentlessly pursuing a defeated enemy. In divergence from traditional Greek warfare and in stark contrast to Asiatic practice, Alexander sought not simply to defeat his enemies, but to annihilate them lest they later discover the temerity to challenge him again. It was in pursuit operations that the inherent ferocity of the Macedonian military found its most terrifying outlet. It is not the least irony surrounding Alexander that in his campaigns – ostensibly undertaken to restore Greek honor, liberty, and fortune lost in persistent conflicts with Persia - he killed more Asian *and Greek* soldiers than had died in the preceding 150 years combined.[8]

For all of the Macedonian Army's extraordinary potential, to be effective, any military force must be well-led and directed, and it was the gifts of military planning and leadership that Alexander possessed in greatest abundance. It was a legacy of traditional Greek warfare that the military commander should put himself at risk by participating personally in combat. Alexander, in this as in so much else, took the "heroic" leadership model to an extreme. He generally placed himself in the thick of the most desperate fighting and plunged into the attack with reckless disregard for his own safety - in the process setting a powerful example for his men. Arrian relates that during a siege of an Indian fortress, Alexander, impatient with the progress of his men storming the enemy wall, impetuously seized a scaling ladder and clambered to the top accompanied by just two companions. In the mad rush to join their commander, the Macedonians over-crowded and broke the ladders, stranding Alexander among the enemy. His men implored him to jump back down into the many arms waiting to catch him, but, espying the enemy commander in the interior court, Alexander instead leaped inside and killed the Indian leader in personal combat. In the process, this tiny group of Macedonians became the focus of the defenders and they were showered with arrows - one penetrating Alexander's lung. Alarmed and enraged, the remaining Macedonians swarmed over the wall to secure what they assumed would be a corpse. That he survived this commonly mortal wound says much about Alexander's physical stamina and toughness (as well as the modern tendency to underestimate the sophistication of ancient medicine). In all, the various sources record that Alexander received a total of eight major wounds in combat - at least two of them very nearly fatal.

Beyond courageous, Alexander was what a modern publicist might characterize as a "soldier's soldier." He extended himself to build bonds of personal comradeship with his men, sharing their privations and hardships, personally attending to their well being, generously sharing the spoils of conquest, and enthusiastically joining in their rough humor and braggadocio. This helps explain the passionate regard – even awe – in which Alexander was for held for so long by his men.[9] However inspiring, camaraderie and heroic personal leadership alone are not enough to define a great commander. Alexander possessed other qualities that, although less romantic, are even more important to a commander's success.

Alexander was gifted with the ability that Frederick the Great called "coup d'oeil," a French term translating to the English "glimpse" or "glance," as in "the stroke of the eye." Frederick defined it as the intuitive (but educated) ability to nearly instantly size up the tactical possibilities of terrain, deployment, and circumstance and to immediately act on this insight to military advantage. Fairly or not, the formal set-piece battle tends to be regarded as the acme of a general's skill and so it is a little surprising to discover that Alexander fought no more than four of them (Granicus, Issus, Gaugamela, Hydaspes) as overall commander of which his rout of Darius' enormous army at Gaugamela is probably the best known example. In all of these, in one way or another, Alexander fought from a position of significant disadvantage on terrain deliberately chosen by the enemy. Invariably, he used his exceptional tactical perception of the ground, the enemy's psychology, faults in deployment, or fleeting opportunities to seize the initiative and to both outfight and outgeneral his opponents.

Alexander's coup d'oeil shows to best advantage in the first battle of his Persian invasion at the Granicus River. The local Persian Satrap (Governor) Artaxserpies had gathered a strong force of local infantry and light cavalry augmented by 18,000 Greek mercenary infantry led by Memnon of Rhodes who had long been an implacable opponent to Phillip's expansionist policy. Memnon, well aware of Alexander's limited resources and the political fragility of the Greek coalition, had cautioned Artaxserpies against a premature showdown with the Macedonians. He advised a scorched earth withdraw, intended to trade space for time, exhaust Alexander's strained logistics, sap Greek moral, and allow reinforcement from the huge military reserves in the Persian interior. Artaxserpies, loath to see such damage done to his rich province and feeling honor (and perhaps politically) bound to a forward defense of his territory, dismissed Memnon's counsel. He elected to confront Alexander from a favorable defensive position on the high eastern bank of the fast flowing Granicus River astride the Macedonian line of advance.

Although Alexander's force was significantly stronger, the speed and depth of the river made it difficult for cavalry and impractical for infantry or to cross in good tactical order. To the experienced Macedonian senior leaders, the strong defensive advantage of the high bank the Persians occupied seemed to render any assault of the position suicidal. General Parmenion (Phillip's most trusted and experienced commander) strongly advised Alexander against attacking and suggested instead that they maneuver south to find a position in which they could exploit their numerical advantage, especially in infantry.

Alexander came to a different conclusion. Strategically, he knew that he had begun the campaign with the slimmest of financial reserves and he was almost out of money. With superior Persian naval forces still dominating the Eastern Mediterranean, his supply lines to Macedonia were threatened, and food and other supplies were already short. Reflecting on his shaky control of the allied Greek coalition, he dared show no sign of weakness or hesitancy in command and he knew he was being closely evaluated by his Macedonian and Greek troops in comparison to his father.

A quick survey of the Persian position also convinced him that it was more vulnerable than it seemed. He noted that the Greek mercenary infantry were poorly deployed and not in position to oppose rapidly a crossing attempt. He sensed that the Persian infantrymen arrayed forward were inexperienced, nervous and comparatively lightly armed. He intuited that, as a result of long habit and their cultural pre-disposition as horse warriors, the Persian leaders would focus their attention on their own and Alexander's cavalry formations. And he knew that none of the Persians had seen Macedonian heavy cavalry in action and were probably unfamiliar with its tactics and abilities. Finally, the Macedonians had arrived at the Granicus in the afternoon and the Persians expected no significant action to take place until the following day.

But rather than wait, Alexander called a hasty meeting with his commanders and staff, sketched out a simple plan and immediately deployed for battle. He engaged the Persian light infantry screen with his missile troops, while his light cavalry made a series of flanking feints north and south along the western bank, causing the Persians to extended and thin their cavalry line. Sensing the opportune moment, Alexander personally led his heavy cavalry in a pell-mell lunge across the river aimed at the junction between the Persian cavalry and infantry on the right. The Macedonian infantry, struggling across the swollen river in bad order but with resolute determination, supported their cavalry as best they could.

Alexander and the Companions, in such formation as they could manage while negotiating the river obstacles, plunged deeply into the Persian line. Alexander personally engaged three of the enemy cavalry commanders before being knocked from his horse by a vicious cut to his neck. He was narrowly saved from a killing blow by the intervention of one of his Noble Companion officers, Cleitus ("The Black") who, at tremendous personal risk, dismounted to defend the prostrate King amid the swirling mêlée. In a few minutes, the lightly equipped Persian cavalry broke and dispersed under the furious onslaught of the heavy Macedonian horsemen. Alexander remounted and wheeled his cavalry to attack the Persian infantry from the rear. Assailed from two sides, the Persians panicked. In moments, organized resistance collapsed and they scattered in an attempt to evade the aggressive pursuit of the Macedonian light forces. In the process they abandoned the relatively immobile 18,000 Greek mercenaries who had hardly been engaged.[10]

Macedonian losses in the battle were between 300 and 400 dead. The Persians left some 4,000 on the field and lost a further undetermined number in the days of pursuit that followed. In a hopeless position, the Greek mercenaries attempted to negotiate surrender. Alexander, outraged by what he regarded, under the circumstances, as their treason and mindful of the message it would send, ruthlessly attacked and killed all but 2,000 of them at no recorded loss to his own force. The surviving mercenaries were sent back to Macedonia as slaves for the state mines.

The Granicus battle displays Alexander's gifts as a tactical commander. It demonstrates his imaginative grasp of the unconventional approach and his intuitive sense of the right moment and place for the decisive stroke. It shows his prowess and recklessly heroic personal leadership and his pitiless, relentlessly aggressive endeavor to destroy any who dared oppose him.

In the perspective of the overarching campaign, the Granicus also reveals another essential attribute of the great commander; the ability to organize a series of tactical engagements and related actions into larger operations to attain a deliberate strategic result. Effective strategic vision is the true measure of supreme command and the most difficult and elusive of all military skills. The strategic commander must set realistic and achievable, if sometimes highly ambitious, grand objectives. He must accurately assess the capabilities and qualities of his own and the enemy's forces. He must be able to predict with reasonable precision the enemy's reactions and responses to his actions, and counter them. He must cope with unexpected enemy actions or unforeseen events without fatally compromising his own strategic design. He must craft his operations to be compatible with the nature and abilities of his forces and the prevailing social, political, and economic conditions and expectations of the larger society or he must alter those conditions to make them congruent with his objectives. The supreme commander wears many hats and must master much more than simple soldiering to achieve his strategic aims. With little practical experience, Alexander demonstrated an astonishingly firm grasp of strategy.

Alexander began the maneuvers that brought him to the Granicus in 334 BC, when he continued Phillip's plan to punish the Persian Empire (allegedly) in revenge for more than a century of depredations and the persecution of the Greek cities in Asia Minor. The stated objectives were to remove the immediate threat to the Greek cities on the Black Sea, secure navigation in the Northeast Mediterranean, humble Persian pride by exacting tribute, and liberate the vassal Greek cities of Asia Minor. Privately, Alexander held or evolved much grander ambitions. He intended to destroy, not merely punish, the Persian Empire, a feat that would gain him immeasurable military glory. He may or may not have had a vision of a grand "Empire of Man" uniting the peoples of the East and West, but he certainly intended to establish his personal authority over most of them.

Beyond unprecedented martial glory, Alexander held another cherished dream. Aristotle had taught a model of geography that posited a world composed of thee small continents—Europe, Asia, and Africa— surrounding the Mediterranean Sea and themselves bounded by a surrounding ocean. Greek philosophers believed the "Great Surrounding Ocean" was the source of all the world's major rivers and that it could (theoretically) be used to navigate between them. Alexander intended to be the first to traverse the breadth of Asia, circumnavigate the Surrounding Ocean and return triumphantly down the Nile as the only man to have literally seen the "world." If he had been confronted by a map of the planet depicting its size and continental scale as we know it to be, Alexander would have been stunned and deeply depressed. Based on his own assumptions, however, a journey of conquest across what he thought was a comparatively small Asia and Africa, seemed plausible (if startlingly ambitious). Alexander correctly perceived his greatest obstacle, as well as opportunity, in accomplishing this grand objective to be the vast and fabulously wealthy Persian Empire to the east.

Although in decline and internally stressed, Persia was still the largest and, at least notionally, the most powerful empire in the world. In 336, after the assassination of his predecessor, Darius III assumed the title of "Great King" and Achaemenid Emperor. Darius was scion of a people known (inaccurately) in the West as Medes. He held tenuous sovereignty over a vast, but often very loose confederation of semi-autonomous Satrapies (Provinces) composed of the many varied peoples of modern Southwest Asia and the Middle East. Darius inherited all the military resources of a large, diverse, wealthy, and long established empire. The Persian elite were originally a Turko-Iranian horse people who migrated from the North during the chaos of the 11 century BC and eventually took control of the areas once dominated by the ancient Assyrian and Egyptian empires and beyond. Their principal military art derived from the light cavalry traditions of the Eurasian Steppe warriors who wore little or no body armor and whose primary weapons were the composite bow and light javelin. They had absorbed the various fighting techniques of their polyglot subjects, but the infantry of these, in keeping with dominant Asian tradition, were much more lightly armed and armored than Greek troops. Both Persian cavalry and infantry retained or adopted the preference for missile engagement practiced by steppe cultures. The Persian elite had grown to appreciate the potential of heavily armored Greek infantrymen and their peculiar, but effective, practice of close quarter shock attack. Such troops, however, were not available among their indigenous populations and they came to depend upon contingents of Greek vassal or mercenary infantry as their most important source of reliable infantry. Ironically, this is how Alexander came to kill more Greek soldiers in his campaigns than had died in previous Persian-Greek conflict. Although it was wanton and cruel, the destruction of Memnon's men proved to be an effective shaping operation. Thereafter, any Greek mercenary would think twice before enlisting in Persian service against Alexander.[11]

Alexander's operations after his victory on the Granicus River demonstrate his strategic ability and judgment. Rather than charge pell-mell into the heart of the Persian Empire, Alexander took pains to secure his rear and develop a strong forward base from which to operate. His next step after establishing an Asian foothold was to proceed with liberating the Ionian Greek coastal cities. This was in keeping with the expectations of the allied Greek coalition and with Alexander's own propaganda. In the process, Alexander also denied Darius the revenue and support of some of his wealthiest and most populous provinces. Simultaneously, seizure of the coast negated Persian naval superiority and the threat to allied communications by means of a land campaign that denied the Persian fleet secure bases in the Eastern Mediterranean. In the event, the major coastal cities proved less than enthusiastic about their "liberation" and remained surprisingly hostile to Alexander and loyal to Darius. Their subjugation absorbed much more time and resources than Alexander had hoped because they forced him to reduce by deliberate siege some of the most formidable fortresses in the world. These included the ancient port city of Tyre, regarded by conventional military wisdom as impregnable if vigorously defended.

Tyre was a well garrisoned and fully fortified island located almost one-half mile offshore, with two large harbors and no easy approaches. It had its own flotilla of active warships and had been lavished with every marvel of defensive engineering its conspicuous wealth could afford. The Assyrians had besieged it in the 6th century for over eleven years without success. But in the end, it proved simply a challenge for Alexander's imagination and the skill of his engineers. During nine months of siege, Alexander defeated and blockaded Tyre's naval forces, systematically cut it off from outside relief, constructed an enormous mole which converted the island into a peninsula, and repelled all counter moves. Alexander culminated his operation with a final assault on the breached walls by the ferocious Macedonian infantry. In addition to demonstrating his consummate engineering skill and imagination, Tyre also reveals the ruthlessness that was a large component of Alexander's success as a conqueror. Perhaps 7,000 defenders, most of them private citizens pressed into their city's service, were killed during the siege and final assault. Following the victory, the entire population, possibly 30,000 men, women, and children, were sold into slavery after the Macedonian troops were given three days of "liberty" to visit upon the hapless Tyrannians what they would. The rape of Tyre was an intimidating message Alexander was sending to any other community that thought to resist his power or chose to dispute him an easy victory.[12]

Following Tyre, Alexander made quick work of the remaining Persian garrisons in Egypt and ordered a short operational pause to reorganize, reinforce, and resupply his main force in preparation for an advance into the Persian interior. Meanwhile, his capable generals conducted a series of successful shaping operations that, in addition to securing important terrain and routes necessary for the main Army's passage, yielded a windfall of Persian treasure and resources that greatly helped to sustain the momentum of the campaign. After several weeks of coastal maneuver to the tip of the Gulf of Issus in Anatolia, Alexander finally confronted a large Persian army.

It had been assembled hastily, but it significantly outnumbered the Macedonian force and was led by Darius in person. Uncharacteristically, Alexander had badly misread the tactical situation and was surprised by strong Persian formations on his flanks. Undaunted, he rapidly adjusted his deployment, aggressively engaged the Persians, defeated and ultimately routed them. Darius was forced into ignoble flight and he abandoned to the Macedonians his camp treasury and personal entourage, including his mother and other members of his immediate family. In the weeks after this defeat, Darius made an escalating series of peace overtures culminating in an offer that included ransom for his family that was larger than the annual state revenue of Macedonia, limited independence for the Ionian Greeks, control of Asia Minor, marriage to a royal princess, and a treaty of perpetual peace and military alliance. Plutarch reports that on reviewing the final proposal, Parmenion said, "I would accept this offer, were I Alexander." To which Alexander replied, "As would I, were I Parmenion." Apocryphal or not, this exchange captures the essence of Alexander's self-confidence, resolution, and his single mindedness in pursuit of his objectives. His was a brand of all-in gambling tempered by keen insight and cool strategic judgment.[13]

After more weeks of maneuvering, Alexander again confronted Darius at the head of an even larger Army at Gaugamela in Mesopotamia.

The enormous Persian force was gathered from the near and far provinces at grave risk to the political integrity of the remaining empire. It was by then nearly devoid of any Greek infantry component, but greatly outnumbered Alexander's field army (possibly by more than two-to-one). This mighty host must have seemed irresistible to Darius. And so it was with dismay that he watched his grand army out-maneuvered, out-fought, and once more routed by the Macedonians. In the face of a personal onslaught by Alexander at the head of his Companions, Darius again fled the field. Soon, in the company of his personal bodyguard commanded by the Bactrian Satrap Bessus, he fled the heart of his lands to the wilds of his vassal provinces Sogdonia and Bactria (modern Afghanistan and Pakistan). Alexander quickly overcame remaining resistance and occupied the Persian capitals of Babylon, Persepolis, and Ecbatana.

For Alexander's allied Greek troops – as indeed for his own Macedonians – this was the fulfillment of the Greek dream of revenge and they expected to soon begin the long trek home, triumphant and very wealthy men. For Alexander's personal dream, however, the capture and plunder of the Persian capitals was only the beginning of his quest for conquest and glory. Somewhere along his journey, Alexander had decided to not just destroy the Persian Empire, but to rule a greatly expanded version of it in his own right as the self-styled, self-made heir to the Achaemenid dynasty. Alexander quickly stabilized his new empire by assuming control of the existing (and uniquely efficient) Persian civil services. He wisely resisted any temptation to sweeping re-organization and left existing infrastructures intact and unmolested. He appointed Macedonian governors to vital positions and dispatched them with competent Asian advisers and trusted garrisons to maintain internal order. He honorably integrated such remaining Persian troops as were willing into his own service and he dismissed the allied Greek forces after enlisting all who choose to stay on as mercenaries. Alexander then gathered reinforcements from home, reorganized his field force, and set out on the next series of operations for which he had begun preparing even before his victory at Gaugamela. Learning of Darius' escape into the hinterlands, Alexander decided his first order of business was to pursue and kill the deposed emperor and prevent a serious rival to his new status as "Great King." These operations drew Alexander's reduced, but still substantial army into some of the most difficult and hostile territory in the world – then or now.

These are areas that should be of particular interest to modern Americans as they are the focal point of our recent interminable conflicts, and the Macedonian experience might well have served as a sobering reminder of the challenges and costs to any outsider who seeks to assert authority there. A common military maxim holds that "amateurs talk about tactics, professionals study logistics."[14] To gain further insight into the military genius of Alexander we have to consider the staggering difficulties he overcame in sustaining his army day to day as an organized fighting force in this barren and hostile environment. Even assuming a significant reduction in forces for what developed into "pacification" operations in the northeast of Alexander's new dominions, we can assess that the problem of providing even minimal daily subsistence to his forces from local resources would daunt the ablest administrator due to the arid and undeveloped nature of the country.

Supposing a total force of no more than 35,000 combatants, 15,000 camp followers, 10,000 cavalry mounts, and 10,000 baggage animals renders a calculated minimum daily requirement for 128 tons of grain, 200 tons of fodder, and 265,000 gallons of potable water. The problem is exacerbated by Alexander's need to maintain dominant mobility. As they moved far inland from the coasts or navigable waterways, the Macedonians became almost entirely dependent on pack animals – horses, donkeys, and crucially, camels – for bulk transport. Effectively, this limited Alexander's advanced logistic parties to foraging in a 60 kilometer radius of a designated marching depot because the utility of grain or forage gathered from distances further than this would be negated by the consumption demands of the additional pack animals required to carry it. While they were operating in conspicuously fertile areas such as the Tigris/Euphrates Valley, sufficient local provisions were available with minimal effort. In more arid climes, however, movement required painstaking advanced logistical planning and preparation.

In the mountains of Bactria, the climate and topography made the challenge of securing sufficient food and forage extreme. Alexander was nevertheless able to maintain a high operational tempo despite very limited local resources– a feat that no Persian force had ever been able to do. Macedonian forces apparently experienced no significant logistic failures or delays due to supply problems – mute testimony to Alexander's military judgment and staff planning skill. It is also a reflection of the sheer competence and professionalism of his subordinate officers. It must also be noted, however, that the passing of Alexander's Army spelt existential catastrophe for the inhabitants of that 38-mile-wide corridor. Those unfortunates would have been stripped of all sustenance and left to starve in a cruel winter with their denuded storehouses, fields, and flocks ruined even before they were needed in the coming spring.[15]

In Sogdonia, Alexander discovered the body of Darius, murdered and abandoned by Bessus and his own bodyguard. Alexander learned that Bessus had declared himself the rightful heir to the Achaemenid throne – a provocation that Alexander could not ignore. In addition to his Persian pretensions, Bessus was a Bactrian prince and he had retreated into what he (vainly) hoped were the safe havens of his people's high mountain fortresses. In addition to the problem posed by Bessus, who was eventually trapped and mercilessly destroyed along with all of his followers, Alexander had to deal with the bewildering array of ethnic and tribal peoples of the Northeast. Those regions had never been more than nominally under Persian authority and were – then as now – fiercely jealous of their independence and prerogatives. This was a situation intolerable to Alexander who was never willing to brook any open opposition to his personal authority over a subject people.

Alexander was drawn into a series of irregular operations that today we might characterize as an "insurgency." That Alexander was able to decisively master this difficult situation in the astonishingly short period of three years suggests that his techniques should be carefully studied by the modern American military as a guide to their own operations in the region. Unfortunately, the tactics Alexander used would be unacceptable in the context of prevailing Western norms and mores. Alexander's success in guerilla warfare was really only an extension of his native inclination to meet all challenges with pitiless aggression and overwhelming force. These methods dovetailed effortlessly with the character of his army that had long relied on its ferocity and hyper-aggression as a powerful tool to psychologically dominate enemies. The army's professionalism soon led it to master the combat techniques of ambush, counter-ambush, and mountain warfare. Alexander's conceptual approach to reconciliation with his discontented new subjects was to divide them politically, buy or otherwise seduce the powerful, terrorize the rest into grudging submission or destroy them with brutal violence. The alternative to peaceful obedience Alexander offered these discontented peoples was to offer them with an "eternal" peace."[16]

A final and perhaps most definitive example of Alexander's military genius is paradoxically one of his least remarked upon, but actually most remarkable achievements. Alone among the Western commander's of antiquity, Alexander managed to decisively defeat a Eurasian horse army on its own terms and on its own ground – a feat that would seldom be equaled by another Western army until the age of gunpowder. To make this interpretation clear it is necessary to explain something more about the art of war as practiced by the various semi-nomadic horse cultures of the Eurasian Steppe of which the Scythians were among the larger and more powerful. The Scythian nobility constituted a small elite of heavily armed and armored horsemen capable, individually, of engaging in close combat with Alexander's heavy cavalry but prevented by both small numbers and long habit from doing so. The vast majority of Scythian warriors were lightly equipped horse archers mounted on tough steppe ponies who relied almost exclusively on long-range missile fire to wear down and destroy their enemies. Their tactics of fluid movement and mobility were utterly asymmetric to the linear formations and tactics of infantry-based armies. At the Jexartes River that described the northern boundary of Sogdonia from the immense Eurasian Steppe beyond, Alexander was confronted by a horde of Scythian warriors in their characteristically amorphous formations of loosely grouped horsemen. At that point, the Jexartes was relatively deep and very wide – well beyond the range of a standard bowshot. The Scythian intentions were unclear, but Alexander was loath to retreat from them lest he leave his hard-won conquests exposed to attack. Nor could he risk having the Scythians fall upon his vulnerable rear elements during the withdrawal. He was also, perhaps, motivated by his reputation of invincibility and simply could not resist attempting to solve a new, even if avoidable, military problem.

Giving full reign to his intuitive imagination, Alexander deployed his siege train and used the powerful engines as field artillery - possibly the first such use in recorded history. The artillery missiles drove the Scythian horseman away from the opposite bank and held them at bay while Alexander crossed over his light troops to establish a bridgehead and cover the Macedonian engineers, now become combat sappers (another possible first), while they constructed ferries to transport the heavy troops. In good time, the main Macedonian force was able to make the crossing unmolested and in good order. In this minor operation Alexander effectively established the tactical principles of an assault river crossing which endure and are taught in military schools today.

Confronted by an unfavorable situation, the Scythians used their superior mobility to move, as individuals and small groups into the interior, tempting their enemy into a heedless pursuit, over-extending, and isolating the pursuers from supporting forces. On cue, the seemingly unorganized Scythian horsemen would subtly wheel, envelop, and destroy their erstwhile pursuers in a deadly trap. Alexander seemed to take the bait and sped his light cavalry on the heels of the "retreating" Scythians, unwittingly, as the enemy thought, positioning it for destruction.

It was really Alexander, however, who had set the trap. The Scythians had badly underestimated the relative mobility of the Macedonian light and medium infantry and the power of Alexander's massed heavy cavalry. The enveloped Macedonian light cavalry gradually fell back toward their advancing infantry and heavy cavalry whose flanks and rear were secured by the stolid phalanxes of pikemen. Too late, the enveloping Scythian horsemen recognized their danger and Alexander's formations were able to surround and annihilate up to a full third of the total Scythian force – probably the worst defeat they had ever suffered or ever expected too. The very next day, a delegation of Scythian leaders came to Alexander to make terms and soon departed northeastward to seek easier foes. In the succeeding decades they, or the domino effect their sudden migration might have had upon the other Eurasian horse peoples, became a serious thorn in the side of the early Chinese Qin dynasty – Perhaps even inspiring the prodigious feats of wall building for which the Qin are celebrated. In any event, Alexander had strategically secured his Northern frontier and freed himself to continue his campaign eastward to the Indus Valley.[17]

Ultimately, all human ambitions have their practical limit and Alexander's were no exception to this rule. In 326 BC on the banks of the Hyphasis River in modern India, after eight years of continuous campaigning, the Macedonian army had had enough. The soldiers were increasingly discomfited by their king's behavior. The Alexander that the Macedonian soldiers served in India seemed a very different man from the boon warrior-companion who had led them across the Hellespont to Asia. For some time, Alexander had been growing more preemptory and contentious. He only infrequently sought the confidence of his Companions and he laid plans to begin arming and training selected Asian troops to perform the heavy infantry and cavalry roles - the unique military identity of the Macedonian soldiers that made them indispensable. He spent more and more time in the company of Asian political advisers and sycophants and he increasingly assumed the attire and manners of his Persian court. Formerly he imbibed alcohol socially and sparingly, but now he drank heavily and was quick to brawl with his former intimates. He declared himself divine and demanded that even Greeks prostrate themselves in his presence after the oriental custom.

During a now-infrequent evening spent drinking with his Macedonians; an intoxicated Alexander began to denigrate their contributions to the new Empire. He speculated that, with himself as commander, he could have achieved all with any army including the Persian. He also dismissed the achievements of his father and the previous generation of Macedonian leaders, among whose sons he was speaking, as insignificant when compared to his own. He mocked his Companions for their limited vision and adherence to their Macedonian ways. Alexander praised the alleged sophistication and superiority of Asian culture particularly as manifest in their granting him what he seemed to believe was his due as the actual (not merely notional) son of Zeus.

Alexander was challenged on these offensive presumptions by a disgusted Cleitus "the Black" – among his ablest subordinates and he who had risked his own life to save Alexander at the Granicus River. Cleitus pointed out the impropriety of the divine decree as applied to Greeks and the disrespect his Persian behaviors implied to the Macedonian troops and Companions, especially when coupled with the increasingly arbitrary and unpleasant duty assignments Alexander gave his Western officers. Cleitus made very plain his contempt for Alexander's growing arrogance and haughty inapproachability. Some sober heads attempted to propel Cleitus forcibly out of the furious King's presence, but, when Cleitus appeared again a moment later, Alexander personally killed the unarmed man in a fit of drunken rage.[18] The soldiers, many of whom by this time had traveled some 15,000 weary circuitous miles in the wake of their increasingly volatile commander, were aware of and distressed by this incident. Cleitus was respected and popular. It called the King's judgment deeply into question. The men were grown homesick and skeptical of where all this endless activity was leading.

They were now in country unknown to even the most learned Greek scholars. In the unaccustomed climate of sub-tropical India, the Macedonian soldiers suffered from the smothering humid heat and died of strange diseases. Despite winning a major victory at the Hydaspes River in the Punjab against the army of the Hindu King Porus, Indian tribal resistance to their advance remained fierce and took a constant toll of casualties. Under interrogation no Indian was able to tell the Macedonians the remaining distance to the Great Surrounding Ocean nor even seemed to know what they were trying to describe. The troops were done. They vigorously petitioned their King to abandon his odyssey and lead them home. They sullenly resisted all of Alexander's passionate attempts at inspiration, persuasion, or promise of reward. Soon they were supported by most of the officers—loyal men with distinguished records who personally owed much to Alexander, but who had grown disenchanted with the commander's quixotic dreams. For a time Alexander, having badly strained the formerly close bonds of comradeship he shared with his men, reacted with angry petulance.

The tension was palpable and explosive. More than affection, the conviction that only Alexander could successfully extract them from deep within a hostile land, was probably all that stopped the mutiny short of regicide. Reluctantly and with ill grace Alexander agreed to abandon his grand vision, but first he extracted from them a concession that he offered as expediency. He would lead his major force home by the indirect route of sailing down the Indus River and back up the Persian Gulf. This "short" way back to Mesopotamia committed the Macedonian Army to further fierce and costly fighting as they slowly descended the Indus in the face of stubborn local opposition. Unnecessarily, the return trip required almost two full years. It also caused many of the soldiers to fall victim to Alexander's only major lapse in operational judgment. Without adequate intelligence or reliable guides, Alexander inexplicably decided to lead a large force on foot across the Gedrosian desert of Southern Iran. In those empty wastes, a great many of his good veterans perished from want and exposure. The rest survived by the barest of margins.

Upon finally reaching his designated capital at Babylon early in 323 BC, Alexander addressed himself to the convoluted variety of duties and problems attendant to managing his enormous and unstable empire. Simultaneously he was planning future military campaigns against Arabia, Carthage, and Italy. Many noticed a marked change in him. Since the mutiny on the Hyphasis, he seemed even more withdrawn, contentious, and frequently embittered with his Macedonians. He was further depressed by the sudden death in Ecbatana of his best and closest friend (and probably lover) the adored Hephaestion. It was remarked that Hephaestion had always been a steadying influence on his personality, but that was over and Alexander was inconsolable. Grief stricken and irrational, he peremptorily ordered all of Hephaestion's attending physicians to be garroted.

Physically, Alexander never seemed fully recovered from the grievous wound he received in the Indian fortress. His skin was sallow and he was uncharacteristically indolent for long periods. Alexander complained of insomnia and a host of minor discomforts that previously he would have ignored. He was short tempered and increased his already heavy drinking. His orders were sometimes capricious and he was even more ruthless and arbitrary in dealing with those whom he believed had failed him. His paranoia became excessive and, on little or no evidence, he ordered the execution or assassination of many, including his own court historian Cleisthenes and the venerable Parmenion, for treason – real or merely suspected. His efforts to integrate and harmonize the leadership of his culturally diverse court were unsuccessful. In a bold attempt at Susa, he orchestrated a mass wedding of his Macedonian officers to Persian brides (which must have seriously annoyed their existing wives in Greece). Few of his officers seemed to take this seriously, however, and most treated their new wives, despite their noble rank and lineage, as merely additional mistresses. Tensions among the various ethnic factions ran high. The Westerners made little effort, out of Alexander's sight, to hide their contempt for the Asians.

In June, after an epic drinking binge, Alexander collapsed, lingered in and out of consciousness for a few days, and died just weeks short of his thirty-third birthday.[19] Arrian claims that when, in a lucid moment on his deathbed, he was asked to whom he bequeathed the Empire, Alexander replied, "To the strongest."[20] Accurate or not, the stark truth is that Alexander's domains had no logical coherence save that provided by Alexander. His Empire was a kind of personality cult that could hold together only under the fear and focus provided by Alexander himself. It literally did not survive the night he died, as his generals immediately fell into hot dispute over the succession. In the end, which was not long in coming, Alexander's suffered the fate of all purely military empires. It fractured into a dozen violently competing successor states and launched decades of chronic warfare among contenders seeking to re-establish control over the others.

What then are the enduring legacies of Alexander? The vast Empire he forged was, like the mythical Camelot, ephemeral. He could be said to have transformed Western warfare in the 4th century BC and set models for tactical engagement that redefined military practice for over two hundred years until they were eclipsed by the even more radical Roman system. But, that is arguably more Phillip's legacy than Alexander's and a strong case can made that it only accelerated an evolutionary process that would have happened anyway. It might be suggested that Alexander's campaigns became a virtual school for strategic design. However, many theorists and practitioners have argued persuasively that strategic acumen is more an inborn talent than an acquired skill. At best it can be refined by careful study, but never imparted where the talent is lacking. Alexander's role in ushering in the "Age of Hellenism" and the lasting effects of Hellenism itself are, as already noted, in profound dispute among serious scholars who have earned the right to an opinion. Alexander failed to found a dynasty or even an enduring state. He failed, ultimately, to unite the many antagonistic peoples of the East and West into a harmonious Empire of Man, nor could he be said to have made much progress in that direction. He failed to reach the Great Surrounding Ocean and circumnavigate the world. Can any commander who failed to meet his grand strategic objectives, even one possessing the demonstrable military genius of Alexander, truly be said to be great?

The evaluation of greatness in history inevitably depends on one's own cultural, political, and personal values. It will always be determined according to the bias of the individual observer. If we evaluate Alexander exclusively from the perspective of military achievement his record is unrivaled. His career offers, however, sobering reminders of the dubious value of military success when it is uncoupled from the political objectives that give it purpose. For the earnest commander of any age, Alexander represents the apogee of military competence. For good or ill, he will continue to be the benchmark by which extremely ambitious soldiers measure themselves. Alexander fulfilled his prophecy as the Invincible Commander, in that eternal glory, more than any other objective, seems to have been Alexander's most cherished ambition. And since we are still analyzing and arguing about him some 2,300 years after his death, we might well agree with the Romans and conclude that, as a military commander at least, Alexander was indeed "Great."

Notes

1.   For a general introduction and survey of the complex issues surrounding the original sources of Alexander historiography see Eugene N. Borza's introduction to the classic biography by Ulrich Wilcken, *Alexander the Great* (New York: Norton & Company, 1967) xxi-xxviii.

2.   For an evaluation of Alexander's reputation in the 4th Century Greek world and his significance to and rehabilitation by Roman historians see Peter Bamm, *Alexander the Great; Power As Destiny* (New York: McGraw-Hill, 1968) 9-22

3.   An objective and accessible integration of the competing interpretations of Alexander's childhood and influences is found in Paul Cartledge, *Alexander the Great; The Hunt for a New Past* (New York: Vintage Books,) 81-90

4.   Alexander's life, accomplishments and historical significance have generated a staggering body of literature over the centuries. Interpreters of the Macedonian can generally be grouped into three broad categories: Apologists (also known as Hagiographers), Moral Critics, and Neutralists. Among the more famous and influential of the modern apologists are: William Tarn (1869-1957), JFC Fuller (1878-1966), Mary Renault (1905-1983), and even Oliver Stone (1946-) who find in Alexander a visionary and enlightened, if flawed, social idealist. The best known of the moral critics include: Hans Delbruck (1848-1929), Will Durant (1885-1981), and Victor Davis Hanson (1953-) who, while giving full appreciation to Alexander's military genius, regard his career and accomplishments as disastrous to his followers, his victims, their societies and to Western culture generally as having established a de facto justification of the "might makes right" school of international relations. Hanson pulls no punches in describing Alexander as an ancient Hitler (Hanson, *The Wars of the Ancient Greeks* (London: Cassell, 1999, p. 190). The neutralists, probably due to both the caution of their conclusions and the understatement of their prose, tend to be less well known. Excellent objective general biographers of Alexander currently in print include Ulrich Wilcken (1862-1944) and Paul Cartledge (1947-) both of whose works are cited above.

5.   For an abbreviated appreciation of the multifarious cultural identities of Alexander and his on-going influence in the transforming societies of the Hellenistic world see Peter Bamm, *Alexander the Great; Power As Destiny* (New York: McGraw-Hill, 1968) 24-68.

6.   Christopher R. Gabel, *Great Commanders* (Fort Leavenworth, KS. 2013) 2.

7.   For an excellent and lavishly illustrated modern interpretation of the Macedonian Army and a general overview of Alexander's campaigns see Nick Sekunda and John Warry, *Alexander The Great; His Armies and Campaigns 334-323 BC* (Oxford: Osprey Publishing, 1998) Passim. Although his conclusions on Alexander's historical significance are dubious, JFC Fuller's reconstructions of

Alexander's battles, operations, and his strategic design, reconciled from the conflicting ancient sources, remain definitive and unequaled by more recent scholars. See, JFC Fuller, *The Generalship of Alexander the Great* (New Brunswick, NJ: Rutgers University Press, 1960) Passim.

8. Victor Davis Hanson, *The Wars of the Ancient Greeks* (London: Cassell, 1999), p. 178.

9. Lucius Flavius Arrianus (Arrian of Nicomedia),*The Campaigns of Alexander*_(Translated by Aubrey deSelin Court, London: Penguin Books, 1958) 313-316.

10. JFC Fuller, *The Generalship of Alexander the Great* (New Brunswick, NJ: Rutgers University Press, 1960) 147- 154.

11. An unparalleled general history of the Persian Empire and its military machine, refreshingly free of the cultural biases that still tend to distort Western oriented interpretations of the Greek experience, is provided by Tom Holland, *Persian Fire; The First World Empire and the Battle for the West* (New York: Anchor Books, 2007)

12. JFC Fuller, *The Generalship of Alexander the Great* ,206-218.

13. Lucius Mestrius Plutarchus (Plutarch), *Lives of the Nobel Greeks and Romans* (Translated by Aubrey Stewart and George Long, New York: CreateSpace Inc., 2011) p. 238.

14. GEN Robert H. Barrow, Commandant, USMC, *Annual Address to the Marine Corps Assoc.*, Proceedings, 1980.

15. The most comprehensive study of the challenges faced by Alexander in resourcing and sustaining his campaigns (and a masterpiece of analytical historical research) is Donald W. Engels, *Alexander the Great and the Logistics of the Macedonian Army* (Berkeley: University of California Press, 1978)

16. Ancient sources made little distinction between what a modern military professional would consider Alexander's conventional and unconventional wars. Using the parlance of his professional generation, JFC Fuller devotes a chapter (Fuller, Chapter 8.) to "Alexander's Small Wars." Among more recent analysts of "counter-insurgency," a stand-out study is Robert B. Asprey, *War in the Shadows; The Guerilla in History Vol. I* (New York: Doubleday, 1975). See also Victor Davis Hanson, *Carnage and Culture* (New York: Doubleday, 2001, pgs. 74-90) for further elucidation (and condemnation) of Alexander's tactics and techniques.

17. JFC Fuller, *The Generalship of Alexander the Great* , 237-242

18. Arrian, *The Campaigns of Alexander*, 213-216.

19. *Ibid.*, 380-395.

20. *Ibid.*, 394.

Chapter 2

Genghis Khan

by Terry Beckenbaugh, Ph.D.

Of all the great commanders in human history, perhaps none rose from more dire straits to greater heights than Genghis Khan. Rising from the poverty of exile, the young boy named Temujin who eventually became Genghis Khan, helped his family survive the harsh steppe climate, grew to a strong and charismatic young man who united the disparate Mongol tribes into a nation, and founded what became the world's largest contiguous land empire. Yet for all his accomplishments, Genghis Khan is probably the least well known of the great commanders. A significant reason for that is the fact that when Genghis Khan founded the Mongol empire, the Mongols had no written language.

The earliest primary sources chronicling the Mongols were the accounts of the peoples the Mongols conquered. Since that conquest tended to be brutal, the portrait of the Mongols that emerges is understandably not flattering. To study the Mongols one must have an extraordinary fluency in a variety of foreign languages. Thus, the scholar can spend a lifetime mastering diverse languages such as Japanese, Korean, Chinese, Vietnamese, Turkish, Russian, Persian, Arabic, Hungarian, German, Latin and Mongolian to study the Mongol conquests. An added handicap for people in the English-speaking world who wish to study the Mongols is that the Mongol conquest never reached the British Isles, nor did significant English-speaking elements serve within the Mongol forces or fight against them. This has the effect of tamping down scholarly inquiry in the English-speaking world, so that the English speaker must have reading comprehension of German and/or Russian to read the best western scholarship available on the Mongol empire.[1] Since very few people have the linguistic ability to truly master the plethora of languages necessary to study the Mongols, those who do overwhelmingly tend to focus on a region the Mongols conquered. This narrows the focus to China, Persia, Arabic-speaking lands of the Middle East and Russia and is much more manageable as a scholarly endeavor.[2] Another issue that hinders the study of the Mongols is the state of Mongol cultural development compared to the subjected peoples' cultural development.

Unlike the Persians, Greeks, Romans and Chinese, who forcibly stamped their culture on conquered peoples, the Mongols over time absorbed the culture of their more developed subjects. The Mongols' military was far more advanced than the sedentary cultures they conquered, but once

Figure 2. Genghis Khan portrait cropped from a page in an album depicting several Yuan emperors at the National Palace Museum in Taipei; 14th Century; author unknown

in control the Mongols often relied upon the administrative machinery of the of the defeated peoples to manage those regions. This left it to those conquered peoples to characterize the Mongols, and while in awe of Mongol military prowess, they were often less kind in describing their conquerors' culture and society. As a nomadic people, the Mongols did not have large urban areas, or a capital complex or governing bureaucracy to aid in governance of the ever-expanding empire. With no capital and no bureaucracy, and the vast majority of Mongols being illiterate, Genghis Khan had no choice but to rely upon the literate members of foreign bureaucracies to staff and document his growing empire. Furthermore, the nomadic peoples of inner Asia were long tempted by the riches of their sedentary neighbors. This was no different with the Mongols who, now controlling those riches, succumbed to them. So it is accurate to say that while the Mongols militarily conquered many sophisticated nations, those same nations culturally conquered the Mongols over time.[3] This makes studying the Mongols a challenge for any scholar, and part of the reason that so much of Genghis Khan's life is shrouded in myth and legend.

The future Genghis Khan was born into the uncertain, violent world of the late twelfth century. The Mongols fought among themselves and paid tribute to the Chin Dynasty in China. They were an impoverished and desperate people yearning for stability and prosperity.[4] Organized on a tribal basis, the various tribes engaged in a vicious cycle of raiding and retaliation among each other that left a trail of corpses and orphans. Genghis Khan's father, a Mongol Chieftain named Yisugei kidnapped Genghis Khan's mother, Ho'elun, and married her. Ho'elun was one of Yisugei's many wives, but she was the senior wife. When Genghis Khan was born, legend states that he held a blood clot the size of a knuckle bone in his right hand—an augur of greatness. At the time of the birth, Yisugei had recently captured a Tartar named Temuchin-uge. Yisugei named the boy Temujin because he was born around the time of Temuchin-uge's capture.[5] Of course when he was born is another matter entirely. The best scholarship on the matter argues that Temujin was born in the mid 1160s.[6] Temujin was the first of four sons and a daughter by Yisugei and Ho'elun. By another wife, Yisugei had two additional sons, Bekhter and Belgutei, half-brothers of Temujin. It is not known whether Temujin was older than Bekhter; sources are incomplete on this issue. Yisugei's extended family lived close to the Onon River in modern-day Mongolia, and this was where Temujin learned to fish, hunt, ride a horse, and shoot a bow-and-arrow. He also made friends with people who later played a crucial role in his rise to power, most notably, a boy named Jamuka. Temujin and Jamuka became *andas*, blood brothers, when they exchanged various gifts and made oaths pledging loyalty and friendship to each other.[7] Yisugei took Temujin on some of his travels. On one of these trips, Temujin was betrothed to the daughter of an Onggirat tribesman, Borte. Betrothal for pre-teens was common among Mongols. Borte's father insisted that young Temujin live with the family until the couple was old enough to marry.[8] Life was going well for the young Temujin, but a tragedy struck that not only changed the boy Temujin's life, it also had a dramatic effect upon world history.

Yisugei, Temujin's father, was poisoned on his way back to the family's camp by Tatars whom he had raided, but had forgotten. They remembered him and they poisoned his food while he shared a meal with them. Yisugei managed to struggle back to the family's encampment before dying, and, with his last breath, directed that young Temujin should come back to lead the family. The death of his father fundamentally changed the direction of Temujin's life. Temujin was still a boy, only nine years old by one account,[9] but as the oldest boy, he was in line to take his father's place as chief of the group. Because nine-year old chiefs do not inspire confidence in people, the rest of Yisugei's small tribe abandoned Temujin and his family, and cast them out on the steppe. This heralded a very difficult period, not only for Temujin, but the entire family. Survival was a family effort, and all the children contributed to feeding and clothing the small group.[10] Finding food and shelter on the steppe was difficult, but Temujin also had to worry about Tatar tribesman hunting him down so he would not take his revenge on them when he reached maturity. Thus, the nine-year old boy had to grow up fast—very fast.

Very quickly Temujin asserted his control of the family by murdering his half-brother Bekhter. According to *The Secret History*, Temujin and his full brother Khasar were fishing with their half-brothers Bekhter and Belgutei. Bekhter stole fish caught by Temujin and Kasar, having previously stolen birds shot by the boys. These acts proved to be too much for Temujin and Khasar, especially when Ho'elun refused to punish Bekhter for his transgressions. Temujin and Khasar ambushed Bekhter, shooting him with arrows until he died. Bekhter's last words were to beg for the life of Belgutei, which was spared. Although Bekhter was not her son, Ho'elun was furious with her boys, calling them, "Killers, both of you!"[11] Considering the family's dire straits, the loss of Bekhter's labor and fruits of his hunting and fishing would have had a catastrophic effect on the family—not to mention that two of the boys in the family were now admitted murderers. However, if there was any doubt before as to who was the male head of the family, Temujin's murder of Bekhter settled things definitively.[12] It also demonstrated that Temujin had a deep ruthless streak and an unsettling willingness to do anything to accomplish his goals. People or things that stood in his way were dealt with harshly and decisively. This was not a boy who equivocated. He, like the harsh environment of the steppe, was unforgiving, and rarely gave second chances.

Shortly after the killing of Bekhter, Temujin was captured by the Tayichi'ut tribe and held as a prisoner. He was held in the Tayichi'ut camp in a cage, guarded twenty-four hours a day. Yet somehow he managed to escape—throughout his life he always seemed able to work his way out from dire predicaments. In this instance, Temujin waited until his guard was a youth, overpowered him, ran to a riverbed and stayed in the river until his pursuers gave up the chase. One of his captors, Sorkan-shira of the Suldu tribe, helped Temujin escape the area and eventually entered Temujin's service.[13] This story illustrates many of the traits that made Genghis Khan a great commander—resourcefulness, charisma (in that Sorkan-shira saw the potential greatness in the boy), and an unwillingness to accept defeat no matter how bleak the situation. Although Temujin never received any formal schooling, his classroom was the steppe, his school the hard life of a Mongolian youth trying to survive. His bravery and charisma attracted followers, and the constant raiding and retaliation gave him an in-depth picture of nomadic politics. For much of the time Temujin was forced to operate from a position of weakness, and this forced him to think long-term and develop his strategic genius. He would need all those skills to unite a Mongol people that focused more on each person's individual tribe than being part of a nation. The Mongol people needed someone to drag them collectively to nationhood.

Genghis Khan's most impressive achievement was the uniting of the Mongol people under his rule in 1206 CE. Genghis Khan possessed tremendous strategic and political gifts, which made his military accomplishments possible. He used force when necessary, negotiation when possible, diplomacy and marriage when convenient, as he single-mindedly pursued his goal of the unification of the Mongol people under his control. To do this he had to work within the Mongol cultural and social system, but eventually he had to destroy elements of that system and become a revolutionary. Unfortunately, solid information from this period of Genghis Khan's life is difficult to ascertain. There were many tales of bravery, stealing horses, recovering stolen horses and raiding other tribes, but as the numbers of Temujin's supporters grew, he had to fight several conventional battles before Temujin could claim the name Genghis Khan.[14]

Before Temujin could even consider raising an army, he needed to ensure his survival. At the age of fifteen, he finally took Borte as his bride and assumed his role as the leader of his tribe, taking over for his late father. Even though viewed as a man by many of his tribesman, he was still a boy with man-size responsibilities. Realizing he needed help, Temujin decided to seek out a protector, but on his terms. This did not mean going hat in hand in the hopes that a powerful tribal chief would take him under his wing and nurture him until he finally was ready to lead. He had to prove immediately that he was a leader, and that anyone who took on the role of mentor understood that it was a symbiotic relationship—having the young, charismatic Temujin as an ally was something to be desired. Temujin had gained allies in his youth, escaping from captivity and rescuing stolen horses. He now called upon these allies to help him, and went to the Kerait Chieftain Toghrul as not just a supplicant, but as a leader or noyan.[15]

Toghrul was a logical choice as an ally for Temujin. Temujin's father, Yisugei, had once helped Toghrul regain his throne as the chieftain of the Keraits. While the relationship between Toghrul and Temujin was as between a lord and vassal, Temujin made sure to remind Toghrul of the connection between the Kerait chief and Temujin's father. Of course, Toghrul had enemies as well, including the Merkits, hostile to both Toghrul and Temujin's late father. The Merkits wanted to see just how deep the connection was between Toghrul and Temujin. Around 1184, the Merkits mounted a large raid on Temujin's camp. While Temujin and the bulk of his family escaped, his young wife, Borte, was captured and taken back to the Merkit camp. Just as Yisugei had kidnapped Ho'elun, the Merkits avenged Ho'elun's kidnapping by the abduction of Borte. Instead of acting rashly, Temujin saw an opportunity to use his relationship with Toghrul to force the Merkits to return his wife. Not only did Toghrul agree to help Temujin regain his wife, but his blood brother from youth, Jamuka of the Jadarat tribe, also pledged to aid Temujin. With Toghrul and Jamuka's aid, the Merkits were defeated decisively and Borte was returned to Temujin. Upon her return it was discovered that Borte was pregnant. During her captivity she had been given to a Merkit as a wife. Now that she returned, was the child she carried Temujin's or her captor's? It was a question never satisfactorily answered, although Temujin treated the child, Jochi, as his own. [16] This affair demonstrated an important trait of the future Genghis Khan—the ability to gain acceptance of those outside his family and tribe.

Thus Temujin rose from a fatherless, poverty-stricken boy to one of the most powerful chieftains of the steppe. A crucial element in his rise was the acceptance into the "tribe" of members from other tribes who willingly gave up their own tribal affiliation to throw in their lot with Temujin. The reasons for choosing to abandon one's tribe to follow Temujin undoubtedly varied widely. However, Temujin's charisma, personal bravery, political acumen, and loyalty to those who helped him surely played a role in prompting many of these young men to switch allegiance. Temujin also chose several other young men as blood brothers—such as Jamuka—whose followers then supported Temujin. The loyalty of these initial followers of Temujin were rewarded by becoming generals in their own right, or being named members of Genghis Khan's Imperial Guard. In addition to his many other gifts, Temujin proved to be a good judge of talent and character. As he built his army, the leadership capabilities of its officer corps were far and away superior to those of any opponent.[17] That core of men surrounding Temujin would soon be sorely tested by one of their own—Jamuka.

For a year or so after the Merkit raid, Jamuka and Temujin remained on good terms, but it was not to last. Jamuka was a charismatic leader in his own right, who came from a more prestigious tribe. It was only a matter of time until the two old friends came to blows. Jamuka's tribe was a tribe of horse-breeders, while Temujin came from sheep breeders. The horse breeders were higher on the steppe social hierarchy than the sheep breeders, and there was animosity between the two groups. Although the two boys were childhood friends, there was not enough room on the steppe to contain both men's ambitions. Conflict between the two was inevitable. Temujin's policy of treating outsiders as members of his tribe paid big dividends, as many dispossessed people came to him seeking shelter and protection, so his tribe grew accordingly. Jamuka was already head of one of the most powerful tribes on the steppes, the Jadarat, and he took a traditional view of not easily accepting members of other tribes.[18] Temujin also understood the value of effective propaganda, and he made good use of it in his struggle with Jamuka. The shaman Teb-Tenegri prophesied that god came to him and said, "I have given the whole surface of the earth to Temuchin and his sons."[19] Superstition ran rife among the Mongol tribes, and Temujin quickly grasped the potential of this bit of propaganda, and used it to attract more followers. He needed to use all of his non-violent means to even the battlefield against Jamuka, probably the most talented opponent Temujin ever faced.[20]

Temujin first moved against Jamuka politically, calling a *quriltai* (election council) to name a leader of all the Mongol tribes. Although he was not nearly the most powerful of the tribal chieftains, Temujin was well known on the steppe. Temujin decided to pit the various tribes against each other, positioning himself as a compromise candidate for the Khanship. Several of the more prominent tribal chieftains were led to believe that Temujin could be controlled by them. Thus, even though the *quriltai* did not include all the Mongol tribes, Temujin was elected the Great Khan and given the name Genghis Khan. The elevation of Genghis Khan to the leadership of all the Mongols—even though the title was mainly in name only, still gave him a powerful propaganda tool in pursuit of his goal of uniting all the Mongols under his rule. This new title was sure to antagonize Jamuka, who still dreamed of uniting the Mongols under his own leadership.[21]

The struggle between Genghis Khan and Jamuka for leadership of all the Mongol tribes reached its climax in 1206 with Jamuka's defeat and execution. Jamuka initiated hostilities by raising an army from the Mongol tribes that were loyal to him and his tribe. The historical record is not clear in how many battles were fought, but it seems that Jamuka more than held his own against Genghis Khan. They would have fought using the same kinds of armies and tactics, but the difference appears to have been one of philosophy. Where Genghis Khan welcomed defeated former enemies into his ranks or tribe, Jamuka refused to do so. Thus, even when he was defeated on the battlefield, as long as Genghis Khan survived, he could rebuild his power base because of his open attitude toward members of other tribes, his fair treatment of them, and his rewarding of merit. Jamuka, who still held traditional views of who could be a tribal member, could not afford a defeat because of the limitations inherent in his concept of the tribe. Genghis Khan was trying to create a nation in the modern sense, where membership was open and not based solely on blood ties. The administration of this nation would come later, but the idea of a Mongol nation came from Genghis Khan—which is why Mongolians today look at him as the founder of the modern Mongol nation.

The struggle between Jamuka and Genghis Khan lasted well over a decade before Genghis Khan was victorious. Jamuka, in one last attempt to defeat Genghis Khan, enlisted the powerful Naiman tribe—a non-Mongol tribe which traditionally fought against the Mongols—to help him recover his position. Genghis Khan soundly defeated the Naimans and destroyed them as a tribe, but incorporated into his tribe those defeated elements willing to swear loyalty to him.[22] With Genghis Khan's already well-established reputation for ferocity toward enemies, five of Jamuka's vassals betrayed him and brought him as a captive to Genghis Khan hoping for a reward. Furious at Jamuka's vassals' treachery, he reportedly had the men beheaded in Jamuka's presence. Genghis Khan wanted his boyhood companion to once again be his friend, but Jamuka realized that as long as he was alive, he constituted threat to Genghis Khan. Recognizing the inevitable, Jamuka requested that his execution not involve the spilling of blood, a request which Genghis honored.[23] With Jamuka's death Genghis Khan was the unquestioned ruler of the united Mongol people. To ensure Mongol hegemony over the steppe, Genghis then embarked upon a vigorous program of cultural and social reform.

Genghis Khan had witnessed firsthand the evils that resulted from the ruinous cycle of raiding and revenge that characterized the relations among various Mongol groups. Accordingly, he instituted measures to discourage such practices. He decreed that no Mongol could own another Mongol as a slave. The practice of kidnapping wives from other tribes, seen sometimes as necessary because of prohibitions of marrying within one's own tribe, was now punishable by death. Stealing livestock and horses also elicited the death penalty.[24] Thus, over five centuries before English philosopher John Locke discussed the concept of natural rights, Genghis Khan moved to ensure that one of those natural rights, the right to property, was guaranteed to the Mongol people. These rights were not declared universal, as Locke's were, but for Mongols only. Still, the inclusive nature of Genghis Khan's idea of who constituted a Mongol was far more radical than contemporary governments in Asia and Europe.[25] Much of the chaos of Genghis Khan's youth was caused by the kidnapping of women for wives. Not only was his own mother kidnapped by his father, but his first wife was also kidnapped. Putting a stop to this practice was obviously a priority of the Great Khan. If his citizens were not pre-occupied with the cycle of raiding and counter-raiding, they had to be kept busy focusing their energies elsewhere. Genghis Khan had an idea of how to keep the men who formed the Mongol nation busy—he turned his war machine against the sedentary cultures of China and Central Asia.

The Mongol army that Genghis Khan led out of Mongolia after 1206 proved to be the best army of its time. No other force on the planet matched the Mongols in discipline, organization, planning, and logistics. While the Mongols initially lacked skill in reducing fortified cities, they quickly adapted and built a siege train that rivaled anything the Romans possessed. Genghis Khan used the basic steppe organization of the decimal system to build his army. A unit of ten men was an *arban,* a unit of 100 men was called a *jaghun,* a unit of 1,000 men was a *minqan*, and a unit of 10,000 men was called a *tumen.* The tumen is analogous to a modern-day corps, even though it was smaller and could operate independently. It performed the basic functions of a corps, and several tumen together formed a Mongol field army, or a *horde.*[26] To supply the tumens with men, horses, and foodstuffs, Genghis Khan expanded his process of breaking up tribes and divided the entire Mongol nation into *aurugs.* Each aurug was responsible for a set number of men, horses, and foodstuffs prior to a campaign. The entire Mongol administrative structure—what little there was in 1206—was tasked with supplying the war effort.[27] In order to further cement his control over the Mongol nation, and ensure a minimum level of training for officers, Genghis Khan established the *keshik.*

The *keshik* originally served as Genghis Khan's bodyguard, composed of the most trusted and skilled followers from his earliest days as a leader of men. Initially a few hundred men, it grew to 10,000 men by 1206.

The institution of the *keshik* was founded on Chinggis Khan's four kulu'ud or heroes, who served amongst its commanders: Boroghul, Bo'orchu, Muqali, and Chila'un. It originally consisted of 80 *kebte'ul* or night guards and 70 turqa'ut or day guards, with an additional *minqan* that escorted Chinggis Khan into battle.[28]

There was evidence that at its height, the *keshik* not only guarded Genghis Khan, but it also acted as a general staff-like entity, doing much of the operational planning for campaigns. It also functioned as an officer-training school. The sons of unit commanders (*noyad*) were put forth by their fathers for service in the *keshik*. It was open to commoners as well as nobles, and promotion was generally by merit. Members of the *keshik* were sent to serve as staff officers for higher-ranking officers. They learned how the army functioned, moved, and was supplied, and how it obtained and processed intelligence, among other things.[29] In short, these institutions gave the Mongol military a basic, but surprisingly modern, military structure.[30] Members of the *keshik* could give orders to any Mongol officer who commanded a jaghun (1,000 men), and it was considered a great honor to be accepted to the *keshik*.[31] It was also a key to the Mongols' military success. In most every battle the Mongols fought against non-steppe opponents, Mongol enemies had superior numbers, weaponry, technology and equipment—but woefully inadequate organization and discipline. The Mongols won the bulk of their battles with superior planning, training, execution and discipline. Part of that discipline came from another, political, function of the *keshik*.

By his destruction of the tribal structure for the Mongol military, Genghis Khan made the Mongol army a more egalitarian force. There were many who resented the loss of privilege and to ensure Genghis Khan's hold on power, the boys who served in the *keshik* were basically hostages. They were well treated, but there was always the chance that an ambitious field officer might want to overthrow Genghis Khan and take the throne for himself. That possibility was made more remote when a son was close to the Emperor. The *keshik* also saw up close how the system of promotion by merit worked and were thoroughly indoctrinated with Genghis Khan's ideas, so that when these boys came of age and assumed their own commands, they generally understood and supported Genghis Khan's radical re-structuring of Mongol society through the Mongol army. So the dual purpose of the *keshik* proved to be absolutely crucial to the establishment of Genghis Khan's conquests and sustainment of the same, as well as to the absolute loyalty of the army.[32] But the *keshik* was only part of the army; it did not form the rank-and-file.

The mere act of survival on the harsh steppe was the chief school for the vast majority of the Mongol forces. Learning to hunt in an area where prey cannot be cornered required a tremendous amount of skill with the bow and arrow, and cooperation among hunters to corral and kill prey. Unfortunately, no Mongol training manual has survived—and perhaps none was ever written. Mongol boys would have learned to shoot the legendary Mongol composite bow at a young age, often learning on a bow with a one-hundred pound pull that they constructed themselves. While many steppe tribes used the bow, generally a bow similar to the Mongol weapon, the Mongols were famed above all others for their archery skills. They learned to shoot small game on the ground, and even birds, because one had to be skilled with the bow to survive on the steppe. A favorite steppe hunting tactic, practiced by the Mongols and others, was the *nerge.* A large number of hunters formed a ring, sometimes several miles in diameter, and then slowly converged, making sure to keep the game within the ring. Eventually the ring would be small enough that the killing could start. To perform the *nerge* required good communication, control, discipline, patience, and teamwork—all valuable military traits.[33]

The Mongol soldier's ability to endure hardship was legendary. Large Mongol forces routinely operated in desert and steppe areas in which armies from sedentary cultures had extreme difficulty surviving, much less moving through. The environment prepared Mongol men and boys for hard campaigning. The steppe climate had wildly fluctuating temperatures, which gave the Mongols an advantage over more sedentary opponents unused to such harsh conditions. The Chinese and Persians were not migratory, and thus did not move sheep and horses over large expanses, so were unfamiliar with how to feed large numbers of animals on the move in dry conditions. The Mongols used their horse for just about everything. The Mongol soldier ate a yogurt made of horse milk. *Kumiss,* or fermented mare's milk, was the national drink, and if desperate, he could drink the horse's blood.[34] Thus, given their small logistical "footprint," the Mongols traveled light and moved faster than any other armies before the Industrial Revolution. But all this does not really differentiate the Mongols from any other steppe force, such as the Huns or Avars. What made the Mongols different—and far more dangerous—was their discipline.

Mongol troops were quite simply the best disciplined troops in the world during the lifetime of Genghis Khan. Where other steppe armies disintegrated when opportunities for rape and plunder presented themselves, the Mongols retained discipline and unit cohesion. This was largely due to Genghis Khan's ideals and ferocious punishments for breaches of discipline. On the one hand, potentially great riches and advancement were there for the taking for the talented young trooper. But plundering was not the way to get ahead in the Mongol army. Even when requisitioning food, Mongols forces could be murderous, but still maintained their discipline. Because of Mongol motivation and discipline, Mongol *tumens* operated as army corps on a widely dispersed front, until enemy contact was made, then the *tumens* would concentrate on the eve of a battle. This gave the Mongols a tremendous flexibility that their opponents often did not have.[35] Discipline was strict, but fair. Even Mongol princes, the sons and grandsons of Genghis Khan, had to obey army commanders. The punishment for disobedience of orders was often death. Yet it took more than just fear to make the Mongols the best soldiery of their day, they were motivated by their loyalty to Genghis Khan, and their realization that even if they could not attain royalty, they could still advance very high in the military command structure because of Genghis Khan's egalitarian impulses.[36] Theoretically, every male Mongol from around sixteen years of age until sixty was eligible for military service. In practice, that number was considerably smaller as enlisting every male Mongol would have had a devastating impact on Mongol society. A more reasonable estimate was that one male Mongol per family served in the military.[37] As a steppe people, the Mongols had no industrial base with which to make swords, armor or anything forged. Mongols made their own bows and arrows, but scavenged battlefields for more sophisticated armor.[38]

The Mongol composite bow was quite possibly the best individual hand-held weapon ever to emerge in the pre-gunpowder era. The Mongol bow was made of horn and animal sinew glued together on a wooden frame, using fish glue, and then lacquered it once the glue had set.[39] When unstrung, the bow looked like an oval, but the composite frame gave it remarkable strength. Learning to use the bow proficiently took years, but Mongol children—both boys and girls—practiced archery from early childhood and by the time they were teenagers were usually adept in its use.[40] The bow was actually far superior to early gunpowder weapons in terms of rate of fire, accuracy, and expense. The problem was that it took years of use to become proficient in the weapon. The Mongol composite bow's main competitor for the best individual weapon in the pre-gunpowder era was the English or Welsh longbow. They had similar capabilities, but the longbow was a fearsome weapon in its own right. The longbow was first used in Wales, and English King Edward I (ruled 1272-1307) brought it back to England after campaigning in Wales. The longbow was made from a single piece of wood, and had an extreme range of 400 yards, and an effective range of 250 yards. Like the Mongol bow, it took years to master, but in the hands of an expert bowman it too could fire much faster than a crossbow or even a primitive musket, when the latter arrived on the scene later. The longbow could penetrate armor at around 100 to 150 yards.[41] It had one significant drawback: It could not be fired from horseback. In contrast, the Mongol bow had a maximum range of 500 yards and was effective at close to 300 yards. Mongol soldiers were extremely skilled at its use, and it too could penetrate armor at around 100 yards. Due to the Mongols' method of firing, they could fire even faster and, likely, more accurately than their English counterparts. Mongol archers used a thumb ring to pull back the bowstring. English archers used three-fingers, the European custom. By using the thumb ring, Mongol archers could fire faster and more accurately with a true release of just the thumb, while the English longbowman had to coordinate the release of all three fingers simultaneously; otherwise it would negatively affect the shot. Like the English, the Mongols used a variety of arrowheads on the battlefield. Some arrowheads were specifically designed to pierce armor, others to whistle or have matches on them for signal purposes. Some arrowheads were designed specifically to stun an attacker.

Finally, there was the Mongol bow's ability to be fired from horseback. This required not only great skill with the bow, but great skill with the horse also. This combination of maneuverability and firepower gave the Mongols a significant edge on the battlefield. The composite bow was not a new weapon, but Genghis Khan was the first steppe warrior to use it in a coherent combined arms doctrine to make it reach its full potential.[42] That doctrine not only made the most of the mounted archer, it made tremendous use of the extra mobility provided by the Mongols familiarity with the horse.

For the average Mongol, the horse was their means of mobility. The most common horse on the Mongolian steppe was the Wild Mongolian horse, or *Przewalski* horse. The Wild Mongolian horse was often smaller than its Chinese, Persian, or Arabic counterparts. It averaged between "12 and 14 hands" tall, which is small for a horse.[43] Although smaller and not as strong as other horses, the one advantage the Wild Mongolian horse had over its counterparts was its endurance. Mongol horses had legendary stamina, in large part due to the training Mongols put their horses through. Zhao Hong, a Song (Chinese) emissary had the following to say about Mongol horse training:

When their horses are only one or two years old they ride them harshly in the steppe and train them. They then maintain them for three years and after that mount and ride them again. Thus they train them early and for that reason they do not kick or bite. Thousands and hundreds form herds but they are silent and are without neighing and calling. When they dismount they do not rein them in and tether them, but they do not stray. Their temperament is very good.[44]

Horses allowed Mongols to manage their herds, made it possible for them to move great distances across the steppe, gave them milk for yogurt, and even provided fermented mare's milk as an alcoholic beverage. As such, horses were highly valued in Mongol society. Mongol children were in constant contact with horses from the time they could walk. Because Mongol training of horses made them docile, they could be trusted with small children. Riding became second nature to every Mongol boy and girl. Such had to be the case, given that the early Mongol forces were essentially all-cavalry armies.[45]

The Mongols took the care and maintenance of their horses very seriously. Genghis Khan specifically laid out how horses were to be treated, when they could be led with a bit in their mouth, and so on. Keeping Mongol horseflesh in prime condition was a top military priority. Each Mongol cavalryman kept between three and five horses with him on campaign.[46] There were even rules for when a horse could be killed. A horse ridden into battle could not be killed for food. If a horse survived a battle but could no longer be ridden in battle, it was put out to pasture. When a Mongol died, his horse was also killed and buried with him so he could ride the horse in the afterlife. The Mongols also valued horses of different colors. The individual units of the *keshik* rode different colored horses to differentiate themselves. White horses were reserved for royalty and were considered sacred.[47] Mongol horses were a key element in Mongol society and the Mongol military. The mobility that horses gave the Mongols played a key role in the development of Mongol strategy, tactics, and logistics.

Mongol armies traveled light, which allowed them to be fast when necessary. The average Mongol cavalry trooper did not carry much on his person, and what he did carry varied by season. Dried meat was a common source of food, as was *kumiss* (fermented mare's milk) and lots of dried mare's milk when in season. The bulk of the average Mongol trooper's diet consisted of dairy products, which were high in protein. Each *arban* carried a primitive mobile mess kitchen, and the majority of non-dairy foods consumed by the Mongols were soups or stews. Soup was easy to make and relatively light to carry. The combination of soup or stew, dairy products, and food scavenged from enemy populations or hunting allowed the Mongol trooper to maintain the necessary 3,600 calories per day necessary for strenuous military activity. Use of the *nerge* for hunting on campaign not only helped procure food, it gave the troopers field training.[48] The procurement of weapons also figured prominently in Mongol campaigns.

In the early period of Ghenghis Khan's reign, most Mongol troopers went into battle with little more than the Mongol composite bow. As time passed, the Mongols stripped enemy dead of their possessions, and this netted them swords, armor, lances and other forged weapons. However, Genghis Khan decided that it was important for the Mongols to start manufacturing weapons of their own when his army changed from an all light-cavalry force to a combined force of horse archers and lancers, and then later incorporated elements from sedentary societies, such as infantry.[49] The Mongols also learned to appreciate the skills of Chinese and later Persian and Arab engineers. Engineers who defected to the Mongols were given large rewards, and when the Mongols captured a city, before the plunder and slaughter started, the Mongols divided up the prisoners into various categories. Artisans and engineers were again highly valued, and were sent to Karakorum to serve the Great Khan. They too, despite having fought against the Mongols, could become wealthy and influential because of their skills.[50] The more the Mongols fought, the more they won, the more adaptable and lethal they became. Initially, walled cities frustrated the Mongols to no end. By capturing and luring engineers to serve with the Mongols, eventually fortified cities proved to be no match for the Mongol forces. The Chinese, Persians, Arabs and Europeans eventually learned this the hard way.

If there was one word to characterize Mongol tactics and procedures, it would be "adaptable." The Mongols, especially in the early days of Genghis Khan's reign, were always on the offensive. Even if the goal of an operation was defensive, the Mongols assumed the tactical offensive. Considering the defensive weakness of an all-cavalry force, this was understandable. Thanks to their superior mobility and greater articulation, the Mongols generally assigned one force to fix the enemy in position and while others struck him in the flanks. Mongol hordes usually attacked in a five-line formation, with the first three ranks consisting of shock cavalry, usually armed with a lance, and the other two lines as missile or light cavalry, armed with the Mongol bow. Clouds of light cavalry skirmishers would be in front of and on both sides of the formation to ensure that it would not be outflanked and also to harass the enemy with a constant stream of arrows. When a Mongol *tumen* came into contact with the enemy main body, it sent word to nearby *tumens* and then began an organized retreat as reinforcements converged. Once the Mongol force concentrated for a battle, it had a bewildering variety of tactics and stratagems available to it.[51]

The Mongols developed their battlefield tactics to fit the type of units that made up the bulk of the Mongol army—horse archers. The Mongols' superior mobility allowed them to outmaneuver their foes. They often used the classic steppe tactic of the feigned retreat. They would entice the enemy into a pursuit, and when the foe was strung out, tired and disorganized, turn on the enemy force and annihilate it. Although the term "horde" often connotates a massive disorganized group, a Mongol *horde* was anything but disordered. Some of the tactics the Mongols used were the arrow storm and rolling barrage. When using an arrow storm on an enemy formation, Mongols fired at long range, not picking out a specific person for a target, but firing at a particular unit. This arrow storm had the effect of a preparatory artillery bombardment. It disrupted and demoralized an enemy force, and attrited it as well, softening it up for the heavy cavalry charge that usually followed. The Mongol rolling barrage was just what it sounds like—a moving arrow storm. It would be used preparatory to a heavy cavalry assault, or as a means of covering a retreat. Thanks to their superior discipline and unit cohesion, the Mongols had the ability to concentrate an arrow storm in a particular place, or on a specific enemy unit. This even extended to siege operations, where a specific section of wall was chosen to receive the concentrated fire of the besieging forces. The Mongols also used a tactic that would later be called by Europeans the "caracole." It involved Mongol light cavalry moving up to enemy lines, shooting their arrows, and then riding back to the protection of their own lines. Since Mongol archers generally carried sixty arrows per man into battle, the number of arrows that could be fired at an enemy was considerable. To fight the Mongols was to face an enemy more disciplined, more mobile, and packing more firepower. Another favored tactic was the double-envelopment, an example of using the *nerge* to fight an enemy army rather than hunt prey. With the Mongols' superior mobility and firepower, they usually seized the initiative. Because of the extended nature of the Mongol force, the enemy rarely had good intelligence on the size of the force facing him. Because of the bewildering nature of Mongol attacks, and attacks that seemed to come from all directions, the natural instinct of an enemy was to pause and try to decipher the situation facing him. That pause often proved deadly, as the Mongols often had already commenced encircling movements to crush the enemy force. [52]

The Mongols even developed a procedure for taking strongly fortified cities by siege. If at all possible, the Mongols tried to lure the enemy force out into the open, annihilate it and pursue closely so that the city might be entered and taken without a siege.[53] If a siege was unavoidable, the Mongols waited until the final stages of the campaign to begin a siege. Any cities or towns in the region that could aid or threaten the Mongols' lines of communication were taken first. Then, the surrounding countryside was scoured for civilians to perform manual labor as the Mongols' engineer corps built a wall of circumvallation around the besieged city, trapping not only the garrison but the city's inhabitants inside as well. The siege train was brought up and a weak point ascertained in the defenses, whereupon the bombardment of the city began. The city was kept under constant attack by not only Mongol catapults, but by individual archers who swept the city walls to keep the defenders under a constant fire. Catapults fired combustible ammunition into the city to cause fires and further weaken the defenders' resolve. When it appeared a breach was imminent, the Mongols herded together the prisoners taken from the outlying areas, and forced them either to fill up the defensive moat, or act as human shields for the Mongol troopers as they neared the city's walls, forcing the inhabitants to kill their own people to get to the attackers. The Mongols also used rams and dug tunnels to undermine the fortifications. Once a breach was made, the assault was swift and brutal.[54] However, the Mongols made good use of intelligence and psychological warfare to get cities to surrender to them without a siege or assault.

Genghis Khan understood the power of propaganda and psychology. The Mongols, and specifically Genghis himself, had a reputation for bloodlust. While the numbers of people killed by the Mongols was certainly significant, Genghis Khan did not order killings for entertainment purposes. There was a method to his madness—Genghis Khan used terror as a tool. It certainly was a blunt instrument, and he was not afraid to use it. Knowing what the Mongols were capable of made conquered areas much less likely to rebel, and it made cities that were considering putting up a strong resistance think twice. If a city did surrender, Genghis Khan treated that city leniently—knowing that while news of a wholesale massacre spread quickly, news of Mongol clemency also spread rapidly. The choice before a city targeted by the Mongols was clear: resistance and annihilation or surrender and survival. Genghis Khan was also a firm believer in deception, and good intelligence. He had an extensive spy networks that provided an accurate gauge of his enemy's strength and dispositions. The Mongols used merchants as spies, and employed the *yam* (the Mongol empire's Pony Express) to ensure a steady flow of information. Little wonder then that Genghis Khan and his successors guaranteed the protection of merchants and made sure the trade routes stayed open. It was safer to travel the Silk Road in the time of the *Pax Mongolica* than it is today. "Information dominance" was always a crucial element in Genghis Khan's campaigns. Not only did the Mongols gather accurate intelligence on a potential enemy, a careful misinformation campaign kept the enemy guessing as to the Great Khan's intentions and resources. Mongol spies routinely—again in the form of merchants—planted ridiculous numbers of the Mongol forces. On a campaign, it was common for each soldier to have a "dummy" he placed on a spare horse to mislead an opponent about the size of the Mongol force. Likewise, Genghis Khan often had his men light more campfires than were necessary, again to fool an enemy regarding the size of the Mongol force. Mongol scouts were sent out in advance of a field army to set prairie fires to obscure Mongol movements.[55] To demonstrate how well Genghis Khan succeeded, in much of the world he was regarded as a bloodthirsty murderer, the epitome of barbarism. Even the word "horde" connotes a disorganized mass of men. The peoples defeated by the Mongols made up tales of the Mongols as masses of people spilling out of Inner Asia and overrunning everything in their path. Nothing could be further from the truth, as Genghis Khan's armies were well disciplined, informed, supplied and often outnumbered. That enduring misperception alone may be the greatest legacy of Genghis Khan's amazingly successful misinformation campaigns.

The first non-steppe empire to feel Genghis Khan's wrath was the Jin Dynasty of northern China. The Jin had, like most Chinese dynasties, played the steppe tribes off each other to keep them from raiding Chinese territory. Spies and defectors painted the Jin Dynasty as dangerously weak, thus a combination of Jin weakness and riches proved to be too much for Genghis Khan to resist. When a new Jin emperor demanded Genghis Khan's fealty, the great Khan reportedly spat on the ground and walked away from the Jin representatives. Such an insult meant war. Although the Mongol forces were steadily improving, defeating the Jin was no small task. The Jin military reportedly boasted 120,000 horse archers and 500,000 infantry, while Genghis Khan mustered merely 75,000 men, all cavalry. As often proved to be the case, Genghis Khan was not cowed by long odds. He sent his *tumens* south in the late spring of 1211 and immediately started taking the outlying towns of the Jin Empire. As Genghis Khan's forces pressed deeper into Jin territory, several Jin commanders defected to the

Mongols' side. The new Jin emperor sent his best general to salvage the situation along the frontier. He, in turn decided to send a trusted negotiator to Genghis Khan to broker a truce between the two sides. The negotiator promptly defected and joined the Mongol army. Genghis Khan accurately interpreted the intelligence about widespread unrest of the peoples under Jin control. After winning several stunning victories and killing literally hundreds of thousands of Jin soldiers, the Mongol hordes stood outside of Zhongdu (modern-day Peking). The long campaign, the extended lines of supply and communication, not to mention fierce Jin resistance as the Mongols closed around the capital, left Genghis Khan's forces depleted and exhausted. Instead of insisting on the annihilation of the Jin, Genghis Khan accepted a peace treaty with the Jin in 1215. Still, the cost was steep: The Jin emperor had to give one of his daughters to Genghis Khan as a wife, tons of gold and silk, 500 male and female slaves, and 3,000 horses—not to mention all the land north of the Yangtze River. Lastly, Zhongdu, the Jin capital, was opened for rape and pillage for a month to the Mongol forces. The Jin Emperor also recognized Genghis Khan as his overlord.[56] Upon his return to Mongolia, Genghis Khan faced several threats to the Mongol nation. His response demonstrated that the Mongols could execute operational planning on a vast scale.

Several tribal groups on the Mongols' western border were in revolt. Additionally, the Jin soon attempted to reverse the verdict from the first Mongol-Jin War. Jin Emperor Xuanzong made peace overtures to his former enemies, the Sung Dynasty to the south. He moved the Jin capital from Zhongdu to Nanjing (Kaifeng)—further south and away from the Mongol menace. Genghis Khan felt sufficiently threatened by developments back in Mongolia to remain there and allow one of his generals, Mukali, to press the campaign against the Jin. Mukali was given a mandate to continue the destruction of the Jin, while Genghis Khan's son Jochi launched a campaign against the forest peoples on the Mongols' western border.[57] That these campaigns were conducted successfully without Genghis Khan's presence on the battlefield speaks volumes about the quality of commanders coming out of the *keshik*. Mongol armies did not suffer from any significant drop in performance and Genghis Khan solidified his control of the Mongol throne. Genghis Khan also benefitted from the defection and capture of many Chinese administrators and engineers, who not only helped improve the administration of conquered territories, but the engineers built the fearsome siege train that later enabled the Mongols to crack fortified cities time and time again. The Mongol war machine was coming into its own, and faced an even more formidable challenge than the Jin.

To the west of the Mongols lay the Khwarazmian Empire, another significant challenge for Genghis Khan. After destroying the Kara Khitai Empire, the region between the growing Mongol Empire and Sultan Muhammad's Khwarazmian Empire, the horde commander, Jochi, Genghis Khan's eldest son, went to great pains to let Sultan Muhammad know that the Mongols did not seek conflict. In fact Genghis Khan wished to open trade with the Khwarazmian Empire. Of the items the Mongols wished to procure, the Khwarazmian Empire produced excellent steel for swords and armor which the Mongols still did not have the ability to produce on their own,.[58] Sultan Muhammad, or Khwarazm-shah, was suspicious of Genghis Khan's motives. In 1218 Genghis Khan sent a caravan of 450 merchants to the Khwarazmian Empire's frontier city of Utrar (Otrar). The governor of the city feared that the merchants were spies—and considering how the Mongols used merchants as spies, the fears were reasonable. The governor rashly executed the entire caravan. Furious, Genghis Khan sent three ambassadors to demand an apology and punishment for the governor of Utrar. The three Mongol ambassadors were mistreated; one was killed outright while the other two had their beards shaved off. This provocation was too much for Genghis Khan and took the mistreatment of his ambassadors as a declaration of war. If the Sultan Muhammad wanted war, Genghis Khan would give him war.[59]

The campaign against Sultan Muhammad was Genghis Khan's masterpiece. It included the destruction of an empire, the death of Sultan Muhammad, and carnage on an almost unimaginable scale. The Khwarazmian Empire was centered on modern-day Iran, but stretched east into Afghanistan and north into Turkmenistan, Kazakhstan, and Russia. This was the Islamic heart of central Asia, and it was about to suffer an almost unimaginable disaster. Sultan Muhammad's empire was restless on the eve of the Mongol invasion. There was widespread dissatisfaction with the Khwarazm-shah's rule, and the Sultan managed to offend the Caliph in Baghdad, thus alienating an important segment of his population. Because of the offense, declaring a jihad, or holy war, against the infidel Mongols was no longer an option.[60] Thanks to his spy network, Genghis Khan had an accurate picture of the Khwarazmian Empire on the eve of the conflict. Sultan Muhammad made a fatal mistake: not trusting his army to fight in the open against the Mongols, and believing them to still be unable to take walled cities, Khwarazm-shah ordered the bulk of his army dispersed around the empire, garrisoning and fortifying cities to prepare them for sieges. Ceding an aggressive commander like Genghis Khan the initiative was a catastrophic mistake; throwing away a large numerical superiority proved to be an even more calamitous decision. Not all of the Sultan's advisors agreed with the decision to distribute the troops. The Khwarazm-shah's son, Jalal ad-Din, forcefully argued that the armies should be pulled out of the cities, and the Mongols met in the western portion of the empire when they were at the end of long supply and communications lines. In the end, he was overruled by his father.[61]

The Mongol armies descended on the Khwarazmian Empire like a thunderbolt. Realizing that Sultan Muhammad's plan was to rely on the walled cities, Genghis Khan divided his army of roughly 250,000 into three separate wings. The largest wing remained under his personal control and made for Bukhara. Another wing, under Genghis Khan's sons, Ogedei and Chagatai, besieged the city of Utrar, while the final wing under Jochi attacked the city of Khojend. Genghis Khan's attack on Bukara was a masterpiece as the Mongol *tumens* crossed a supposedly impassable desert and captured Bukara with ease. This flabbergasted Sultan Muhammad, because Bukara was south and west of the capital, Samarkand. How on earth could the Mongols have gotten *behind* his forces already? It seemed as if the Mongols were attacking everywhere at once. Genghis moved his horde to Samarkand, where he was joined by Ogedei and Chagatai after their successful conclusion of the siege of Utrar. The miscreant governor who abused the Khan's ambassadors paid for his crimes—he had molten gold poured down his throat as his means of execution.[62] Chaos and fear gripped the Khwarazmian Empire and Genghis Khan exploited it to sow further confusion and terror.

One of Sultan Muhammad's advisors defected to Genghis Khan and informed him of tensions within the ruling family. Genghis Khan decided to forge letters written by various leaders, specifically playing on the tensions between the Sultan and his mother. The letters were allowed to fall into the Sultan's hands and the response was near panic, as the letters implied that large numbers of his troops were deserting because of his ill treatment of his mother. The ruse worked spectacularly and much of the organized resistance to the Mongols collapsed. As field armies further dispersed, Sultan Muhammad fled with a group of hand-picked troops, leaving Samarkand and its 60,000-man garrison to its fate. The leading religious figure in Samarkand, Sheikh al-Islam feared what would happen if the Mongols stormed the city. He too had heard the rumors and agreed to surrender the city on March 17, 1220. The Shaykh managed to protect 50,000 people of Samarkand's original 500,000, but the bloodbath was extensive. The city's citadel continued to hold out, and the Mongols wanted to make an example of Samarkand. The fortifications were destroyed, the population was divided into groups of tens and hundreds, and the survey of the population began, along with the looting of the city. Genghis Khan added 30,000 skilled workers to the list of captives to be sent to Mongolia. Many more were to be used as fodder in further attacks upon fortified cities, and many, many more were simply executed.[63] Time and time again, the leaders of the Khwarazmian troops fled, leaving their men to an awful fate. Was it any wonder that resistance to the Mongols was ineffective given such poor leadership? In contrast, Genghis Khan continued his pursuit of the routed Khwarazmian forces, who in addition to trying to ensure their own escape, had to deal with crowds of terror-stricken refugees also fleeing the Mongols. The Sultan's own escort was whittled down by Mongol attacks or just plain desertion. The relentless Mongol pursuit followed the Sultan to an island off the coast of the Caspian Sea, where in December 1220 he died of natural causes.[64] Although the Sultan was dead, the war continued.

Sultan Muhammad's son, Jalal ad-Din, refused to surrender. He raised another army and tried to defeat the Mongols. Where fear and paranoia consumed his father, Jalal ad-Din was determined to fight the invaders. Jalal ad-Din raised a large army in what is now modern-day Afghanistan and met the Mongols head on. He defeated a Mongol force of three *tumens* under the command of Genghis Khan's adopted son Shigi-khutukhu. This defeat caught the full attention of Genghis Khan, who hurried into Afghanistan in full pursuit of Jalal ad-Din with five *tumens*, and the remnants of Shigi-khutukhu's force. He caught up with Jalal ad-Din and soundly defeated him at the Battle of the Indus, destroying his army. Jalal ad-Din escaped capture by jumping his horse off a cliff in plain view of Genghis Khan, who expressed his grudging respect for Jalal ad-Din. Jalal ad-Din eventually made his way to India and despite a vigorous pursuit by the Mongols, was never captured. While Jalal ad-Din represented the last organized resistance of the Khwarazmian Empire, the rest of the empire felt the full weight of the Mongol fury.[65]

The number of those killed by the Mongols in the destruction of the Khwarazmian Empire is in dispute; what is not in dispute is that it was catastrophic. David Morgan's analysis is worth discussing here. Morgan states:

Contemporary historians were unanimous when they wrote about the horrors that accompanied the Mongol invasion of Khwarazm-shah's empire…the figures that these writers quote for the numbers of people massacred are beyond belief. Sayfi tells us that 1,600,000 were killed in the sack of Harat [Heart], and 1,747,000 at Nishapur. Juzjani puts the Harat death toll even higher, at 2,400,000.[66]

While those numbers are astounding, Morgan then continues to say that they cannot be taken literally. The cities could not have sustained populations that great, even considering it was wartime and they were most likely flooded with refugees seeking shelter. What can be examined is the Mongols' effect on Persian agriculture and the landscape. Persians relied on the *qanat*, a system of underground irrigation channels, to ensure that farms received water. If the farms did not have water, the desert would re-take the land. The *qanat* requires extensive maintenance to continue bringing water to the cities and farmland surrounding them. The Mongol invasion either wrecked the *qanat* or so depleted the population that it could no longer be maintained adequately, and much of that area reverted back to desert. The cities of the region that survived were not nearly as large as they had been before the invasion. Even today, much of that land is still desert.[67] After the destruction of the Khwarazmian Empire, Genghis Khan returned to Mongolia.

In the summer of 1226 CE, Genghis Khan embarked on what would be his last military campaign, a war against the Tangut Empire of China. The Mongols eventually bested the Tanguts, but Genghis Khan died during the campaign in August 1227. There are many stories of the Great Khan's death, but none is definitive, and even the Great Khan's gravesite is not known—other than that it is somewhere in modern-day Mongolia—as the Mongols went to great lengths to make sure his resting place remained undisturbed.[68]

Genghis Khan has to be considered one of the greatest commanders in human history. He built an army, a government, a nation, gave the Mongol nation a written language, a legal system and raised a relatively insignificant steppe tribe into a major world power. To do just one of those things would have made Genghis Khan a noteworthy individual in human history. To do all of them speaks volumes about his brilliance and charisma. He was literally centuries ahead of his enemies in terms of discipline, organizational structure, psychological warfare, siege warfare—and the list goes on and on. He combined brilliance with ruthlessness and cruelty, but even the cruelty had a purpose. The Mongol conquests were indeed ferocious and bloody. Stories of pyramids of skulls and the total razing of cities were not fables. One estimate suggests that Genghis Khan's campaigns were responsible for approximately 40 million deaths during his twenty-one year reign.[69] Killing, looting, and raping his way across the Eurasian landmass, he established an empire that eventually reached from Central Europe to the South China Sea, from Siberia in the north to India in the south, and lasted for over 200 years. Genghis Khan's legacy is more than just as the founder of a nation, a brutal warlord, or an enlightened despot; it also is a record of military excellence and charismatic leadership that few individuals have ever equaled.

Notes

1. David Morgan, *The Mongols*, 2nd edition (Malden, Massachusetts: Blackwell Publishing, 2007. Originally published in 1986), 5.

2. Morgan, *The Mongols*, 2nd edition, 6.

3. Morgan, *The Mongols*, 2nd edition, 5-8.

4. Paul Ratchnevsky, *Genghis Khan: His Life and Legacy* (Malden, Massachusetts: Blackwell Publishing, 1991), 12. Translated into English and edited by Thomas Nivison Haining. Originally published in 1983 in German.

5. Ratchnevsky, *Genghis Khan: His Life and Legacy*, 16-17.

6. Ratchnevsky, *Genghis Khan: His Life and Legacy*, 17-19. Considering the other events in Genghis Khan's lifetime, how early Mongol youth marry, and putting them on a timeline, Ratchnevsky's estimate makes the most sense; Morgan, *The Mongols,* 2nd ed., 49. The Mongolian People's Republic celebrates the year 1162 as the year of Genghis Khan's birth.

7. Ratchnevsky, *Genghis Khan: His Life and Legacy,* 19-20.

8. Ratchnevsky, *Genghis Khan: His Life and Legacy,* 20-21.

9. Morgan, *The Mongols,* 2nd ed., 51.

10. Ratchnevsky, *Genghis Khan: His Life and Legacy,* 22-23.

11. Paul Kahn, *The Secret History of the Mongols: The Origin of Genghis Khan* (Boston: Cheng & Tsui Company, 1998), 18-20. First expanded edition, originally published in 1984. The quote is from page 20.

12. Ratchnevsky, *Genghis Khan: His Life and Legacy,* 24.

13. Kahn, *The Secret History of the Mongols,* 20-25; Ratchnevsky, *Genghis Khan: His Life and Legacy,* 25-27

14. Kahn, *The Secret History of the Mongols,* 20; Ratchnevsky, *Genghis Khan: His Life and Legacy,* 28-31; Morgan, *The Mongols,* 2nd ed., 49. Morgan is considerably more skeptical of *The Secret History* than either Kahn or Ratchnevsky. Much of the section describing the unification of the Mongols will come from Ratchnevsky.

15. Ratchnevsky, *Genghis Khan: His Life and Legacy,* 31-32.

16. Ratchnevsky, *Genghis Khan: His Life and Legacy,* 31-37.

17. Morgan, *The Mongols,* 2nd ed., 53.

18. Ratchnevsky, *Genghis Khan: His Life and Legacy,* 37-38.

19. Ratchnevsky, *Genghis Khan: His Life and Legacy,* 41.

20. Ratchnevsky, *Genghis Khan: His Life and Legacy,* 41.

21. Ratchnevsky, *Genghis Khan: His Life and Legacy,* 43-44; Morgan, *The Mongols,* 2nd ed., 54-55. Morgan says that Genghis (or as Morgan spells it, Chinggis) Khan means Oceanic or Universal Khan and is not sure if Genghis Khan received the title before his struggle with Jamuka, or after his final victory over Jamuka.

22. Ratchnevsky, *Genghis Khan: His Life and Legacy,* 84-87.

23. Kahn, *The Secret History of the Mongols,* 109-114.

24. James Chambers, *The Devil's Horsemen: The Mongol Invasion of Europe* (Edison, New Jersey: Castle Books, 2003), 53-54. Originally published in 1979.

25. Just to be clear, the author is not arguing that Genghis Khan was democratic in his thinking by modern standards. He was not, and in a different time and place he would be called an Enlightened Despot. Yet for his time and place the ideas were revolutionary.

26. Timothy May, *The Mongol Art of War* (Yardley, Pennsylvania: Westholme Publishing, 2007), 31; R. Ernest DuPuy and Trevor DuPuy, *The Harper Encyclopedia of Military History: From 3500 B.C. to the Present* (New York: HarperCollins Publishing, 1993), 4th edition, 367.

27. May, *The Mongol Art of War,* 29-32.

28. May, *The Mongol Art of War,* 28. Italics are in original.

29. May, *The Mongol Art of War,* 32-35; DuPuy and DuPuy, *The Harper Encyclopedia of Military History,* 367-373.

30. Chambers, *The Devil's Horsemen,* 51.

31. Morgan, *The Mongols,* 2nd ed., 79-80.

32. May, *The Mongol Art of War,* 33-34.

33. May, *The Mongol Art of War,* 46-47.

34. Chambers, *The Devil's Horsemen,* 56-57.

35. May, *The Mongol Art of War,* 46-49.

36. May, *The Mongol Art of War,* 49.

37. May, *The Mongol Art of War,* 28.

38. May, *The Mongol Art of War,* 49-50.

39. Chambers, *The Devil's Horsemen,* 56-57.

40. May, *The Mongol Art of War,* 50-51.

41. DuPuy and DuPuy, *The Harper Encyclopedia of Military History,* 359; Mike Ashley, *British Kings & Queens: The Complete Biographical Encyclopedia of the Kings and Queens of Great Britain* (New York: Barnes & Noble Books, 2000), 588-594. Originally published as *The Mammoth Book of British Kings and Queens* in 1998.

42. May, *The Mongol Art of War,* 50-51.

43. Louis A. DiMarco, *War Horse: A History of the Military Horse and Rider* (Yardley, Pennsylvania: Westholme Publishing, 2008), 122-123.

44. May, *The Mongol Art of War,* 55-56. The quote is on page 56.

45. Chambers, *The Devil's Horsemen,* 58.

46. May, *The Mongol Art of War,* 54.

47. Chambers, *The Devil's Horsemen,* 58-59.

48. May, *The Mongol Art of War,* 58-62.

49. May, *The Mongol Art of War,* 63-64; Jack Weatherford, *Genghis Khan and the Making of the Modern World* (New York: Crown Publishers, 2004), 94-95.

50. Weatherford, *Genghis Khan and the Making of the Modern World,* 94-95.

51. DuPuy and DuPuy, *The Harper Encyclopedia of Military History,* 369-371.

52. May, *The Mongol Art of War,* 70-77.

53. DuPuy and DuPuy, *The Harper Encyclopedia of Military History,* 370-371.

54. May, *The Mongol Art of War,* 77-79.

55. May, *The Mongol Art of War,* 69-71.

56. Ratchnevsky, *Genghis Khan: His Life and Legacy,* 105-115.

57. Ratchnevsky, *Genghis Khan: His Life and Legacy,* 115-118.

58. Weatherford, *Genghis Khan and the Making of the Modern World,* 105-106.

59. Morgan, *The Mongols,* 2nd ed., 60.

60. Ratchnevsky, *Genghis Khan: His Life and Legacy,* 123-125.

61. May, *The Mongol Art of War,* 116-117.

62. J. J. Saunders, *The History of the Mongol Conquests* (Philadelphia, Pennsylvania: University of Pennsylvania Press, 2001), 56-57. Originally published in 1971. See also May, *The Mongol Art of War,* 117. Saunders states that the governor of Utrar was killed by having molten gold poured down his throat, May says that he had molten silver was poured down his throat, and into his eyes and ears.

63. May, *The Mongol Art of War,* 119.

64. J. J. Saunders, *The History of the Mongol Conquests,* 59.

65. DuPuy and DuPuy, *The Harper Encyclopedia of Military History,* 366.

66. Morgan, *The Mongols,* 2nd ed., 65.

67. Morgan, *The Mongols,* 2nd ed., 69-71.

68. Ratchnevsky, *Genghis Khan: His Life and Legacy,* 142-144.

69. Matthew White, *Selected Death Tolls for Wars, Massacres and Atrocities Before the 20th Century.* Accessed 5 June 2012 at [http://necrometrics.com/pre1700a.htm#Mongol].

Chapter 3
Napoleon Bonaparte
by Mark T. Gerges

"...my argument is that war makes rattling good history; but peace is poor reading. So I back Bonaparte for the reason that he will give pleasure to posterity."

Thomas Hardy, *The Dynasts*[1]

Napoleon Bonaparte's legacy still resonates to this day. He is part of our cultural literacy, a common image still invoked to suit our own ends. A recent Super Bowl commercial showed a tiny French car, winding its way through Paris to the strains of an upbeat French tune. The voice-over was a computer-generated voice from a GPS, directing each turn and then announcing arrival at Saint Cloud. The scene then cut to a tree lined avenue, French Imperial Guardsmen and their horses in serried ranks, coming to attention as a diminutive Napoleon jumped from the vehicle, GPS in hand, which he suddenly thrust into his shirt, his familiar pose now complete. His image in the form of busts grace home design stores and provide a link to the French emperor that somehow denotes class and sophistication to our 21st century lives. The derogatory term "Napoleonic complex," referring to a short person driven to high performance in compensation for his diminutive height is in common use despite not being at all accurate— at five feet seven inches tall, Napoleon was of average height for 19th century Europe. So why does Napoleon Bonaparte, dead for almost 200 years, still have such a draw on our popular consciousness?

In many ways, an accurate version of Napoleon remains difficult to determine and depends on one's perspective. Even before his death, some used and manipulated his image and historical legacy for their own purposes. Immediately after his downfall, early writers tore down the image, showing Napoleon's faults and assigning every action to ulterior and nefarious reasons. Later, others tried to latch onto Napoleon's greatness, hoping that by copying the structure and imagery of the French First Empire, its greatness and glory would reflect upon their own later governments. The sheer number of books devoted to him is daunting— over 200,000 volumes since his death in 1821 and 200 in the past four years alone.[2] One book, Peter Geyl's masterful *Napoleon: For and Against*, is a bibliographical essay on the struggle to use Napoleon's legacy over the past two centuries but as the book was written in the 1940s, a much expanded version is needed today. Much of what we understand in the

Figure 3. "The Emperor Napoleon in His Study at the Tuileries," 1812, painting by Jacques-Louis David; National Gallery of Art, Washington, D.C.

English-speaking world about Napoleon comes from his archenemy, the British, who may not be the only side one should consult if attempting to find an accurate view of the French emperor. Yet, despite the arguments over his legacy, the nature of his rule, and motivations for his policy, some common threads remain undisputed. His performance as a battlefield commander ranks among the greatest, and Napoleon is often the first mentioned among history's finest leaders. Why?

Napoleon was born Napoleone di Buonaparte in Ajaccio, Corsica on 15 August 1769, just a year after the Republic of Genoa sold the unruly island to the Kingdom of France. He was the second surviving child of the eight born to the family of Carlos and Lietizia Buonaparte. His father's connections as a lawyer working for the new French government on the island allowed the family to avail themselves of the educational opportunities open to the minor nobility (*la petite noblesse*) in pre-revolutionary France. At the age of nine, Napoleon followed his older brother Joseph to schooling on the mainland to learn French at Autun and five months later attended the military academy at Brienne-la-Château. Brienne was one of twelve military schools preparing young men for the military academy in Paris. Brienne consisted of 120 students; sixty from the older, noble families of France, *le grand noblesse*, and sixty from *la petite noblesse*—Napoleon was part of the latter group and attended on a scholarship.[3] His time at Brienne was not a particularly happy period. Marked by his heavily accented French, an accent he never lost, he focused on studies and reading. He excelled in mathematics and spent his free time reading history, in particular the campaigns of what were considered the great commanders—Frederick the Great, Alexander, Caesar, Marlborough, Turenne. He made no close friends at Brienne and was a bit of a loner during his five years there. He passed his exams in 1784 and then transferred to the École *Royal Militarie* in Paris.[4] The École *Royal Militarie* was a new school, founded in 1776, and designed to more closely align the nobility in France with service to the King. Each student held a warrant personally signed by the monarch to attend the school. The cost of living in Paris was more expensive than Brienne, and increased the strain on the family's modest income. His financial straits were one of the reasons he completed the two-year curriculum in a single year and, after passing his final exams, became a lieutenant in one of the most famous artillery regiments in the Royal army, *Régiment de la Fére*, at the age of sixteen.

His early career did not show any hints of the greatness that was to follow. He was hardworking, studious, with few friends during his time at the military academy. If his peers were not drawn to him as a leader, his teachers at least recognized his abilities and commented on them in his academic reports. One unusual fact does emerge, however. The schools at Brienne and later the École *Royal Militaire* were designed to tie the nobility to the Bourbon regime, and they did an admirable job of providing the young officers needed to run the *Ancien Regime's* army. When the revolution came to France in 1789, of all the artillery graduates of the École *Royal Militarie*, only one, Napoleon, sided with the revolutionary government. Napoleon's siding with the revolutionaries marked him as politically astute and not tied to the existing structure of the French state. None of the other officers in *Régiment de la Fére* joined the revolutionary cause.[5]

Were it not for the upheavals of the French Revolution, Napoleon Bonaparte would have remained a junior officer in the French army, a minor and forgotten figure. Of all the branches in the *Ancien Regime's* army, the artillery and engineers required the most education, an unappealing requirement to nobility who viewed themselves as born to lead men. Therefore, more commoners and minor nobility went into these technical branches.[6] As an artillery officer, Napoleon could expect a long career in the *Ancien Regime*, leaving the service as a captain, his further promotions blocked by his minor noble birth. After arriving at the *Régiment de la Fére,* long absences to return to Corsica marked his early career, with 32 months leave in the first six years.[7] On leave in Corsica after the French Revolution began in 1789, Napoleon became involved in the efforts of Corsican independence. He met a childhood hero, Pauli, a Corsican nationalist who had fought for Corsican independence twenty years earlier, but after Pauli invited British troops to occupy the island, Napoleon and his family fled to mainland France in July 1793.   During the siege of Toulon in 1793, Bonaparte's rise to national prominence began. The summer of 1793 was a tumultuous period for France. The National Convention removed the king, Louis XVI, from office the previous fall, and sent him to the guillotine in January 1793. War loomed with all of Europe and civil war threatened France. The Vendée rose in rebellion, and several large cities, including Marseille, Lyon, and Bordeaux created armies to protect themselves against the revolutionary government in Paris. The great seaport city of Toulon, home to the French Mediterranean fleet, invited the British into the harbor, and soon British troops and an Anglo-Spanish fleet protected the rebellious town. The crisis of the late summer led to what became known as the Reign of Terror, or in French simply *la Terreur,* when a committee of twelve in the National Convention ruled France and led it to more extreme measures in order to save the revolution's accomplishments.

Napoleon, upon his return to France, wrote a pro-revolutionary tract,

Supper at Beaucaire, and his pro-revolutionary ideas caught the attention of Representatives Augustin Robespierre and Antoine Christophe Saliceti. Augustin was the younger brother of Maximillien Robsespierre, the *de facto* leader of the Committee of Public Safety and Saliceti, a fellow Corsican. They appointed him a lieutenant colonel and commander of the artillery in the siege of Toulon.[8] The siege's commander, General Jean Baptiste François Carteaux, formerly a painter, wanted to assault the city, but Napoleon looked at the ground and determined that a peninsula of land, dominated by Mont Caire, was the key to the harbor. Napoleon believed that capturing the peninsula would force the British fleet to depart. The problem with Napoleon's plan was that the French revolutionary army besieging Toulon had only four siege guns and a handful of smaller pieces, so he scoured southern France for artillery that he ordered to Toulon on his own authority.[9] On 22 September 1793, Carteux, thinking this assault a waste of effort, gave Napoleon only 600 soldiers, and with the few guns collected, the young officer assaulted the peninsula. The British reacted first and smashed the assault, and now aware of the danger, built Fort Mulgrave, an earthen fort with 24 guns, nicknamed "Little Gibraltar."[10]

Despite this setback, Napoleon collected the necessary supplies and arms to assault the position again. Carteux was relieved, and after a second political appointee, a doctor, was relieved, the command of the siege was given to a professional soldier, General Jacques François Dugommier, who saw the value of Napoleon's plan. Napoleon continued to collect guns from across southern France. One of the elements of Napoleon's greatness emerged at this juncture. His ability to understand the common soldiers and talk with them as comrades created intense loyalty throughout his reign. Scenes of Napoleon, on the eve of some of his greatest victories, sitting around a campfire, suffering the same hardships as his men, talking to them as equals despite the differences in rank, marked this talent. This ability to understand what motivated soldiers was on display during the siege. One battery, key to shelling Fort Mulgrave, was exposed to heavy return fire and the daily casualties made it difficult to find artillerymen willing to expose themselves to near certain injury. Napoleon did not react with speeches appealing to their bravery, nor a commitment to the revolution, or their peers and compatriots. He had a simple wooden sign made and placed at the entrance to the battery's position. The sign read "battery of men without fear." There were never problems finding volunteers for that battery again.[11]

With 100 guns scrounged to support the assault and 6,000 men from General Dugommier, on 17 December Napoleon acted again, this time with sufficient forces. The assault on the peninsula lasted for thirteen hours of bitter fighting, in which Napoleon was wounded in the thigh but Fort Mulgrave fell to the Revolutionary troops. The next day, the French placed ten cannons in the fort firing on the harbor, and realizing the hopelessness of their position, the Anglo-Spanish fleet abandoned Toulon, ending the siege.[12]

The Committee of Public Safety rewarded the 24 year old with promotion to brigadier general, and appointment as artillery commander for the Army of Italy.[13] Waiting for final approval of his appointment, army headquarters sent Bonaparte to inspect coastal fortifications along the Mediterranean coast. He developed a plan for an offensive against the Kingdom of Sardinia's army in Piedmont. Given to the representatives on mission from the Committee of Public Safety, the representatives ordered the commander of the Army of Italy to execute the plans, which were successful and led to the capture of Tenti pass, key to the Maritime Alps.[14] Through the success of his campaign plan, the army began to know Napoleon's name and the government sent him to Genoa to determine the attitude of the rulers toward the French government. However, while he was there the Committee of Public Safety fell from power in the Coup of 9 *Thermidor*, and his patrons, the Robespierre brothers, were guillotined.[15] Napoleon's letters to the Robespierre brothers during his time in Genoa became known, and on his return to France, he was imprisoned. For two weeks, Napoleon did not know whether he would join the Robespierre brothers at the guillotine, but the fury of the *Thermidorian* reaction calmed and General Bonaparte released.

In May 1795, while awaiting assignment in Paris, Napoleon worked in the Topographic Bureau, an early plans section for the French military. While there, he drew up a plan for an assault on Austrian and Sardinian positions in northern Italy, but his refusal, on grounds of ill health, to serve as an infantry brigade commander in putting down the Royalist revolt in the Vendée, caused his dismissal from the service. He and his closest friends, in particular future marshals of France Joachim Murat and Andoche Junot, spent their time in the coffee houses in Paris. After the end of the Reign of Terror, the government, known as the Directory, ruled France but other than ending the extremism of the Committee of Public Safety, did little to commend itself to the people. In the summer of 1795, the two-thirds law of *Fructidor* expelled 500 of the 750 members of the National Convention. This law in particular affected Royalist representatives who had returned to the Convention after the fall of Robespierre and hoped to regain power through the elective process. The countryside and Paris seethed at the new law, and on 5 October (13 *Vendemiare*) a crowd began to converge on the National Convention's hall, and the members feared for their lives. One of the members of the Directory, Paul Barras, who as a representative on mission had observed Napoleon in action at Toulon, remembered the out-of-favor general and put him in command of the troops defending the National Convention. Napoleon had been in Paris when the King's Swiss Guards were massacred in 1792, and remembered what a mob could do if not stopped. Napoleon sent a cavalry troop under Murat to bring the cannons near the Place de Carrousel to the Tuileries Palace. Firing on the approaching mob, within 30 minutes the "whiff of grapeshot" was over, the mob dispersed, and the Directory government saved. The cannon fire killed nearly 200 Royalist supporters and wounded at least that many; it was the first time the regular army fired on the crowd in Paris since the fall of the Bastille, and was an important step in bringing Napoleon to the attention of the government.[16]

Napoleon's campaigns over the next few years showed him as a brilliant commander, but even then, he was still only one successful general among a handful of successful Revolutionary generals. Each campaign deserves more space than can be devoted here.[17] His challenges taking command in Italy in 1796 were particularly stark. Then a twenty-six-year-old general of division, the other generals in the army saw his appointment to command the French Army of Italy as a political move. The army was stalemated in the Maritime Alps, had not been paid in six months, and was poorly supplied. Half the army was in the hospital or had deserted. The division commanders, Major Generals André Masséna, Pierre Augereau, and Jean-Sérurier Mathieu, all much older and experienced men, were skeptical of this young political general. Improving discipline within the unruly ranks, Napoleon's Italian campaigns were a model of maneuver of a more agile, smaller force against larger ones, each time concentrating greater numbers on isolated Austrian detachments, defeating them in detail. At one battle, Lodi, Napoleon earned his nickname "the little corporal" from his soldiers for his role in sighting thirty-six cannons to fire on the Austrians, since the emplacing of the piece was normally the responsibility of a gun corporal.[18] Between April 1796 and April 1797, Napoleon knocked the Piedmontese out of the war, captured all of northern Italy from the Habsburg Empire, and defeated Austrian armies attempting to regain northern Italy.

General Bonaparte was becoming very popular with the French people while the Directory government remained unpopular, and in 1798, the Directory gave Napoleon an army to invade Egypt, removing the popular young general from France. The Egyptian campaign was unusual because of what Napoleon brought with him--not only an army, but also160 scholars and scientists who established the Institute of Egypt, a lasting and important research facility that began modern Egyptology.[19] Napoleon closely controlled what information Paris received from Egypt, thus the French lauded his victories but were unaware of disasters such as the siege of Acre.

Europe by 1799 was exploding. The foreign policy of the Directory government was aggressive, and unease over French policy, such as deposing the Piedmont king and incorporating his lands into France, and reorganizing Switzerland and the Low Countries into republics allied to France, led to a second coalition coalescing against France. Russian armies moved through Switzerland towards France, Austrian armies fought in northern Italy and along the Rhine, and the military conquests of the last four years were in jeopardy. It was into this crisis that Napoleon returned from Egypt, leaving behind his army and arriving with a small band of close advisors. Those politicians seeking to replace the corrupt and inefficient Directory government were looking for a "sword;" a successful general who could guarantee that the military would accept a coup. It is important to remember that at this point Bonaparte was one of a handful of successful Revolutionary generals, including Jean Baptiste Bernadotte and Jean Baptiste Jourdan, both known from their campaigns along the Rhine. Not all the conspiratorial dealings that caused General Bonaparte to be the candidate can be recounted here; the people's joy upon his return to France led to the election of Napoleon's younger brother Lucien to head the Council of 500, the lower house in the government. This allowed Napoleon to play a key role in the coup of 18th *Bruimaire* (9-10 November 1799). This coup ended the Directory government and in its place created the three-man Consulate.

The coup of 18th *Bruimaire* marked the end of the French Revolution and beginning of the Napoleonic era with Bonaparte's rise as one of the three consuls. Thirty years old in November 1799, Napoleon was the 'sword' in the new government, insuring military support. The two other consuls, Abbie Seiyes and Roger Ducos, were both older and more experienced in the tumultuous politics of the past decade and planned to marginalize the inexperienced general. However, they did not reckon on the abilities of the young General Bonaparte. The French people had grown tired of the constant shifts in government and ministers lining their pockets for personal profit; they feared that the extreme aspects of revolution could return without some sort of stabilizing efforts. In his role as counsul, Napoleon Bonaparte was not so much an innovator as someone who could improve and make efficient the existing structures. Most of what he did as the First Consul and later as Emperor was not new. What made Napoleon stand apart was his ability to look at a problem, determine the causes, implement changes, and systemize the procedures. This is what he did brilliantly in the next four years.

The immediate need was to write a new constitution to legitimize what had occurred on 18th *Brumaire*. As the debates began on the form of the new government, two figures emerged on opposite sides of the debate. Seiyes formed one side while Bonaparte opposed him. Napoleon, with no experience as a politician, won more and more representatives over to his side through the strength of his argument. The new constitution bore Napoleon's personal stamp. The constitution retained the three consuls, but one was clearly primary—the First Consul, who approved all laws. This centralized the true power into the hands of the First Consul, who of course became Napoleon. In return for a constitution that limited democratic participation, the people accepted political involvement of a smaller electorate, built upon age and property restrictions in exchange for stability and an end to the violence.[20]

The next four years saw a rash of activity with first a campaign into northern Italy to recapture the lands lost to the Austrians in 1799, which secured his political position after the victory at Marengo. Then Napoleon turned to a host of economic and societal reforms that systemized the accomplishments of the French Revolution. The list is impressive, and each item shows Napoleon's mark: the *Code Napoléon*, in which he personally participated in over half the meetings; reform of the financial system and establishment of the Bank of France; peace with the Habsburgs and later Great Britain, which led to the first period of peace since 1792; restoration of the Catholic Church in French life; ending the civil war in the Vendée and Brittany; amnesty which encouraged *émigrés* and Royalists to return to France; reform of the education system establishing a system of *lycees* and secondary schools; creation of the departments of France to simplify local administration; and the list goes on. These accomplishments alone would have marked Napoleon as one of the great statesmen of his day and among the greatest of France. He kept the trappings of a republic, but the French government by 1804 could best be termed an enlightened despotism, and with his coronation as emperor on 2 December 1804, any final pretenses of France being a republic ended with the creation of the French Empire. Overall, the Consulate years were beneficial. The France that emerged from the four years of the Consulate government had the rule of law again in place, most internal divisions healed, and was a strong, stable power able to take its place on the European stage—a leading role, as Europe was about to discover.[21]

The Peace of Amiens between France and the United Kingdom brought peace to Europe and a wave of English tourists to Paris. However, each side looked at the peace not as a permanent state, but as a trial armistice. The expectation was for further negotiations to resolve outstanding issues such as trade but these meetings never occurred. Each side violated aspects of the treaty. Great Britain refused to evacuate Malta and South Africa, and supported a Bourbon prince's attempt to overthrow Napoleon, then the Consul for Life. France's reorganization of the German states and the Low Countries hardened Great Britain's attitudes when war resumed. France assembled an army along the Channel coast from Hanover to Brest, a threatening posture to England only a few watery miles away.[22] To carry the army across to England, France built fifty-foot barges with a 35-ton carrying capacity, and all that was needed was control of the English Channel for a few days.[23]

The army that stood poised for the invasion of England reflected revolutionary changes in the military arts. Napoleon himself was not an inventor, but rather an improviser. His fame relied upon his ability to see what needed to be done and then innovate and adapt to overcome an obstacle. His methods were not new. His techniques on campaign derived from his extensive reading of history as a young man, which continued as emperor. Developments such as marching divided and then combining on the battlefield to overwhelm one's opponent were discussed by writers such as General Pierre-Joseph Bourcet, Comte de Guibert, and Victor-François, duc de Broglie in the 1760s through 1780s.[24] The French Revolution allowed these ideas to reach a receptive officer corps, desperate for any advantage and not hidebound by past experience. Napoleon's greatness was in taking the best of these ideas and systemizing them, creating a regulated approach in everything he did.

With the responsive organization of the army, Napoleon could react when he erred, which at least one author argues is how every one of his campaigns began.[25] The creation of all-arms formations—brigades and divisions with commanders at each level having their own staffs, and elements of infantry, cavalry, artillery, and supporting arms such as engineers, wagon train, and ambulances combined under one command were all discussed by French writers before the Revolution and then put into practice during the tumultuous days of the 1790s. Napoleon took these organizational reforms to the next logical level at the camp at Boulogne. He created seven infantry corps and a cavalry corps; a marshal, part of the new meritocracy of France, commanded each. For the 1805 campaign, the *Grande Armée* totaled 210,000 soldiers with an additional but much smaller French army in Italy.[26] In addition to a staff to assist the commander, each corps contained two to three divisions of infantry, a brigade of cavalry, one or two batteries of artillery, and engineer, medical, and transportation units. This simplified the span of command and control. Napoleon now issued orders to seven corps commanders, who in turn oversaw and commanded five to seven elements themselves. Each corps, with all the assets of a mini-army, moved on separate routes, separated in time and space by a day's march from the nearest supporting corps. This eased the question of supply for an army that lived off the land for much of the men's rations, but also dispersed the *Grande Armée* over a much larger area, meaning it would make contact with the enemy, and then rapidly concentrate.

Formed in June 1803, the *Grande Armée's* encampments, centered on Boulogne, were more than just a lodgment. The *Grande Armée* trained incessantly for over a year. A typical training week saw progressive larger unit training each day, beginning with company and battalion drill, then brigade and division until culminating at corps level maneuvers that capped the week, followed by a day of rest before repeating the cycle. Of the infantry, forty-three percent had combat experience, and over fifty percent of the cavalry were veterans. One-third of the officers and non-commissioned officers had at least six years service.[27] By the summer of 1805, the *Grande Armée* was the best-trained army in the world, filled with experienced senior officers and idealistic recruits.

The men to command the seven corps were all experienced warriors from the earlier campaigns of the revolution, proven on the battlefield and rewarded for that success upon the creation of the marshalate in 1802. Marshal Jean-Baptiste Bernadotte commanded First Corps. A pre-revolutionary enlisted man, he was an extreme Jacobin. He made his name in the French Army of the Rhine during the wars of the Revolution. Brave, but not trusted by Napoleon, he later became the king of Sweden.[28] Marshal Louis Nicolas Davout commanded the Third Corps. One of the greatest battlefield commanders, Davout had been a pre-revolution cavalry officer who stood with the revolutionaries but was then dismissed from the service because of his noble birth. Returning to the army during the crisis of 1794, he made his name along the Rhine and then in Egypt under Napoleon. Known as the Iron Marshal, he was a strict disciplinarian, incorruptible, intelligent and well studied in the art of war. His corps was considered the best trained in the army.[29] Nicolas Jean de Dieu

Soult commanded Fourth Corps. This pre-revolution non-commissioned officer was calm and intelligent, fair but hard and known as a skillful looter.[30] In many ways, Marshal Jean Lannes, commanding Fifth Corps, epitomized the opportunity offered during the revolution. Uneducated as a child, he studied several hours each day, reading military history to improve himself. He made his name under Napoleon first in Italy and then Egypt, and was one of the few subordinates who dared to offer Napoleon frank advice—often uninvited.[31] Commanding the Reserve Cavalry was Napoleon's brother-in-law, and former cavalryman from the 9th *Bruimaire*, Marshal Joachim Murat.[32] The final element of the *Grande Armée* that was to play an important role at Austerlitz was the Imperial Guard under Marshal Jean-Baptiste Bessieres. Son of a surgeon, he was known for his calmness and bravery, and commanded the mounted guides first organized to protect General Bonaparte in 1796.[33] Probably the most important man next to Napoleon himself in pulling all these strong personalities together was the chief of staff, Marshal Louis-Alexandre Berthier. He had been a pre-revolution engineer officer and served in America during the American Revolution. One of the few people who could read Napoleon's hurried handwriting, Berthier had an incredible attention to detail and was essential to the working of the French military machine.[34]

The French term *coup d'oeil* translates as the stroke of the eye. *Coup d'oeil* is the ability to take in a military situation at a glance, to recognize the possibilities of a position or to have an eye for ground.[35] For a commander on the battlefield, it is the ability to see beyond the noise and confusion and understand what is actually happening. This ability to see and understand the key point was one of Napoleon's greatest strengths. With his immediate grasp of the situation, he rapidly and unhesitatingly came to a decision and then carried through those actions without second-guessing, delaying, or changing the initial dispositions. To translate those directions into orders for the *Grande Armée*, Napoleon as head of state and commander-in-chief created an imperial headquarters that allowed him to function as both when on campaign. There were two sections—the *maison*, and the general staff. A third element, the *Intendant Général,* or quartermaster-general, was technically not part of the imperial headquarters, and dealt with army supply and logistics.[36] The personal staff, known as the *Maison Militaire de l'Empereur*, was the smaller element of the two. There were three parts: his aides-de-camps, the *cabinet,* and the *officers d'ordonnance*. Historian John Elting describes the aides, all handpicked officers and experts in their fields as "men for all missions, leading improvised task forces to meet unexpected emergencies, massing artillery to support a decisive attack, clearing snarled supply lines, conducting large scale reconnaissance, and sometimes handling minor diplomatic assignments."[37] The *cabinet* dealt with spies and the collection of intelligence on the enemy. The *cabinet civil* also was often attached to run the civil government of the empire. The last element of the *maison*, the *officers d'ordonnance*, or orderly officers, were junior officers who conducted inspections in the emperor's name, collected information, and then reported those results back to the emperor.[38]

The *grand etat-major général*, or army staff, was the domain of Berthier. The first modern staff with specialized staff functions, it was a large organization dealing with all aspects on intelligence, topography, movement, and written orders. During the 1805 campaign, the *grand etat-major général* grew to 400 officers and 5,000 men.[39] It had but one function—turn the orders of Napoleon into clear, well-written, instructions for the *Grande Armée*. Not even Napoleon would interrupt Berthier and his aides as they worked on producing an order.[40]

The system to support Napoleon was well defined. Two hours after dusk, each corps sent a staff officer to the Imperial headquarters with the latest reports. Later more detailed corps summaries, containing the location, strength, logistical situation, and commander's estimate, were due to Napoleon by midnight.[41] Eighteen-hour work-days, both on campaign and at peace in Paris, were normal for Napoleon and began with the arrival of these summaries. Rising at midnight, Napoleon read the reports, dictated replies, issued changes of orders, prioritized reports, and when he finished near dawn, would retire for an hour's rest. He would rise again by 6 a.m., dress and breakfast, then receive important personages, consider future movements, and then sit down at his desk where he read the carefully sorted documents and dictated replies.[42] By 10 a.m., new documents and orders based on his earlier instructions were ready for signature, and then he would call for his horse. Napoleon would head off to visit corps headquarters and inspect units. These visits gave him the opportunity to "disperse a little more of the hypnotic attraction he could wield at will over almost all his men. The easy familiarity which he permitted the rank and file made him genuinely beloved."[43] He took soldiers into his confidence to tell them his plans, or recognized soldiers by name who previously performed some act of bravery; all this tied the soldier to him. After the day's ride, he returned to headquarters, read more news, issued orders, or conducted interviews. The day's meals were haphazard affairs, often taken in silence and rapidly eaten in under twenty minutes. By 8 p.m., he went to sleep for four to five hours, protected by his Mameluke servant Roustam sleeping across the door's threshold.[44]

As the renewal of hostilities loomed in 1805, a new coalition emerged. The Third Coalition against France was the brainchild of the British Prime Minister William Pitt. To the British, a Europe dominated by France threatened British trade with the continent, their colonial interests and empire through the rebuilding of the French fleet. The French meddling in Italy and the German states had reduced the power of the Habsburg empire as a counter-weight to French expansion. Great Britain devoted £5 million to subsidize other nations to oppose France.[45] The first to join the British were the Swedes, followed soon after by a much more important power, the Russians. Upset at the Imperial Recess that aligned German states more closely with France and Napoleon's overtones to the Shah of Persia, the British promise of £1,250,000 per 100,000 Russian soldiers fighting Napoleon sealed the deal.[46] Austria joined, upset at French claims in Italy and Napolcon's crowning as thc king of Italy and whilc Grcat Britain pressured Prussia to join, the Prussian government remained noncommittal.

The allies knew that Napoleon had made his reputation in Italy and therefore decided that northern Italy would again be the main theater of war. Austria sent its largest army of 95,000 men under the Archduke Charles there to defend its interests.[47] A second Habsburg army of 58,000 men under the nominal command of Archduke Ferdinand went to the German states; the chief of staff and defacto commander was Lieutenant General Karl Mack von Leiberich.[48] This army was to be reinforced by Russian forces—first 38,000 under Field Marshal Mikail Kutusov, then another 40,000 under General Fredrich Wilhelm von Buxhowden, and a final 20,000 under Levin August, Count von Bennigsen.[49] These detachments marched east as they organized to join with the Habsburg army near Ulm before commencing combined operations. A final 20,000-man army under the Archduke Charles was in the Tyrol, linking the two theaters of war.[50] An additional 55,000 Swedish and later British troops were promised to join the coalition along the North Sea coast, making the total facing France at least 331,000 in the fall of 1805. France had 210,000 in the *Grande Armée*, and another 50,000 under Marshal Andre Massena operated in northern Italy, plus 20,000 in Naples, and another 30,000 that remained at Boulogne.[51]

Once, when an aide asked Napoleon for more time to deliver a message, he replied, "you can ask me for anything—except time!"[52] Time was the one unyielding aspect that Napoleon could not control, and looking at the situation in 1805 he knew that the longer he waited, the more time this gave the allies to combine their forces and increase the odds against

France. Before deciding on marching to central Europe, a key aspect of the 1805 campaign was supposed to be the French fleet. An elaborate series of maneuvers and feints were designed to draw the British fleet from the English Channel to the West Indies to protect their sugar trade. Once the British fell for the feint, the French fleet was to race back to Europe, win naval superiority in the channel, and allow the *Grande Armée* to cross to England on their barges. However, all of this took time, and Napoleon refused to wait. On 24 August 1805 he issued orders to his corps assembled at Boulogne; on 26 August they began their movement instead toward the Rhine River and Black Forest. It would not be until October, long after the army had left Boulogne and was deep inside of Habsburg territory that the decisive naval battle of Trafalgar occurred, smashing a combined French and Spanish fleet and ending any thoughts of attacking England directly. [53]

Within three weeks, the *Grande Armée* approached the Rhine. The Austrian troops had not been idle; Mack, analyzing Napoleon's early campaigns determined that his speed and boldness were the keys to the French success. Mack copied the French methods, and pushed his troops rapidly forward, invading the Duchy of Bavaria on 2 September and marched to the city of Ulm.[54] However, once there they waited for the Russian troops who had promised to arrive by 15 October. Mack had no further objective, suggesting his hope that rapid marching in and of itself would somehow translate into a purpose. To the west of the Black Forest, acting as if it was screening the movement of the entire French army, was the Reserve Cavalry under Murat. Making contact with the Austrians on 6 October, aggressive patrols kept the Austrian eyes focused west. The Austrians expected that the French could not push large bodies of troops through the Black Forest until the end of November. The weather contributed to this impression in the first half of October. Heavy rains turned the roads to mud while flooded streams limited the possible crossing sites. Napoleon wrote "the Danube has overflowed with a violence unequalled in one hundred years."[55] Despite the poor weather, the *Grande Armée* averaged twelve miles a day, closing the trap on Mack.[56] By 10 October, Bernadotte's First Corps and Davout's Third Corps were at Munich, eighty miles behind Mack's position and the fingers of the *Grande Armée* began to close around Ulm.[57]

Mack became uncomfortable in his positions, and sent 25,000 men across the Danube River to see if the way was still clear. On 11 October, they ran into 4,000 French troops who held off the Austrians for an entire day.[58] Over the next three days Mack sent out more small detachments from his army in various directions, but each met French units closing the noose tighter around Ulm. French bombardment and surrender negotiations began and on 19 October, Mack agreed to surrender if no support arrived within ten days. Since the Russians and Habsburgs agreed to be in Ulm on 15 October, Mack expected relief any day.[59] What he did not realize at the time was that the Russians were still operating on the Julian calendar while the Austrians and the rest of Europe were on the Gregorian. According to the Russian timetable, twelve days behind the rest of Europe, the Russians, marching through Poland, still had time to arrive at the agreed-upon meeting.[60] When Mack realized that no assistance was near, he surrendered.

So far, the campaign had not developed according to any grand plan; Napoleon no more foresaw Mack's surrender at Ulm than did Mack anticipate this outcome for the campaign. Historian Owen Connelly in his book *Blundering to Glory* argued that Napoleon's greatness was not in his plans. Never does a campaign unfold as expected since the enemy is a living, thinking opponent, acting to foil one's plans as much as one may act on his. Connelly argued that what made Napoleon great was his ability to improvise with what was at hand, reacting more rapidly than the enemy.[61] Napoleon's *coup d'oeil* gave him an advantage since the thousand little details did not distracted him from focusing on the truly important actions. In the *Grande Armée*, Napoleon had a tool that was more flexible and responsive than his opponents. This army marched more rapidly than expected and with units containing all arms, was able to fight outnumbered and hold its own against larger foes.[62] Finding the Habsburgs stationary at Ulm, Napoleon directed the army to mass there; the individual corps commanders knew that French support was always within a day's march, so they act aggressively, attacking much larger enemy formations. French soldiers, noting that the vast majority of the army had not seen the enemy, much less fired a round, commented "Our Emperor, said they, has found out a new way of making war; he no longer makes it with our arms but with our 'egs [sic]."[63]

Over the next few weeks the French pursued the scattered Austrian units that escaped Ulm and chased the Russian forces who began to arrive piecemeal.[64] Not everything went the French way. Near Braunau, Murat and Lannes had the opportunity to destroy an isolated portion of Kutusov's forces but instead headed to Vienna.[65] The Russians found a division of Mortier's newly formed corps isolated of Dürrenstein, and nearly destroyed it—3,000 of the 5,000 French soldiers engaged became casualties.[66] By 12 November, French troops arrived in Vienna. After Russian officers tricked Murat into an armistice that was then renounced by the emperor, the French pursuit continued until 23 November when the exhaustion of the French troops and the last chances of destroying the Russian forces piecemeal vanished, forcing a halt.[67]

By the last weeks of November, Habsburg troops under the Emperor Francis and Russian troops under Tsar Alexander and Field Marshal Kutuzov arrived near the Moravian village of Olmütz (modern Czech Republic) numbering 86,000 soldiers.[68] The French, dispersed for foraging, were near the town of Brünn (modern Brno). Napoleon faced a dilemma, and the situation worsened each day. The *Grande Armée* was at the end of a logistical tether that extended back to France. The area was not productive, making prolonged foraging impossible. The temperatures dipped into the 20°s Fahrenheit, and the army was miles from any major city. After three months on campaign, the infantry were tired, foot worn, and needed rest. Napoleon needed a major victory to conclude this campaign and prevent additional countries, such as Prussia, from joining the anti-French coalition. Napoleon had to lure the allies to attack him on ground of his own choosing.

Central Moravia is gently rolling farmland with few dominant features. To the north, the Moravian mountains restrict large-scale movement. A major east-west road ran between Olmütz and Brünn. Just south of the road, a gentle plateau known as the Pratzen Heights extended from northeast to southwest, ending above the village of Tellnitz. The Pratzen Heights rose 35-40 feet above the surrounding farmland. Looking at the Pratzen from the east, it was a steep climb, and an excellent position for defense. However from the west, the plateau rose gently over two to three kilometers and offered no impediment to movement. As Napoleon looked over this terrain in the last week of November, he saw the value of the terrain and told his staff to study the ground carefully because it would be the site of a great battle. [69]

Only 56,000 French troops were in the Brünn area; the rest were scattered across the route of the *Grande Armée* in occupation duties. Bernadotte's corps of 10,000 was to the north, guarding the approaches from Prague. Davout's corps was in Vienna, 80 miles away.[70] Napoleon began setting the conditions for this battle by showing French weakness. Understanding that the Austro-Russian army would be looking for revenge after Ulm, he sent his aide General Anne-Jean Savary to discuss a possible armistice; a Russian aide Count Dolgoroukie, a young hot-headed member of Tsar Alexander's entourage, came to the French camp to deliver a list of demands that insulted the French emperor. Dolgorouki reported to the Tsar that the French troops looked demoralized and weak.[71] On 21

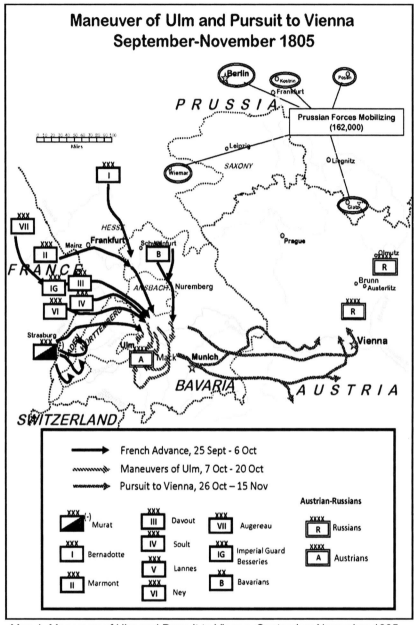

Map 1. Maneuver of Ulm and Pursuit to Vienna, September-November 1805.

November, Napoleon advanced one-third of his army towards Brünn, taking possession of the Pratzen Heights and Austerlitz. The majority of the French army was located in the north along the Olmütz road, with only a single division extending the line southward. On 30 November,

Napoleon pulled Murat's cavalry and Soult's Fourth Corps off the Pratzen, abandoning the best defensible position in the area. With 86,000 Austrian and Russian troops, Napoleon expected that the opportunity to destroy a portion of the French army would be irresistible to the allies.[72]

The next day, the Austro-Russian army occupied the vacant Pratzen Heights. The Austrian chief of staff, General-Major Franz von Weyrother, developed a plan that would cut the French off from Vienna, trapping them against the Moravian highlands, and destroying the army. It was a complicated plan and required the Austro-Russian army to divide in seven elements, timed to hit the French at various critical moments in the battle.[73] Two small detachments from the Austro-Russian army would fix the French into position; one would attack along the Olmütz to Brünn highway and the other hold the center of the position along the Prazten Heights. The main body, 59,300 strong in four columns, formed on the Prazten, would attack the weakly held south, cutting the road to Vienna, and then swing north, trapping the French and destroying them against the mountains.

It was a complex plan, dependant on moving columns from the Pratzen through a small opening between the villages of Tellnitz to Sollnitz before shifting north. Complicating the plan was the need to translate it from German into Russian and getting the orders to the commanders in time to execute it on 2 December. It was not until 1:00 a.m. of 2 December that the commanders assembled for the orders briefing. In *War and Peace*, Leo Tolstoy describes the order process in the allied headquarters that night. Packed into a small dining room in a simple farmhouse, dimly lit by candles, the Austrian chief of staff droned on in German, which the majority of the Russian commanders did not understand. Weyrother presented the order "like a college teacher reading a lesson to young scholars."[74] Sitting in the front row was the nominal army commander, Field Marshal Mikhail Kutuzov, 72 years old and sleeping through the orders brief. He lost his influence with the Russian Tsar because of his recommendations that they wait for additional troops to arrive.[75] Only when the briefing ended in the early morning hours did the orders go to the troops; most did not reach the units before the time scheduled for movement to begin. Columns cut through stationary ones still waiting for their orders creating confusion before the first shot.

The scene in the French camp was vastly different, and Napoleon's understanding of ground, time, space, and his enemy's attitudes were key. The Austro-Russian plan to destroy the French army was exactly the one that Napoleon wanted them to adopt. Napoleon had sent orders on

28 November for Davout's Third Corps, 80 miles away in Vienna, and Bernadotte's corps, to march to Brünn; by 1 December Bernadotte's corps had arrived but not Davout.[76] The rest of his army rested along the shallow Goldbach brook. In the north, Lannes' Fifth Corps and the Reserve Cavalry defended a small hill, the Santon, oriented along the Olmütz Road. The center contained Bernadotte's First Corps, the Imperial Guard, and Soult's Fourth Corps, all hidden from allied view by the fog along the Goldbach, augmented by the campfire smoke that hung in the valley. The *Grande Armée* received its orders the previous day and spent the night keeping warm. Napoleon spent 1 December and part of the night visiting the troops, particularly after a skirmish developed in the south in the early morning hours. The soldiers, seeing their emperor among their camps in the early morning hours, cheered *"Vive l'emperor"* and lit straw torches to light his way; his aides ordered the troops to quiet down lest they alert the enemy to his presence. The rest of the night, he spent in the Imperial Guard's camp, sitting on a bay of hay, his feet on a drum, keeping warm by a fire. The contrast between the hectic and confused the Austro-Russian camp and calm French camp was marked.

The Austrian advance began at 6 a.m. in the south with a thrust toward Solkonitz.[77] As the pressure against the French right flank built, Napoleon refused to reinforce it with any troops from the center of his line. The line threatened to break several times, but at each moment of crisis, reinforcements from Davout's corps arrived to stabilize the front. Third Corps had marched 80 miles from Vienna in 50 hours, and went into the desperate fighting often from the march.[78] By 8 a.m., 12,000 French there were holding back 35,000-40,000 allies, and additional allied troops moved from the Pratzen Heights to support the assault and seal the Austro-Russian victory.[79] The fog was clearing, and from Napoleon's headquarters, he could see the dense mass of Russian columns moving off the Pratzen as hoped. As the allied ranks pressed into a narrow, dense mass in the south, the French line there slowly bowed backward, and the Pratzen appeared nearly empty as Austrian and Russian army cleared the heights to add their weight to the attack in the south.[80]

Behind the Goldbach stream, Napoleon waited with his staff and Marshal Soult, whose troops would execute the main attack. The fog and smoke in the valley continued to hide the mass of French troops; Napoleon on the Zuran Hill could see the crest of the Pratzen and watched as Austrian and Russian forces moved south until the crest of the hill was nearly bare. Turning to Soult, Napoleon asked him how long it would take his troops to reach the crest, to which Soult replied "less than twenty minutes, sire." "Then we'll wait a further quarter of an hour," was Napoleon's rejoinder.[81] The plateau cleared of the final allied units until just a few knots of headquarters personnel, watching the deployment, marked where the allied army had been.

Napoleon gave the order and two divisions began to advance from the fog up the plateau. At that moment, the cloud cover parted and the sun shone through—the sun of Austerlitz was a favorable omen that many of the French participants would comment upon later.[82] The Russian tsar and his staff on the Pratzen suddenly heard the French bands come alive; a few moments later to their amazement the lead French units appeared out of the fog.[83] Kutusov ordered the only troops available—the Russian Imperial Guard, east of the heights—to attack, as well as recalling units to return to the Pratzen.[84] It was too late. Heavy fighting both to the north between Lannes and Bagration as well in the center on the Pratzen itself led to the crisis between 9:30-11 a.m. Despite desperate fighting between the guard infantry and cavalry of both sides, the greater numbers and superior position of the French were too much. By 2 p.m., with the commitment of Bernadotte's corps on the Pratzen, the allied center ceased to exist.[85] After clearing the center of the heights, the French wheeled south, and then artillery began to fire into the flanks and rear of the now panicking allied troops. Some fled across the shallow fishponds to the south. The story of thousands of Russians and Austrians sinking to their death is myth; the ponds' ice did break, but the shallow ponds contained few dead the next spring.[86] Instead, the ponds created bottlenecks to the fleeing soldiers, destroying unit cohesion, therefore increasing the panic in the Austro-Russian army. By dusk, around 4 p.m., the battle was effectively over. In the north, the outnumbered French counterattacked the Russians along the Olmütz road; French cavalry pursued broken Allied units, furthering the panic and destruction. Tsar Alexander, heartbroken over the loss, rode away in tears and left Austrian territory. The allied army lost heavily—12,000 captured and 15,000 dead. Fifty stands of regimental colors and 180 cannons were captured compared to French losses of 8,000 men dead and wounded.[87] Napoleon spent the night in the Austerlitz castle where he wrote Josephine one of the great letters of understatement: "I defeated the Russian and Austrian army commanded by the two emperors. I am slightly tired..."[88]

Speaking to his soldiers the next day, Napoleon said *"Soldats! Je suis content de vous."* ("Soldiers! I am pleased with you").[89] The victory effectively destroyed the Third Coalition. William Pitt, hearing the news of the victory declared, "Gentlemen, roll up that map of Europe. We will not need it the next ten years."[90] Austria signed a peace within the month, losing nearly one-sixth of its territory including lands in Italy given to the Kingdom of Italy and in the Balkans to France, and lands in Germany to Bavaria, Wurttemberg, and Baden. Bavaria became a kingdom as a reward for the duke's support of France. The Holy Roman Empire ceased to exist, and the next year Napoleon created the Confederation of the Rhine which looked toward France for leadership. Napoleon's soldiers received rewards—each man at Austerlitz received 200 francs; widows of the fallen received large pensions and their children, officially adopted by the state, received a free education and could add the name "Napoleon" as a baptismal or family name.[91]

Napoleon considered Austerlitz his greatest battle. After most victories, marshals who played key roles received titles to commemorate their efforts, but after Austerlitz no titles were given—Napoleon thought the battle too closely identified with himself to allow any sharing of the honor. The battle showed the key elements of Napoleon's greatness. This included his *coup d'oeil*, his ability to see the terrain and understand the role it would play, his close personal connection with his soldiers, and his clear communication of orders.

Despite humiliating the Austrians and Russians in 1805, the Prussian armies in 1806, and then defeating the rebuilt Russian army in 1807, peace in Europe was fleeting for Napoleon. The French Revolution overturned the old order, making France the dominant nation that other powers sought to counter-balance. The desire to strike at archenemy Great Britain led Napoleon to invade Portugal, and then observing the decadent Bourbon regime in Spain overthrew and attempted to rationalize that country. The Spanish people never accepted his brother Joseph as king, leading to a six-year war that Napoleon termed his "Spanish ulcer." The Continental System, an economic embargo of all trade with Britain, led to war with Russia in 1812 and finally war in the German states in 1813. In these latter wars, the dynamics of warfare had changed—armies became huge, unwieldy, and with large supply trains since such numbers could not live off the land. These armies were unresponsive to the quick maneuvers that led to Napoleon's earlier successes. His opponents changed too, adopting some of the improvements that made the French army so resilient. Only during the allied invasion of France in 1814, did flashes of Napoleon's early brilliance return. The dynamic once again changed; the French army was smaller and Napoleon displayed the flexibility and rapid reading of the ground that made him so successful earlier in his career. However, the large allied armies, acting together, meant that this was a hopeless cause. Waterloo the next year was just as hopeless, and decisively ended

Napoleon's attempts to control France's destiny.

Napoleon's legacy loomed over the 19th and 20th centuries. Immediately after his second abdication and exile to St Helena in 1815, the first authors tried to distill the essence of Napoleon's greatness. Two of the most significant military writers, Baron Antoine Jomini and Major General Carl von Clausewitz, spent their lives determining why warfare changed during the French Revolution and how its greatest practitioner, Napoleon, used it. Through their writings, Napoleon's legacy became embedded in western military thought despite the fact that today, most soldiers would be hard pressed to identify that influence. For example, in 1810, American Colonel Alexander Smyth wrote *Regulations for the Field Exercise, Manoevres [sic], and the Conduct of the Infantry of the United States*, which was nothing more than a translation of the infantry manual of Napoleon's army.[92] Immediately after the Napoleonic wars, the young American military academy at West Point sent officers to Europe to buy military manuals and books to create the USMA library. During the 1820s, the library at West Point contained more books in French than in English, the majority being memoirs and correspondence of French officers.[93] Through this effort, Jomini and other French authors on the Napoleonic military shaped West Point. The USMA engineering textbook, used from 1817 until 1838, was by a French engineer Gay de Vernon, and approved by Napoleon in 1810 for use in the French army's schools.[94] A Napoleon Club founded by students and faculty in the 1850s, studied and dissected Napoleon's campaigns. Membership of this club reads like a virtual Who's Who of Civil War generals.[95] In the Civil War, conventional wags stated that officers in both armies went to war with a copy of Jomini, and by extension Napoleon, in their knapsack. Today, concepts such as principles of war, lines of operation, and center of gravity are key elements of modern doctrine and have a direct connection to Napoleon as seen through his interpreters.

Napoleon still captures the imagination. Forty major battles in the space of twenty years is normally what is remembered, yet his civil accomplishments play a key role in his legacy. The ideals of the French Revolution—a career open to talent instead of birth, the rule of law, the rationalization of civil administration and scrapping of elements from medieval European law were carried across Europe on the bayonets of the *Grande Armée*. Those states nearest France, and incorporated the longest into the French Empire had the most significant elements of the revolution become part of their identity. The Civil Code, or *Code Napoléon*, is a major influence on European law codes as well as those in South America

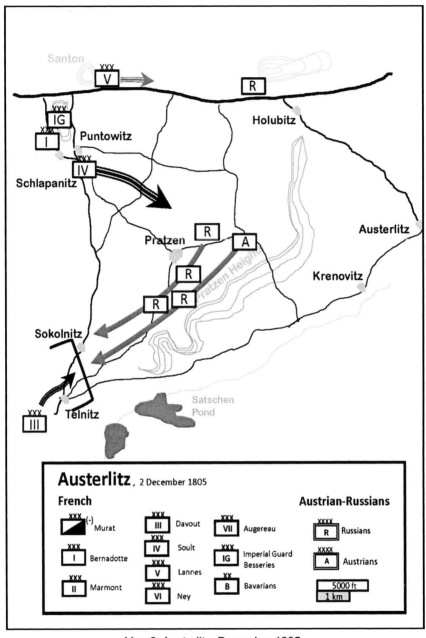

Map 2. Austerlitz, December 1805.

and portions of North America. The *Code* forbade privileges based on birth, instituted equality before the law, insured freedom of religion, and required that government positions be filled based upon talent, codifying those ideals of the French Revolution.

Through the publication of Napoleon's correspondence, dictated on St Helena before his death in 1821, and published beginning in 1823, Napoleon refought his battles and justified his actions. The correspondence was a major influence in how people immediately following his reign interpreted Napoleon's legacy. In 1815 the Congress of Vienna tried to put the revolutionary genie back into the bottle, but the revolutions in France in 1830 and then throughout Europe in 1848 showed that once out, these ideals were impossible to suppress. The creation of the Confederation of the Rhine was the first and a major step on the path to German unification as were the reforms in Italy in leading to its unification. It is not a coincidence that the Italian flag mimics the French flag's design.

Because many of the civil reforms relate to Napoleon's wars, they have lost some of their luster. Some view Napoleon as a monster, bent on world domination, but forget the context of European power politics. The other European states would not accept France's expanded role, and continued to confront the French Empire.[96] His legacy as a military commander and the glory he brought France has generally lost its appeal in the late 20th century revulsion to war. Napoleon's alluring legacy should be of someone who, without the benefit of birth or position rose to the pinnacle of power by sheer talent and ambition. Though the statement is probably apocryphal, Napoleon supposedly said that he was not made emperor but rather found the crown in the gutter and picked it up with his sword. Perhaps his greatest legacy is showing how far a person with talent could rise.

Notes

1. Thomas Hardy, *The Dynasts,* (London: MacMillan and Co, 1904), Part First, Act II, Scene V, page 87.

2. This claim was made by Professor Charles Esdaile during his lunch presentation at the Consortium on the Revolutionary Era in Lakeland, Florida on 20 February 2005. For his full presentation, see *Consortium on the Revolutionary Era: Selected Papers 2005,* (NC: High Point University Press, 2007) 1-12.

3. Stephen Englund, *Napoleon: A Political Life*, (New York: Scribner, 2004), 22.

4. Englund, 23.

5. Englund, 27.

6. David Chandler, *The Campaigns of Napoleon*, (New York: Scribner, 1966), 8-9.

7. Chandler, 13.

8. J. C. Herold, *The Age of Napoleon*, (New York: American Heritage Publishing Co., 1963), 45.

9. Chandler, 22.

10. Chandler, 23.

11. In French, "*batterie des hommes sans peur.*" Chandler, 26.

12. Chandler, 29.

13. Englund, 65.

14. Chandler, 30-31.

15. The coup against Robespierre occurred on 9 *Thermidor* of the Year II, or 27 July 1794 in the Julian calendar. In establishing a republic, the French revolutionaries thought a new era had begun, and counted from that date, 22 September 1792. The calendar removed the Greek and Roman month names, instead replacing them with months based on the seasons and harvest, such as *Thermidor* (heat), *Ventôse* (month of wind-March) or month of the harvest (*Fruitor*, October). The confusion between the Julian calendar and Revolutionary calendar led to its demise in 1806 on Napoleon's orders. Events during this period are known by their revolutionary calendar names.

16. Chandler, 39.

17. Chandler, 53-93, is a detailed discussion on Napoleon's command challenges and execution of the Italian campaigns.

18. Chandler, 84.

19. Tragically, during the riots on 17 December 2011 in Egypt, the Institute of Egypt, located on Tahrir Square, burned, destroying many priceless and irreplaceable documents of Egyptian history. *The Guardian*, 19 December 2011, page 17.

20. Englund, 169.

21. See Herold, 123-164, for a detailed description of the accomplishments of the Consulate.

22. Paul Thiébault, *The Memoirs of Baron Thiébault*, trans Arthur John Butler, (London: Smith, Elder & Co., 1896), II: 123-4.

23. Englund, 223-4, 253-6.

24. Chandler, 159.

25. Owen Connelly, *Blundering to Glory*, (Maryland: Rowman and Littlefield Publishers, Inc 2006), ix.

26. Chandler, 384.

27. John Elting, *Swords around a Throne*, (New York: Simon and Schuster, 1988), 60.

28. Elting, 127.

29. Elting, 132-3.

30. Many of the senior officers were not above enriching themselves while on campaign by seizing artworks as payment for the "liberation" by the French army. Elting,150.

31. Elting, 136-7.

32. Etling, 143.

33. Elting, 130.

34. Elting, 125.

35. Cornélis de Witt Willcox, *French—English Military Technical Dictionary*, (Washington: Government Printing Office, 1917), 295.

36. Elting, 85.

37. Elting, 84.

38. Elting, 84.

39. Chandler, 367.

40. Elting, 84.

41. Chandler, 97.

42. Chandler, 374.

43. Chandler, 375.

44. Chandler, 376.

45. Herold, 169.

46. John Holland Rose, editor, *Select Despatches*[sic] *from the British Foreign Office Archives Relating to the Formation of the Third Coalition against*

France, 1804-1805, (London: Spottswoode & Co., Ltd., 1904), 267; Chandler, 330-1.

47. Chandler, 382.

48. Chandler, 382.

49. Connelly, 78; Chandler, 383.

50. Chandler, 382.

51. Chandler, 384-5.

52. R. M. Johnston, The *Corsican: A Diary of Napoleon's Life in His Own Words* (Boston and New York: Houghton Mifflin Company, 1910), 168.

53. Herold, 170-1.

54. Englund, 272.

55. George Eberle, "March Performances of Napoleonic Armies," U.S. Army Command and General Staff School Student Paper, (Fort Leavenworth, KS: The Command and General Staff School, 1934), 8.

56. Eberle, 14.

57. Chandler, 400.

58. Chandler, 399.

59. Chandler, 399-400.

60. There is an argument whether this lack of synchronization of calendars was the cause of Mack's defeat. Clearly, the French army and Mack's inaction were the causes of his defeat. Whether the reinforcement by the Russians would have changed this seems doubtful as later actions in this campaign show.

61. Connelly, ix.

62. The average of twelve miles a day in poor weather and while fighting skirmishes and battles is impressive. The U.S. Army's Field Service Regulations of the 1930s stated a rate of eleven miles a day for a 1930s U.S. Army division when not in combat. Eberle, "March Performances of Napoleonic Armies," 33.

63. Adolphe Thiers, *History of the Consulate and the Empire of France under Napoleon,* (Philadelphia: Claxton, Remsen, and Haffelfinger, 1879), II: 42.

64. Connelly, 83.

65. Murat and Lannes tricked an Austrian commander by announcing that an armistice had been signed, and then crossed the bridge with their troops. A few days later, Murat failed to exploit this opportunity by signing an armistice without authority. Napoleon immediately renounced it. Connelly, 84-5.

66. Chandler, 406.

67. Connelly, 85; Chandler, 408.

68. Connelly, 85.

69. Chandler, 412.

70. Chandler, 410.

71. J. David Markham, editor, *Imperial Glory: The Bulletins of Napoleon's Grande Armée, 1805-1814*, (London: Greenhill Books, 2003), 30th Bulletin of the *Grande Armée*, 3 December 1805, 51.

72. Chandler, 410.

73. Connelly, 86.

74. Theirs, V:159.

75. Leo Tolstoy, *War and Peace*, trans Ann Dunnigan, (London: Penguin Books, 1968), 595-601.

76. Berthier to Davout, 28 November 1805, *Operations of the 3rd Corps*, trans Scott Bowden, (Boalsburg, PA: Military History Press, 2006) 5. Davout received the order at 4:00 p.m. on 29 November.

77. Chandler, 425.

78. Davout to Berthier, 3 December 1805, *Operations of the 3rd Corps*, 14.

79. Chandler, 425.

80. The Pratzen was not as empty as it appeared. A strong allied force, delayed in marching due to the confused orders, was still on the far side of the heights. Christopher Duffy, *Austerlitz: 1805*, (London: Leo Cooper, Inc., 1977), 106.

81. Chandler, 425.

82. Duffy, 102.

83. Chandler, 425.

84. Duffy, 135.

85. Chandler, 431.

86. Markham, 54.

87. Chandler, 432.

88. Napoleon to Josephine, 3 December 1805, as cited in Claude Manceron, *Austerlitz: The Story of a Battle*, (New York: Norton, 1966), 55.

89. Markham, 55.

90. James Richard Joy, *Ten Englishmen of the Nineteenth Century*, (New York: The Chautauqua Press, 1902), 3.

91. Markham, 61-2; Chandler, 439.

92. Michael Bonura, *Under the Shadow of Napoleon*, (New York: New York University Press, 2012), 44.

93. Bonura, 71.

94. Bonura, 76.

95. Bonura, 112.

96. Much of the demonization of Napoleon started with contemporary British sources and should be treated carefully. The political context in Europe during this period was much too complex to blame on one country or man—each state was playing power politics to maintain their status. For example, Napoleon's invasion of Russia in 1812 was a result of Russia renouncing its Treaty of Tilsit obligations not to import British goods; Russia mobilization of her army began in 1811, before Napoleon decided on invasion. The threat of the Grand Duchy of Warsaw, a nascent Polish state allied to France, which existed only because the Napoleon took the Polish lands occupied by Russia, Prussia, and Austria in the 1790s and returned them to Poland, threatened Russia and weakened Prussia.

Chapter 4
Warrior of the Waves
Nelson's Legacy to Naval Commandership
by John T. Kuehn, Ph.D.

The Battle of Trafalgar occurred off the coast of Southern Spain on the morning of October 21, 1805. As battles go, Trafalgar numbers among the most decisive in modern history and remains a monument to the superior training, tactics, organization, and—especially—the leadership of the Royal Navy of the period. This chapter examines the supreme commander of the British Fleet at Trafalgar, Admiral Lord Viscount Horatio Nelson, Baron of the Nile. Nelson left a profound legacy to command at sea that still affects how navies, and especially the United States Navy, operate today.[1] Nelson codified for the Royal Navy and all other navies the guiding principle of pre-battle centralized planning and decentralized, violent execution in combat. All of Nelson's operations and battles highlight these simple principles, but none more so than his masterpiece off Cape Trafalgar over two centuries ago.

$$* \quad * \quad * \quad * \quad * \quad * \quad * \quad * \quad *$$

In order to best understand Nelson as a commander we must fast forward to the eve of the Battle of Trafalgar and examine him at his absolute best in embodying the style of centralized personal command and decentralized execution. The period before the actual battle has much to teach us about "The Nelson Touch."[2] Lord Nelson's victory did not rely upon his personal direction of the bulk of the actual combat. Very early in the battle Nelson was mortally wounded and exercised little direction upon subsequent events; however, prior to his wounding he had ceased to exercise much control beyond the bridge of his flagship HMS *Victory*. To understand why we must give him the lion's share of the credit (the other recipients being of course his men and ships) we must go back to the days before the battle, when he laid the foundation for his overwhelming victory.

Nelson understood, perhaps better than many of his contemporaries in the Royal Navy, the importance of preparation before the battle. When he rejoined his fleet blockading the Franco-Spanish force off Cadiz in late September 1805 he immediately convened a meeting with his subordinate commanding officers onboard his flagship. He had already sent a letter to all of them explaining his intention to trick the French Admiral Pierre de Villeneuve into battle. Once battle was imminent, he would attack with

Figure 4. Captain Horatio Nelson, 1781, age 33; painting by J.F. Rigaud.

two columns of ships with the intent to break the traditional battle line of the enemy into three groups: the van, the main body, and the rear. Of these groups, those in the van would be effectively unavailable for the initial phases of the fight since they would have to sail back into the wind (tack) to reach the battle, by which time Nelson intended to have defeated the other two groups of ships. In this way Nelson would rectify any numerical superiority that the enemy might have as well as deny him the ability to refuse battle with the entire fleet (see figure 1). Nelson explained all of this in further detail in person aboard his flagship to his captains. It was a supreme example of a commander making known his intent to his subordinates in a collaborative and accessible fashion. It bears many parallels to a similar dinner that Napoleon held with his generals prior to Austerlitz.[3]

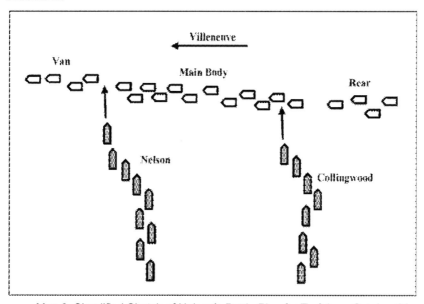

Mao 3, Simplified Sketch of Nelson's Battle Plan for Trafalgar, October 21, 1805. Figure created by John T. Kuehn.

Nelson reiterated his intent in a famous memorandum written on 9 October after his conferences and dinners aboard the *Victory*. Nelson's memorandum emphasized the Royal Navy's key institutional advantages that would bring the victory—superior gunnery and seamanship. Nelson outlined for his captains that he did not intend to form new lines of battle once they sighted Villeneuve's fleet. In order to take advantage of superior British seamanship and trap Villeneuve he intended to waste no time forming up for battle but rather his ships' positions—what was called their order of sail—would also be their order of battle. This would give him speed. Second, he wrote that "...no captain can do very wrong if he places his Ship alongside that of an Enemy." This instruction emphasized his belief that his fleet was ship for ship and man for man superior to that of the French and Spanish. It was also written to emphasize to his captains that if signals could not be seen from the flagship they had complete autonomy to engage the enemy as they saw fit. Close combat would also maximize his ships' advantage in weaponry at point blank ranges through the use of their devastating carronades to inflict maximum death and destruction upon his enemies. Nothing Nelson ever wrote has emphasized the principle of decentralized execution as cogently. Finally, his intention was no mere victory but rather "annihilation" of the entire enemy fleet.[4]

Centralized planning and conveyance of his intent complete, Nelson turned his mind to the battle-readiness of his fleet and detached several his battleships to escort a convoy of supplies for the fleet bound from Malta through the strait of Gibraltar. In fact, procuring fresh meat and vegetables for his scurvy-weakened sailors consumed much of Nelson's time as he attempted to get these items out to the fleet on station off Cadiz on the southern coast of Spain. Nelson also employed what we might today call operational deception.[5] Finding the fleet in a close blockade off Cadiz he decided to move it over the horizon so that the French and Spanish would not be aware of its precise location. He maintained watch on Cadiz with his frigates, which could also intercept and turn back snooping Spanish or French ships attempting to gather intelligence. Nelson meant to lure Villeneuve to sea, knowing that if the Frenchman could see his fleet he might not attempt a breakout for the Mediterranean. Once Villeneuve emerged, Nelson's intention was to intercept and destroy him, but until he judged the wind and time ripe he would remain just out of sight over the horizon paralleling Villeneuve's course.

Events conspired to cause Villeneuve to finally nerve himself to sortie from port. Through intelligence sources of his own he knew that the British force had detached several battleships and was now inferior to his own. He also knew that if he did not sail, he might not have a fleet to command in any case since he knew a replacement was on the way to relieve him. Napoleon had removed Villeneuve from command but his successor (and rival) Vice-Admiral Francois Rosily was still traveling via the overland route through Spain to Cadiz to take command. Now all was in the hands of the weather, specifically the winds. On 18 October the wind blew favorably and Villeneuve ordered his fleet to unmoor. On 19 October the first ships began to leave the harbor, although the wind occasionally died which made it necessary for Villeneuve to have several of his battleships towed out of port. Nelson's frigates signaled the good news that Villeneuve was finally leaving port, bound for Toulon and the Mediterranean in accordance with Napoleon's orders.[6]

Nelson had twenty-seven battleships to thirty-three for Villeneuve, but this quantitative disadvantage was more than compensated for by the superior morale, planning, seamanship, gunnery, and, leadership of Nelson's fleet. Nelson continued to stalk Villeneuve the next day as the Frenchman proceeded east-southeasterly toward Gibraltar with the combined fleet, however the pace of the French and Spanish advance was so slow that Nelson outran Villeneuve and had to bring his entire battle line around 360 degrees in order to fall back into a correct position vis-à-vis the combined fleet. Villeneuve by now had learned he was being stalked. Despite his numerical superiority at 0730 on the morning of 21 October he ordered his fleet to "wear" back toward Cadiz and began a gradual turn of the entire fleet back to port. This movement also gave him the correct disposition for battle based on the winds.[7] He was literally running away from battle. This did not affect Nelson's plan appreciably, the only difference being that Nelson's column would strike near the main body of the combined fleet's line while Collingwood's would now strike the rear.

Nelson had prepared for the light and variable winds that made the collision of the two fleets an agonizingly slow process. He had directed his captains to approach with all sail, including studding sails (auxiliary sails that take advantage of every last bit of available wind for motive force). In this way Nelson would maximize his speed of approach to the enemy which would minimize the amount of time his ships were under fire before they could respond. Once they pierced the enemy line-of-battle the British sailors were to cut these sails away, which would have the double effect of slowing them down (for close engagement) and eliminating these sails from tangling up the standard rigging. Nelson also employed tactical deception by having his own column feint toward the enemy van of ships to confuse them as to his real intention and then turning at the last possible moment toward Villeneuve's flagship (*Bucentaure*) in the main body. This action forced the van to maintain its line ahead and delayed its turning back to come to the aid of the rest of fleet (see figure 1).

Nelson then added a final edge to his fleet's fighting mettle when he sent, sequentially, two significant signals, neither of which was tactical but rather inspirational, as a means to give his men a combat edge. The first signal elicited a spontaneous outbreak of cheering throughout the fleet: "England expects every man will do his duty." This signal was passed a quarter of an hour before the first gunfire and nearly five hours after Nelson had ordered the turn toward the enemy. He followed this with a signal for his captains: "Engage the enemy more closely." This signal might be regarded as Nelson's final turnover of the battle to the discretion of his captains. After this point Nelson's fleet was now in the execution phase of the battle which relied relatively little on Nelson's personal direction and almost wholly on his subordinates.[8] At this point a return to the start of the story is in order to examine how this extraordinary man got to this point in his life.

His name was Horace—not Horatio. His older brother Horatio had died in infancy and it was by this name, in 1777 at the age of 21, that Nelson began to refer to himself. Horace Nelson was born to the Anglican rector Edmund Nelson and his wife Catherine on 29 August 1758 in Burnham Thorpe, a small town located in Norfolk just inland from the coast. The circumstance of his birth placed him squarely in what today would be labeled the middle class—he earned his titles in battle rather than receiving them by birth. The sixth of eleven children, his mother died shortly after his ninth birthday. Catherine Suckling Nelson came from a prominent family whose illustrious ancestors had included a prime minister of Great Britain, Robert Walpole after whose son, Horace Walpole (also a prime minister), the young Nelson received his first name. Catherine's brother, was Captain Maurice Suckling of the Royal Navy.[9]   T h e Sucklings were a prominent family and Maurice and William, Catherine's brothers, had both done well for themselves, Maurice in the Royal Navy and William in the government customs service. In 1771 Maurice, a highly intelligent and competent officer, received command of the 64-gun battleship *Raisonable*. This event prompted Edmund Nelson to send his son, who had already evinced a desire to go to sea, off to become a midshipman under his uncle's tutelage.[10]

The Royal Navy that young Nelson joined in May 1771 deserves some description. Despite draconian discipline the fleet was very much "England's Navy" and not the King's, as was the Royal Army. Commissions were not purchased as in the Army, but rather obtained through connections and family—usually from the gentle and merchant classes for the non-aristocratic applicants. Advancement through the ranks of the naval officer corps was obtained mostly through merit and performance due to the requirement to master math and navigation, the weeding out as a result of the rigors of life at sea, and a long tradition of meritocracy. In Nelson's day the Royal Navy would literally become the "people's navy" much as the French Army became the "people's army" during the French Revolution, although the Navy had been on this path for some time prior to Nelson's arrival. The Royal Navy reflected the nation of Britain every bit as much as the French Army under the Revolution and Napoleon came to reflect France.[11]

Despite this national character, life in the Royal Navy was particularly grim for its enlisted ratings and was a harsh school for midshipmen. The truism that the Royal Navy ran on "rum, sodomy, and the lash" still had some validity in the late 18th Century. But things were changing. Captains and officers who did not balance discipline with enlightened leadership might find themselves like Captain Bligh, set adrift in boats in the south seas, or facing massive mutiny, as indeed happened infamously off Spithead and at Nore during Nelson's life in 1797. The issue at Spithead, however, was not revolutionary fervor but pay, which had not been increased for over 100 years for the enlisted men. Even so, the mutineers made clear they would set aside their grievances and fight England's enemies should the need arise.[12] The captain who took care of his men while maintaining strict but fair discipline was as a rule more successful. Nelson embodies the type of command leadership that helped make the Royal Navy the dynamic and successful institution it was. Like Napoleon, Nelson's men would revere and follow him to the gates of hell because he cared for them both at sea and ashore.[13]

But all this lay ahead of the lad in a bobbing "Johnny-boat" that now approached the great man-of-war commanded by his uncle. *Raisonable* lay anchored in the Nore, the middle road of the Thames Estuary below London and site of the famous mutiny in 1791.[14] War with Spain threatened as Suckling took the new midshipman under his wing. One of the key things that any successful commander must have is luck, and now Nelson's connections with Suckling combined with good fortune to propel and develop him as both a skilled seaman and budding young leader.

The first event that might be termed luck occurred when the war scare with Spain over the Falkland Islands abated and the crew of the *Raisonable* was paid off. Suckling was transferred to the command of the larger *Triumph* (74).[15] Suckling worried that the new midshipmen might get caught up in the dull routine of the larger warship in port. He also knew that cliques and cabals formed among the midshipmen and officers on the larger ships that could plague a young officer for the rest of his career. Accordingly he paid the apprenticing fee and sent Horace to the smaller merchant vessel *Mary Ann* shipping out for Jamaica and the West Indies. Nelson would serve essentially as a common sailor and "learn the ropes" from the keel up aboard the smaller ship without his uncle's patronage influencing how he was treated. After a year he returned from the Indies a much saltier midshipman with real seamanship skills and a keen insight into his enlisted charges, because he had actually served as one.[16]

For the next five years, when Horace was not under his direct supervision, Captain Suckling continued this program of indirect mentorship, sending Nelson out with associates on long cruises. Nelson traveled into Arctic waters in 1773 and then from 1774 to 1776 he made an 18-month cruise aboard the frigate *Seahorse* (24) around the Cape of Good Hope to the Bengal shore and then back again and into the Red Sea.

In March 1776, with war breaking out in North America, he contracted the first of the many chronic tropical diseases that plagued him (in addition to his constant problems with seasickness). It was probably malaria. He shipped back home, arriving in London at the end of August having recovered his health during the return voyage.[17]

Nelson's timing and luck continued to hold. By this point Suckling had moved ashore as the comptroller of the navy and head of the Navy Board that examined qualifying midshipmen (those with six years' service) for their lieutenant's commission. Also, the war in America meant that the big warships now needed more officers, so the time was ripe for both action and opportunity. Suckling decided that Horace should study a bit more before standing for the exam and assigned the young man to another of his associates, Captain Mark Robinson, commanding the *Worcester* (64) as an "acting" fourth lieutenant.[18] Robinson's ship embarked another Suckling patron, Vice-Admiral Sir James Douglas, and was bound for convoy protection duty in the Bay of Biscay against the burgeoning American privateer threat. Nelson met both men, whom even at that young age he impressed. The harsh seas and frequent down-time allowed Nelson to both hone his watch skills and catch up on his studies for the lieutenant's exam. In particular he impressed Robinson, at least according to Nelson, who wrote:

In this ship [the *Worcester*] I was at sea with convoys till April 2nd, 1777, and in very bad weather. But although my age might have been a sufficient cause for not entrusting me with the charge of a Watch, yet Captain Robinson used to say, 'he felt as easy when I was upon deck, as any Officer in the Ship.'[19]

Worcester docked at Spithead in April and Nelson immediately returned to London to stand for his exam, which was administered by Suckling and two other senior post captains. As might be expected, Nelson passed with flying colors and was commissioned a lieutenant in the Royal Navy, having already proved himself as "An Able Seaman and Midshipman."[20]

Suckling immediately secured Nelson's assignment as second lieutenant aboard the frigate *Lowestoffe* (32) commanded by the learned Captain William Locker, who had served under the legendary Admiral Edward Hawke at Quiberon Bay. It was probably from Locker, and indirectly from Hawke, that the young Nelson acquired his preference for aggressive tactics and close combat as the keys to victory in the age of sail. It was at this time that Nelson began to call himself by his dead brother's name. Parker became Nelson's patron and from this point on

Nelson advanced rapidly, gaining his first command as a lieutenant in of the small brig *Badger* (14) at the age of nineteen.[21]

Thanks to Parker's patronage, the American Revolution, and Nelson's talent and luck, he rose to the rank of post captain in command of the frigate *Hinchinbroke* (28) on 1 September 1779. Nelson had just turned 21 and became one of the youngest post captains in the service, if not the youngest, at the time of his appointment. His time in the Caribbean, just as his cruise in the Indian Ocean, was cut short by disease, probably a combination of typhoid fever and his recurring malaria. Parker dispatched him home to recover. Nelson arrived at Spithead in late 1780 and went immediately to Bath for further treatment. Upon his recovery, none other than the famous Earl of Sandwich, First Lord of the Admiralty, appointed him over numerous unemployed and more senior captains to the command of *Albemarle* (28).[22]

From this point on until he was put on half-pay in Norfolk in 1787 Nelson commanded only one other ship—*Borias* (28)—and then was appointed Senior Office in the Leeward Islands in 1786 while still in command of that ship. Most of his duty had involved convoy escorts protecting British trade against American, Dutch, French, and Spanish privateers and warships. He gained a reputation for excellent leadership and fearlessness as well as for putting the interests of his men first. By this time he had also captured his first prizes and endured a variety of combats, both ashore and at sea. As Senior Officer, his final command, he had battled vested interests and corruption in the West Indies, but had actually undermined his support among certain senior officers by his crusading. He had also found a wife. Nelson first met the young widow Frances ("Fanny") Nisbet in May 1785 on the island of Nevis in the West Indies. Fanny had a young son and her uncle was quite wealthy. They waited until March 1787 to marry, with the King's son Prince William Henry as best man. Shortly after, Nelson's health again in decline, they both shipped home to Norfolk and Nelson went on half-pay in the post-war period of economizing under William Pitt the Younger.[23]

Nelson now led, by all accounts, a settled but restless life for the next five years, his career at a standstill during the time of extended peace after the American Revolution. But revolution came again, this time in France. By 1792 it was certain that Great Britain would become embroiled in the titanic changes sweeping France and rocking all of Europe. In Great Britain, measured support for France's political reform and move toward representative government was replaced with horror when King Louis XVI and Queen Marie Antoinette lost their heads on the guillotine in January

1793. Engaging in a sort of collective insanity, the French Republic, now under the control of mobs and opportunists, declared war on Great Britain the following month.²⁴ The ill-fortune of Europe became Nelson's good fortune. The Royal Navy constituted the nation's first line of defense and now it must put to sea with newly commissioned ships and full-up crews—including captains.

Horatio Nelson profited directly by these events, and from his many influential, high ranking patrons and his good record. Recalled to active duty, Nelson became captain of the brand new ship-of-the line, HMS *Agamemnon* (64). This posting also meant a promotion for the still-young officer (34) to a fourth rank captain. Nelson's own significant odyssey now began. He would command *Agamemnon* until June 1796 just prior to his first major act on the stage of history at the battle of Cape St. Vincent.²⁵ Nelson joined the fleet of Admiral Viscount Samuel Hood. Hood, a hero of the American war, had become one of Nelson's patrons while both served in the Caribbean and he brought Nelson into the fold of his operations in the Mediterranean. This theater of what became a world war would dominate the rest of Nelson's life.²⁶

The French Navy that Hood and Nelson faced was no longer the dangerous and sometime successful opponent they had faced fifteen years earlier. The Revolution hit *La Marine's* officer corps, composed almost entirely of aristocrats, especially hard. Learning how to sail and "fight" ships significantly differs from the requirements of land warfare. Navies cannot be improvised in the same manner that the French Republic was able to do with its armies in the early years of the revolution. Too, social policies that eliminated class distinctions and hierarchy, especially the elimination of the "'undemocratic rank' of master gunner" resulted in a precipitous decline in French gunnery that resulted in the Royal Navy's almost permanent advantage right through to Trafalgar.²⁷

Toulon, the great French naval base, was especially hard hit by the policies and neglect of the Revolution and actually surrendered to Hood's fleet in 1793. The analogy here might be the Confederacy's loss of New Orleans to the North during the American Civil War. At one stroke Britain obtained the most valuable port and base on the French Riviera while at the same time denying the French their most important shipbuilding facility with all of its naval architects and specialized workers. Unlike the case of New Orleans, however, the captors soon lost this prize. Hood quickly realized that without an army to control the heights surrounding the city it would fall to any competently-led army. He dispatched Nelson to Naples to procure more troops from the British ally there. Nelson returned with 2,000 badly-led Neapolitan troops. While in Naples he made the acquaintance for the first time of Lady Emma Hamilton, the young, beautiful wife of the Ambassador Sir William Hamilton. Also, for the first and last time, Nelson had his only direct encounter with the man whose nemesis he would become—the young captain of French artillery Napoleon Bonaparte. Bonaparte, sent by the government in France to oversee the siege of Toulon, had effectively seized control of operations, gained control of the heights and then expertly emplaced his beloved cannon to blast the Royal Navy and its Spanish allies from the city. Nelson noted the accuracy of the shooting and in his memoir noted that, "Shot and shell [were] very plentiful all over the harbor." For the first and last time Napoleon bested his British counterparts, driving them from the city and bringing a bloody "liberation" soon after. Worse, only three of the twenty or so French battleships that were captured when Toulon capitulated were brought away and what remained now served as the nucleus for a new French Mediterranean fleet. Toulon would remain French for the rest of the wars.[28]

Hood's loss of Toulon compromised his position in the Mediterranean. He proceeded to Corsica, which was in revolt against France, in an attempt to re-establish a base there on Napoleon's home island, initiating sieges of the fortresses of Bastia and Calvi. It was during the siege of Calvi, while observing the bombardment of the fortress on 8 July 1794, that Nelson received his first combat wound from shell fragments to his right eye. The damage was permanent and over time Nelson lost all useful sight in this eye, sometimes wearing a patch to hide the disfiguration that occurred due to poor medical treatment and harsh active duty after the wound. Calvi eventually fell, due in no small measure to Nelson's assistance, although his actions at Bastia were critical to the capture of that place.[29] In the meantime, Nelson missed the first major British naval victory of the war at which many of his later captains and admirals (e.g. Cuthbert Collingwood) fought—the Glorious 1st of June as it still is known to the British. Here, Admiral Richard "Black Dick" Howe, brother of the famous general Lord Howe, laid low a French fleet escorting a convoy of grain into Rochefort, killing more than 1200 French sailors and wounding 8,000 more while capturing six French ships and damaging numerous other vessels. However, the French fleet was still very much in being and the British blockade still loose enough that the grain made it into port.[30]

At this point Admiral Hood returned to England leaving the fleet in the hands of Admiral William Hotham. Under Hotham's command the principal goal was to prevent the still dangerous French from recapturing

Corsica, and this he accomplished although he refused battle (against Nelson's advice) with the superior French Fleet once it had turned back to Toulon. By early 1796, however, a more dynamic admiral assumed command of the Mediterranean Fleet and of Nelson—Sir John Jervis. Jervis, who had fought with Wolfe at Quebec, took immediately to the fiery young Nelson and soon became another of his many important patrons and mentors. Jervis's presence "transformed the spirit of the Mediterranean Fleet." Jervis also promoted Nelson to the most senior rank possible for a captain, commodore, since Nelson now routinely commanded more ships than just his own. Nelson also transferred his flag to a new battleship, the *Captain* (74).[31]

By now the Spanish had switched sides in the war and become allied to the French. French sea power now included the formidable Spanish fleet (and soon the Dutch fleet, which the French captured with a cavalry charge when it became unexpectedly icebound that winter). The year 1796 was a low point for Great Britain on land as well. Bonaparte's unexpected victories in Italy that year turned that theater's operations into the decisive campaign. All of Italy was lost (including Naples) to the rampaging armies. With powerful Spanish and French fleets in play the British pulled out of the Mediterranean as the Austrians sued for peace in early 1797. The war now assumed an entirely naval character and Jervis's fleet (and Nelson) now concentrated on preventing the Spanish fleet from combining with the French and ferrying Bonaparte's victorious legions across the channel from Boulogne.[32]

One of the last groups of British ships to leave the Mediterranean belonged to Nelson. Temporarily in command of two captured French frigates (*La Minerve* and *Blanche*), he had miraculously sailed through the main Spanish Fleet at night in the fog. He then proceeded directly to Admiral Jervis whom he found on 13 February 1797 off Cape St. Vincent on the Portuguese coast (across the Gulf of Cadiz and north from Cape Trafalgar). He gave Jervis the critical news that the Spanish Fleet had entered the Atlantic. The next day Jervis made contact with the superior Spanish Fleet under the command of Admiral Don Jose de Cordoba. Cordoba outnumbered Jervis by almost two to one in battleships (twenty-seven to fifteen). Jervis formed line of battle and made strait for the approaching Spanish Fleet, saying "The die is cast and if there are 50 sail of line, I will go through them." The Spanish fleet was divided into two groups which were trying to mass, one windward (upwind) and one leeward (downwind) from the British. Nelson and his good friend Collingwood brought up the rear in *Captain* and *Excellent* (64).[33]

At the key moment in the battle Nelson's portion of the line was closer to the Spanish than the head of the column as Jervis took his ships into a turn to keep the Spanish divided. Nelson, disobeying the famous standing battle orders, wore out of the line without orders and sailed straight for the middle of the Spanish column where the most powerful ships sailed, including Cordoba's massive flagship *Santissima Trinidad* (140). Nelson's aggressiveness and ability to act independently had been known in the fleet, but now they were on display for all to see. Jervis aboard the *Victory* (100) saw Nelson now engage seven enemy battleships with his one. He approved the action and signaled Collingwood and *Excellent* to support him. He then sent out the same signal to the remainder of his ships that Nelson himself sent from *Victory* at Trafalgar, "Engage the enemy more closely." Nelson's ship should have been obliterated as he endured the close but inaccurate fire of the Spanish. Elated by close combat, he rammed *San Nicholas* (80) which had become fouled close aboard with another Spanish battleship *San Josef* (112) and boarded her. Nelson personally led the boarding party aboard *San Nicholas* and took her in violent close-quarters fighting. The next action he took was unprecedented and sealed his fame—with *San Josef* still close aboard he continued with his boarding party across the *San Nicholas* and took the larger *San Josef* as well. Meanwhile, Collingwood had pounded three more Spanish ships to pieces and taken one of them. Of the four Spanish ships taken, two belonged to Nelson. It was a spectacular victory and earned Nelson a Knighthood (of the Bath) and promotion to Rear Admiral. The King made Jervis "Earl St. Vincent" in honor of the great victory. Spanish sea power remained cowed until peace was signed in 1802 at Amiens.[34]

There still remained French and Dutch fleets to fight as well as the Nore and Spithead mutinies of 1797. Once the mutinies were resolved Admiral Duncan managed to demolish the Dutch Fleet as a threat at Camperdown (11 October 1797). This was a victory nearly as great as Trafalgar with the British capturing 13 enemy vessels. Nelson, in the meantime, had been sent by Jervis on his first independent assignment as an admiral to seize the port of Santa Cruz on Tenerife in the Canary Islands. Disaster resulted. Nelson's audacity had not yet been tempered with real failure and he soon found it at Tenerife. He made the classic mistake of underestimating his foes and overestimating his own power to prevail in leading what was essentially an amphibious assault. He took his landing force into an ambush. One of his closest friends was killed in the assault and Nelson almost bled to death when his right arm was shattered by a musket ball. He was saved only by the quick-thinking of his step-son

Josiah who stopped the bleeding with an improvised tourniquet. Nelson was rowed back to the nearest ship, ironically named *Seahorse*, where the surgeon immediately amputated the limb. Ashore things went from bad to worse with the remainder of the operation a bloody repulse.[35] The wound did not heal properly and Nelson liberally imbibed opium for the pain. He returned to England an opium-sedated wreck who believed his career had ended with the loss of his right arm, writing to a friend, "I am become a burthen to my friends and useless to my Country."[36]

Nelson arrived in England to be met at Bath by his wife Fanny and his father on 3 September 1797. His right eye was disfigured, his right arm gone, and his hair prematurely gray. Fanny immediately took to the task of nursing her broken husband back to health and into a fighting fettle. Her actions and his response to them make more difficult to understand his later behavior after his great victory on the Nile when he repudiated his devoted wife in favor of his beautiful mistress, Lady Emma Hamilton. All the major biographers agree, however, that Lady Fanny Nelson deserves the bulk of the credit for nursing her husband back to health and helping him recover. A.T. Mahan was among the first, though, of his biographers to perceptively note the relationship between Nelson's recovery and subsequent cold abandonment of his wife and his "…unseemly susceptibility to extravagant adulation…"[37] This change in character would manifest itself in both his personal and professional lives after 1797; the end result was a commander who could be extremely brutal and callous to those he regarded as enemies, be it the French, his wife, or anyone who supported her in her efforts to regain her husband's affections.

Nelson's record at Cape St. Vincent ensured his assignment to the critical theater of the war in 1798 under Jervis, the commander-in-chief of the Mediterranean Fleet. Nelson raised his flag on *Vanguard* (74) in late March and set sail for the Gulf of Cadiz. Jervis's confidence in Nelson was unbounded. As soon as Nelson arrived to join the fleet on blockade duty off Cadiz Jervis detached him on an independent command with a small squadron to enter the Mediterranean and keep an eye on the French fleet in Toulon. Jervis forwarded another eleven battleships to Nelson in May 1798, an unprecedented command for such a junior admiral that caused much grumbling among the many admirals senior to him who were without sea command. Jervis instructed Nelson to intercept an invasion fleet embarking the army of Napoleon Bonaparte and suspected to be bound for Egypt. Napoleon's plans to invade England had been stymied by the destruction of the Dutch at Camperdown and a fierce hurricane at Boulogne in 1797. Napoleon's strategy focused on bringing Britain to a negotiated peace through severing her line of communications with the East Indies by capturing Egypt and then continuing, perhaps, on to the real prize—India. Nelson's plan was simple: intercept the invasion fleet and destroy Napoleon and his army at sea.[38]

Jervis's faith in Nelson was rewarded, but not immediately. Nelson's impatience almost did him in, but he was tenacious in pursuit of his quarry. Nelson had been off Toulon prior to his reinforcement but had sailed off and then had his small squadron scattered by a storm. On May 19 Napoleon, escorted by the French fleet under Admiral Brueys, departed. Nelson was desperately short of frigates (he had only 3) to provide him intelligence and he decided Napoleon's destination was Naples. Napoleon instead went to Malta and conquered it. Nelson realized his mistake and decided that Napoleon's next objective was Alexandria, Egypt. He rushed off arriving off Alexandria on 29 June and found nothing. Brueys and Napoleon had taken a different route via Crete and sailed far slower than Nelson imagined. Nelson missed a great chance by not waiting off Alexandria, second-guessing himself and sailing north to Turkey. While Nelson sailed north the French arrived and began to debark their troops. It seemed that Nelson had lost the game of cat and mouse and missed the golden opportunity to destroy both a French army and a French fleet.[39]

Nelson did not give up. Off Sicily he learned of his mistake and doubled back to Alexandria. Late on 1 August he arrived and found the transports empty, but Brueys' thirteen battleships and many smaller warships lay anchored close in to shore in the shallow and treacherous (or shoal) water of Aboukir Bay. Brueys had unwisely sent half of his gun crews ashore to assist Napoleon with the land campaign (Napoleon had won his own great battle of the Pyramids on 21 July). He also thought himself unassailable so close in to the shore. The final nail in his coffin was the late hour of the day. Surely Nelson would not attack in such dangerous waters in the dark! Nelson instantly decided to attack.[40]

Nelson had 15 battleships to 13 of the French, but the French had the heavier weight of gunnery (bigger ships and bigger guns). His orders to his captains show both his seamanship and his confidence in theirs. He sent a signal that required them to engage the French by sailing in the barely navigable water where the French line lay anchored. As if this wasn't hard enough, he instructed all of them to anchor by the stern. This meant that his ships would be anchoring under fire but once anchored they would be at a dead stop and be able to blast their opponents to pieces. Anchoring by the stern was not normal practice and difficult for trained crews to do. It was hard enough to ask seaman in that day and age to do this in the daytime in normal waters, but at night, in shoal water and under fire, reflected a level of confidence in his men and himself that still amazes one today. The execution was not without some hiccups. The famous Captain Troubridge on *Culloden* ran aground just north of the French on the approach. Several ships performed the anchoring maneuver badly and paid with heavy casualties as a result of being out of position. But Nelson's other captains served him well—the lead ship *Goliath* led part of the line inside the French line, creating a double envelopment of the French ships in the first part of the line. The French vessels further down the line were anchored solid and could not help them. The night sky of Alexandria lit up with the din and spectacle of burning French ships as Nelson pounded the French fleet to pieces as his ships proceeded down the line. Only Admiral Pierre Villeneuve in the rear escaped with two battleships and two frigates. The rest of the French fleet—including 11 battleships--was destroyed or taken. Nelson, in the thick of the fighting as usual, received a nasty head wound. He had not lost a single ship and had fewer than 900 casualties, including himself. He had effectively checkmated Napoleon's strategy by stranding the French army in Egypt. When Napoleon attempted to fight his way through Ottoman Turkish territory in order to gain passage to Europe or even India, he was confounded again by that other great naval hero, Sir Sydney Smith, who successfully led the defense of Acre, forcing Napoleon to turn back. In 1799 Napoleon abandoned his army and withdrew to France where he took over the government in a *coup d'etat*.[41]

After the Nile Nelson's fame reached unparalleled heights. The Sultan of Turkey presented him with an elaborate diamond spray that Nelson wore on his impossibly large bicorn hat. The King rewarded him with a peerage as Lord Nelson, Baron of the Nile and his income doubled while he received from the grateful East India Company a ten thousand pound gift. He was the darling of the press and had reached what today is known as "rock star" status. All of the complaining against both Nelson and Jervis ceased, Jervis feeling more than vindicated by his decision to give the young admiral a chance to strike a key blow. Many historians consider the Nile Nelson's most important victory, strategically and tactically. The British position in the Mediterranean remained secure for the rest of the wars to 1815. The French themselves think the Nile his greatest feat—a 1988 scholarly study declared, "[Nelson's victory marked] the end of the French navy as a force capable of counterbalancing British power. It could not be put together again and Aboukir carried within itself the germ of Trafalgar."[42]

Nelson returned to Naples where he was *feted* by the King and

Queen and his friends Sir William and Lady Emma Hamilton. He had not seen the Hamiltons in over five years. His superstar fame now went to his head. Historians are agreed that his behavior now betrayed the ruthless and self-serving side of his character. In addition to beginning a very public (and thus for Fanny, humiliating) affair with the beautiful Lady Emma Hamilton, Nelson allowed himself to be manipulated by the scheming Bourbon monarchs of Naples, especially the sister of Marie Antoinette, Maria Carolina the Queen. In 1798 the French had completed their conquest of Italy and declared a republic in Naples, forcing the Bourbons to take refuge in Sicily and on Nelson's ships.[43] With the return of the Allies to Italy under Marshal A.A. Suvorov in 1799 the Bourbons reoccupied Naples and used Nelson to imprison, mistreat, and execute many political prisoners. It was possibly the lowest point of Nelson's career as he carelessly trifled with his mistress while he let his men and ships be used for political repression and murder by the amoral and corrupt Bourbons. Meanwhile he had impregnated Emma, who was still married to Sir William. Nelson and Emma decided, after Napoleon's victory a Marengo, to return to Great Britain by land through central Europe. Nelson relinquished his command on 12 July 1800. He and the Hamiltons, accompanied by a large retinue, then embarked upon a self-serving "grand tour" through Austria and Germany, Nelson receiving accolades wherever he went. The party finally arrived in England in early November. It had been more than two years since his great victory yet everywhere they went the strange *ménage a trois* of Nelson and the Hamiltons received wild and adulatory receptions. Only at Blenheim Palace were they snubbed by the Duke of Blenheim, scion of the famous Churchill family. Perhaps the best comment on Nelson comes from his former army comrade Sir John Moore, who remarked upon seeing him in Genoa prior to his grand tour, "He is covered with stars, ribbons and medals, more like the Prince of the Opera than the Conqueror of the Nile. It is really melancholy to see a brave and good man, who has deserved well of his country, cutting so pitiful a figure."[44]

Fortunately for Nelson, French victories in Italy and then Germany caused the Russian Tsar, the unstable Paul I, to abandon his alliance with Austria and Britain and declare a League of Armed Neutrality among the Baltic states that was clearly aimed at the highhanded actions of the British Navy and the way it treated neutral ships and impressed their sailors. The Tsar was further irritated that the British refused to acknowledge his claim to Malta, which the British had recaptured from the French in 1800. Of these states the most important was Denmark, with a large and well trained fleet of 23 battleships. Too, the Baltic region provided the balance of naval stores for Great Britain, thus any interruption of these supplies threatened the materiel basis of British naval power.[45] The Admiralty recalled Nelson to active duty and in early 1801 assigning him as second-in-command of a fleet commanded by Vice Admiral Sir Hyde Parker. Parker's orders from the Admiralty advised caution and instructed him to apply gentle pressure by way of a blockade while negotiations took place. He was to avoid giving offense and causing Sweden, Denmark and Russia to combine their fleets, which would outnumber him over four to one. Parker kept Nelson in the dark about his plans and refused to share his thoughts with his famous subordinate. Only after the Danes rejected an ultimatum to leave the League did Parker consult his admirals, although they had intelligence that the Danes were fortifying Copenhagen and preparing for battle.[46]

Parker and Nelson approached Copenhagen in late March in two divisions, the van commanded by Nelson and Parker with the main body. Some of the fortresses at the end of the approach shelled them, but most of the batteries within range remained silent as Parker and Nelson took stock of the situation. Between them they had 19 battleships. Nelson had finally gained Parker's confidence during the voyage and Parker wisely gave the balance of the force, 11 battleships and 18 other smaller warships to Nelson, leaving the planning for an attack, should the need arise, to Nelson. Nelson installed himself on *Elephant* (74), command by the audacious Captain Foley who had sailed inside the French line at the Nile on his own initiative. Nelson's plan to attack the neutral Danes was simple and violent. He would approach the anchored Danish Fleet from the south while Admiral Parker's ships remained to the north to reinforce success or ward off the Russians and Swedes. He relied on a frigate to sound out the channel for the main body. The battle was very much like that at Aboukir, a bloody pounding at close range, but the Danes fought much longer and harder. During the height of the battle the worried Parker sent Nelson a signal of recall and Nelson famously clapped his telescope to his blind eye saying out loud, "I really do not see the signal!" At the same time as his fleet smashed the Danish ships and shore batteries to pieces his bomb ketches sent fiery salvos into the city, setting it afire and indiscriminately killing and wounding civilians along with military defenders. (This might be regarded as the first instance of "strategic bombing" in modern history.) The Danes finally agreed to a cease fire when Nelson threatened to set afire several floating batteries he had captured and used to hold his Danish prisoners. The Danes suffered forty per-cent casualties in their fleet and land defenses. The British suffered almost 1000 casualties, including

253 killed. Tensions remained high for the next five days as Nelson negotiated with the Crown Prince of Denmark and his advisors. After five days he threatened to bombard Copenhagen again, whereupon the Danes capitulated and signed an armistice.[47]

It had been a messy battle, Nelson's sloppiest. Three of his ships had run aground. It had also been his riskiest, but the outcome caused the League of Armed Neutrality to collapse and precipitated the assassination of Tsar Paul, who was replaced by his son Alexander. Nelson's willpower and ruthlessness were rewarded as he replaced Hyde Parker as commander-in-chief. Nelson graciously defended Parker against those who wanted a court of inquiry. Afterwards he returned home and during the period of negotiations with the French prior to the peace of 1802 commanded the defensive forces in the channel, launching an ill-conceived commando raid against Boulogne to destroy parts of the French invasion fleet and bateaux. The French Admiral Louis Latouche-Treville expected him and the result was similar to Tenerife, except that this time Nelson did not lead the landing force personally but remained on his flagship. Neither did he lose an arm. Over 150 men were killed and wounded. However, Nelson was so famous and beloved by this time that nothing could dim the shine of his star. With peace he returned to the settled domestic country house he had set up with Emma and their young daughter Horatia, his break with Fanny complete.[48]

The peace between Great Britain and France lasted barely a year. On 14 May 1803 Great Britain declared war on France. Nelson was appointed commander-in-chief of the Mediterranean Fleet and assigned to watch his old enemy Admiral Latouche-Treville the same day. Two days later he boarded *Victory* (100), Jervis's flagship at St. Vincent, and hoisted his flag.[49] He was back with the fleet he loved and that loved him.

Napoleon's strategy aimed at gaining temporary command of the narrow seas of the English Channel in order to cross with an army of over 150,000 of the finest troops in Europe. However, gaining command of the sea meant that the French Navy must defeat or damage the Royal Navy—or perhaps deceive it and draw enough of it away—so that the invasion would have a reasonable chance of success. Simply put, the French strategy was an invasion that would enable Napoleon to dictate terms to a conquered British nation. British strategy was equally simple—to blockade the French, and later Spanish, fleets in their ports so they could not escort the invasion flotilla.

On 26 August 1805 Imperial French Headquarters issued orders to the *Grande Armée* (now some 210,000 troops) to turn east and abandon its positions along the English Channel for the invasion of Great Britain. Napoleon's decision to do this had occurred even earlier. Since Trafalgar was some two months distant in the future one can categorically state that Trafalgar was not the reason for the suspension of the cross-channel invasion. The Royal Navy's blockade was the decisive element that defeated Napoleon's strategy—given its art and elegance it was surely a military operation that the subtle Sun Tzu would have appreciated.[50] The British strategy accomplished its successful result not with a naval battle for the ages, but rather with the slow, steady application of superior sea power over a period of two years. This in turn was augmented by the relentless offensive energy of admirals like Nelson, who literally hunted down any French or Spanish ship concentrations that managed to slip by the blockade into the open sea. In the end, it was the systemic effects of the British blockade combined with the superior training, tactics, and leadership of the Royal Navy that accomplished this result.

One must give both the French Navy and Napoleon due credit for operationally creating the conditions which might have given the invasion force a fighting chance. The great operational problem for the French and Spanish fleets was their inability to mass due to the blockade. If the majority of the separate fleets at Brest, Toulon, Cadiz, and other points could only combine they might be able to defeat, or at least drive away, the British fleet guarding the English Channel. The only way to do this would be to try to divide the British fleet and then during the period of separation enter the Channel and do battle with the isolated element there. This would be difficult, since the British had large squadrons of battleships blockading all the major ports, under a number of very competent admirals: Nelson, Cornwallis and Keith in particular. The main British fleet—the Channel Fleet—was not even under Nelson but under Admiral Cornwallis with another strong squadron under Admiral Keith in reserve. Nelson's task was to watch the French under Admiral Villeneuve bottled up in the Mediterranean port of Toulon on the south coast of France. Villeneuve had replaced the more competent Latouche-Treville who had died in August 1804.[51]

Admiral Villeneuve had done battle with Nelson before—off the Nile. Recall that Villeneuve's *Guillaume Tell* was one of only two battleships to escape Nelson after the battle. Upon the resumption of hostilities in 1803 Villeneuve was in command of a squadron in the West Indies. He later commanded the French Squadron based out of Rochefort on the French Atlantic coast. He was actually junior to Admirals Denis Decrés and Joseph Ganteaume. Ganteaume had the main French fleet at Brest. However, despite Villeneuve's junior status and deep respect, perhaps fear, of Nelson, he was to be the instrument to obtain command of the sea in the English Channel.[52]

Napoleon needed a way to diminish or remove the British naval dominance from the Channel and devised a daring plan to divide the British fleet. Nelson and the Admiralty believed that Napoleon would again try to attack their lines of communication between Britain and the East Indies by attacking either Malta or Egypt (as he had done in 1798) as one way to distract the Royal Navy. Instead, Napoleon ordered Villeneuve to break out of Toulon and sail west in order to threaten the British colonies in the West Indies, a tactic the French had employed during the American Revolution. En route, Villeneuve would combine his fleet (eleven battleships and 6,400 troops) with a Spanish fleet under Admiral Carlos Gravina. It was hoped that Nelson would follow Villeneuve across the globe. If all went well Villeneuve would combine his force with whatever other French ships had broken out and made it to the Indies. In the meantime, it was hoped that the main fleet under Ganteaume would break out and proceed into the channel to cover the invasion. If Ganteaume did not break out on his own Villeneuve's return with a combined Franco-Spanish fleet might be the agent for concentration of all three fleets, which would then press into the Channel either for battle or to cover the invasion, whichever occurred first. Unfortunately, Napoleon never sat his admirals down and explained the entire scheme to them, so that they often knew only the bare minimum of the details and then only after they had put to sea and opened their sealed orders. This was a recipe for disaster.[53]

Napoleon's plan had many moving parts and relied on almost perfect synchronization between the various French and Spanish squadrons in order to mass in the correct place and at the correct time. It also relied on Nelson taking the bait and proceeding to the Indies in hot pursuit of Villeneuve. It came very close to success in achieving the desired concentration. By early 1805, many of the British ships had been at sea for over a year and were in need of repair and the crews were in need of rest. It was at this opportune time that Villeneuve made his first attempt to execute Napoleon's instructions. However, poor weather and the poor condition of the French ships, which had been cooped up in Toulon for over a year, forced Villeneuve to return to Toulon. However, Villeneuve's first attempt had caused Nelson to make a grave error. He assumed that Villeneuve was sailing for Alexandria in Egypt as Napoleon had done in 1798. By February 7, 1805 Nelson and his thirteen ships-of-the-line had arrived off Alexandria, but they were in very poor condition. This was not only a result of their lengthy time at sea since the outbreak of war, but also due to the Admiralty's failure to perform hull-maintenance on many of them during the respite offered by the Treaty of Amiens.

When the French fleet was not found, Nelson pressed back across the Mediterranean, still convinced that Villeneuve's objective was Egypt. It was because of this notion that Villeneuve's second attempt to break out and join with the Spanish succeeded. Nelson had precious few frigates to watch for Villeneuve and he chose to use these to watch the routes to the east and only one route to the west. Villeneuve cagily slipped out of Toulon on March 30 and then passed north of the Balearic Islands. By 9 April his slow moving ships were in Cadiz, Spain and had combined with the Spanish under Gravina. This combined fleet now proceeded to Martinique in the French West Indies. The combined Franco-Spanish fleet had eighteen battleships and over 5,000 troops—a month later it was in Martinique.

Meanwhile Nelson had again proceeded east to pursue a phantom French Fleet he thought was bound for Egypt. He was in the Central Mediterranean when he finally received word that Villeneuve was bound for the West Indies. Nelson immediately gave chase and by 4 May, 1805 he was at the Strait of Gibraltar taking on stores for an Atlantic crossing. Villeneuve had a month's head start and it seemed almost sure that Napoleon's plan must work. It was now that British seamanship and French indecision played their fateful roles. Villeneuve had secondary orders to attack Barbados but waited until 9 June to double back across the Atlantic and join up, hopefully, with Admiral Ganteaume to cross the Channel.

Nelson and his fleet were in the meantime accomplishing the impossible, pressing across the Atlantic in three weeks in their leaky under-maintained ships—an act of incredible seamanship. They shaved off critical weeks from Villeneuve's head start. In fact, Nelson arrived on June 4 and was already hunting for Villeneuve. Once Villeneuve learned of Nelson's presence, he set course for the Bay of Biscay and a hoped-for juncture with Ganteaume. Although this was probably the right strategic move, it lowered the morale of the Franco-Spanish fleet, which saw only that they were again running away. Nelson soon learned of Villeneuve's departure and immediately dispatched the brig *Curieux* across the Atlantic to inform the Admiralty of Villeneuve's impending arrival, perhaps in the Channel itself. Again, superior British seamanship prevailed and *Curieux* passed word to the Admiralty of Villeneuve's approach as well as Nelson's own return (he had provisioned and set sail about a week after he dispatched the *Curieux*.) It was at this point that Nelson temporarily drops from the story.

With Nelson's intelligence in hand, Admiral Cornwallis raised his blockade of Brest and dispatched a subordinate squadron of ships under Admiral Sir Robert Calder to intercept Villeneuve. Villeneuve collided with Calder in the fog off Cape Finisterre (northwestern Spain) on 22 July in a tactically indecisive action. Its results, however, were strategically decisive. Superior British gunnery caused the surrender of two French ships. This was enough to cause Villeneuve to pull back into the Spanish port of Vigo. Ganteaume, unaware that Cornwallis had raised the blockade serenely remained in port so that by late July any hope of a juncture with Villeneuve was gone. Ironically, Calder was criticized for his strategic victory because he had not captured or sunk more enemy ships. He bore the stigma of having *not destroyed* Villeneuve's fleet for the rest of his career.[54]

Not long after these events Nelson, again sailing across the Atlantic quicker than a French frigate might, returned to the European waters. He had been constantly at sea for over two years, sailing over 10,000 nautical miles in 1805 alone. Villeneuve and Gravina remained united but blockaded in Cadiz (to which they had moved on August 20) and Ganteaume remained under blockade in Brest. Nelson now took the opportunity to try to repair his worn ships and rest his tired seamen while maintaining his vigil off Cadiz.

Finally, it must be emphasized that Napoleon's aggressive actions in Europe combined with the jealousy and resentment these created among the other great powers of Europe. Napoleon's aggrandizing actions in no small measure contributed to the achievement of a long-term goal of British diplomacy—the formation a Third Coalition composed of Austria, Russia, Great Britain and several lesser powers to renew the continental conflict with France. Had this coalition not formed Napoleon might have remained with this army along the English Channel. However, he now had threats to his strategic backdoor, as it were, and had to completely recast his strategy in the light of new realities. The long blockade operations which stymied Napoleon's strategy vis-à-vis Britain had contributed substantially to the favorable political environment of 1805. Nevertheless, the Royal Navy did not rest on its laurels and Nelson, especially, planned for the destruction of Villeneuve's component of Franco-Spanish sea power.

Historians have argued that Trafalgar was won before the first shot. This is probably true based on the discussions above, nonetheless some hard fighting had to be done and so we return to Nelson's masterpiece to see how it all played out in execution.[55]

The last minutes of the approach were harrowing as the lead ships of each column traveled under the heavy and concentrated fire of the combined fleet . Nelson was in *Victory* at the head of the northwestern column and Collingwood was in *Royal Sovereign* (100) at the head of the southeastern one (the French were heading north, back to port). This provides more evidence of the superiority of the British system since the loss of both ships would mean the loss of the two flag officers—however, they were no longer absolutely necessary for success in the overall battle and became more or less fighting members of the crew of the ship they were on. Collingwood won the race and *Royal Sovereign* crashed into the rear portion of the French-Spanish fleet just past noon. He had minimized his casualties by having his sailors lie down during the final minutes of the approach so he would have every man possible to work the guns and deliver the first devastating broadsides, simultaneously, into the ships on his left and right as he pierced Villeneuve's line. This tactic, combined with the excellent British gunnery accounts for the extremely high casualties aboard the French and Spanish ships as the British cannonballs traveled the entire longitudinal expanse of their opponents' ships. The French and Spanish could reply only with the relatively few guns mounted on the bow and stern of their vessels.[56]

The battle now became a melee as Nelson's *Victory* plowed between Villeneuve's flagship *Bucentaure* (80) and the battleship behind her, *Redoubtable* (74). The French gunners had had much better success against *Victory*, which lost many of her sails and had had her helm shot away, yet her momentum carried her ahead as planned. *Victory's* point blank broadsides into the two French ships caused horrendous casualties. Not long after, a sharpshooter aboard *Redoubtable* (74) sighted the be-medaled Nelson, who had refused to take cover below decks, took a bead, and fired. The ball hit Nelson in the left shoulder and then ricocheted through his lung, finally lodging in his spine. This mortal combination of wounds led to Nelson's slow and painful death. *Redoubtable* now prepared to board the ailing *Victory* but her boarding party was wiped out by a devastating broadside from the *Téméraire* (98), following in line behind *Victory*.[57]

Much of the remainder of the battle followed this same pattern of devastating close combat, but in all cases the British had the better of it up and down the line. Meanwhile, Villeneuve was frantically signaling his van under the French Admiral Dumanoir to come about to assist in the battle. Dumanoir did not see the initial signals due to the smoke of battle and continued sailing toward Cadiz. It was only at 3 PM that he came about. By this time about fifteen ships of the combined fleet had struck their colors (surrendered), including Villeneuve aboard *Bucentaure*. Virtually all of them were blazing charnel houses full of dead and dying men. What remained of the French van, unable to affect the outcome of the battle, fled to Cadiz. Not a single British vessel had been lost. Nelson died around 4:30 PM, but he died with the knowledge that his men had won the most complete victory at sea ever obtained by a modern sailing fleet.[58]

In total, the British captured ten French and ten Spanish ships, however a subsequent storm damaged or sank many of these and the British were only able to salvage four battleships and add them to the Royal Navy's order of battle. British casualties at Trafalgar numbered 449 killed and 1,241 wounded. French and Spanish casualties, including prisoners, were almost ten times that of the British, to include over 4,000 killed alone. Several days later, four of the French ships that had escaped Nelson sortied from Cadiz, were intercepted, attacked, and captured by the British Admiral Sir Richard Strachan.[59] Thus the Royal Navy gained eight new battleships as a result of Nelson's and Strachan's battles.

* * * * * * * * * *

Nelson lusted for battle with his country's enemies, there is no better word for it. The way he crafted his plans, inspired his subordinates, and executed his operations and battles also reveal a remarkable intellect. However, like Alexander the Great, he seemed actually to enjoy close combat—whether as a young lieutenant or as Britain's most famous and esteemed fighting admiral near the end of his life.[60] His legacy to admiralship, then, consists of energetic decision in action, animated by enlightened leadership, moral courage, calculated ruthlessness, and intellectual and technical mastery of the art of war at sea. This remains a tall order for any would-be commander, general or admiral, today and in the future.

However, in another way he simply represents the extreme type of a tradition of aggressive British admirals in the age of sail. These include peers like Sidney Smith, Cornwallis, St. Vincent, Duncan, and of course the incomparable second-in-command Collingwood as well as an illustrious string of earlier admirals such as Hawke, Rodney, Hood, and Howe. No one has ever captured this better than the defeated Villeneuve who remarked on the impact of Nelson's death:

To any other nation, the loss of Nelson would have been irreparable; but in the British fleet off Cadiz, every captain was a Nelson.[61]

Notes

1.   Julian Corbett, *Some Principles of Maritime Strategy* with an introduction and notes by Eric J. Grove (Annapolis, MD: Naval Institute Press Reprint, 1988, originally published 1911), 318. Sir Julian Corbett defines command of the sea in this classic work and is, along with Captain A.T. Mahan, one of the founders of modern naval theory. Corbett was among the first to imply that Nelson's legacy had some long term negative effects on British naval officer corps, see 162-163 in the same book.

2.   These were Nelson's own words for his battle plan for Trafalgar relayed to former British Prime Minister Henry Addington in the summer of 1805. See Colin White, *The Nelson Encyclopaedia.* (London.: Chatham Publishing, 2002), 236; as well as the biography entitled *The Nelson Touch* by Terry Coleman that also came out in 2002.

3.   See *The Pursuit of Victory: The Life and Achievement of Horatio* Nelson (New York: Basic Books, 2005), 501-508. Knight includes a picture of Nelson's original hand drawn sketch for the battle. The account of Napoleon's conference with his Marshals can be found in David Chandler, *The Campaigns of Napoleon* (New York: MacMillan, 1966), 422.

4.   Knight, 506-507; 139-140. Carronades were large caliber short range guns that could fire more rapidly than standard naval artillery and were nicknamed "smashers" in the fleet. They were useless at even medium ranges but deadly in close.

5.   Peter Hore, *The Habit of Victory* (London: The National Maritime Museum, 2005), 178-180.

6.   Knight, 510-511.

7.   Knight, 511-512. "Wearing" is different than "tacking" into the wind, tacking requires better seamanship and could lead to a more confused formation if executed improperly. However, wearing was a slower, easier technique involving a gradual turn. In executing the slower maneuver Villeneuve last valuable time. See John Keegan, *The Price of Admiralty* (New York: Viking, 1988), 60. Keegan believes Villeneuve was trying to escape Nelson, Knight, on the other hand, assesses that the Villeneuve's response was also the correct one based on the direction of the winds and of Nelson's approach.

8.   Knight, 514.

9.   Tom Pocock, *Horatio Nelson* (New York: Alfred A. Knopf, 1988), 1; Knight, 3-7.

10.   Knight, 8, 11, 15. This paper uses the term battleship to apply to ships-of-the-line. These were the largest ships and the determining factor was their number of guns, usually any amount of 50 or more heavy guns would earn a ship this classification.

11.   Knight, 14-15; only a third of midshipmen from 1771-1782 came from

the aristocratic class.

12. Hore, 139-142.

13. Knight, *xxxiv*.

14. Ibid., 25-26.

15. Ibid, 26. The standard convention of listing the number of guns for ships in parenthesis will be used for the remainder of this paper. In this case *Triumph* had 74 guns, making her a medium sized ship of the line.

16. Ibid, 26-27.

17. Knight, 27-39.

18. Ibid, 39. Lieutenant is the first commissioned rank in the royal navy and seniority determined pecking order. Normally a ship of *Worcester's* size rated only three lieutenants, but with an Admiral aboard it was not uncommon to assign another, in this case Suckling used his connections to get Horace the job if not the title so as to give him real lieutenant experience that he knew would help him for the oral examination.

19. Knight, 25, cited from 'Sketch of my Life' by Rear-Admiral Lord Nelson and published when he became famous after the Battle of the Nile.

20. Ibid, 41, 682. A post captain is a captain of the sixth rank, that is a captain of a frigate or larger warship.

21. Knight, 43-44, 47-49. The battle of Quiberon Bay in 1759 was to the Seven Years' War what Trafalgar was to the Napoleonic era. Hawke entered shallow and dangerous shoal waters with his fleet to defeat the French fleet that thought itself safe. Nelson would replicate this feat to a much greater degree at the Nile.

22. Knight, 54, 59, 62-64.

23. Ibid, 96-98, 114, 565-569.

24. Arthur Herman, *To Rule the Waves: How the British Navy Shaped the Modern World* (New York: Harper Collins, 2004), 330-331; Knight, 118, 133.

25. Knight,144, 606.

26. Herman, 333; Knight154-155, 645. Many have said that had Hood commanded at the Virginia Capes, Yorktown might have been a hollow victory for Washington as Cornwallis might have escaped by sea, see A.T. Mahan, *The Influence of Sea Power Upon History, 1660-1783* (Boston, MA: Little Brown and Co., 1894), 476.

27. Herman, 333.

28. Herman, 333-336. Knight,157, 165. Admittedly, this nucleus was small. Nine French battleships were burned by Sir Sidney Smith, next to Nelson probably the second greatest British naval hero of the age. He and Nelson loathed each other. Hood tried to evacuate as many civilians who wanted to avoid the slaughter

as possible, taking some 7500 refugees (Herman gives 15,000) with him on his ships that were already packed with troops.

29. Pocock, 113, 118.

30. Herman, 340-341.

31. Pocock, 121, 126-127, 345.

32. Herman, 342-343, 345. An earlier attempt to invade Ireland had been frustrated by a single frigate under Captain Edward Pelew of *Horatio Hornblower* fame and foul weather.

33. Pocock, 128-129; Herman, 345-36.

34. Herman, 346-349; Pocock, 130-133, 148; A.T. Mahan, *The Life of Nelson: The Embodiment of the Sea Power of Great Britain*, Vol, I. (Boston, MA: Little Brown and Co., 1897), 271-275.

35. Herman, 353; Pocock, 135-145. The British lost over 150 men killed in this fiasco. The Spanish were shocked at the scale of their victory and generously returned all Nelson's wounded to him under a flag of truce.

36. Cited in Mahan, *The Life of Nelson*, 306.

37. For representative examples see Pocock, 148; Knight, 557; and, especially, Mahan, 314-316.

38. Knight, 266-267; Herman, 353.

39. Herman, 353-356; Knight, 577.

40. Ibid., 356-357; Hore, 150.

41. See Knight, *xxxi-xxxv,* for a detailed description of Nelson's famous signals at the Nile. See also Chandler, Part IV for a complete discussion of Napoleon's Egyptian campaign.

42. Knight, 302-303, 307; see also Richard Natkiel, *Atlas of Maritime History* (New York: Facts on File, 1980), 90.

43. Herman, 360-365; Knight, 307-345.

44. Herman, 360-365; Knight, 307-345. For a discussion of Suvorov's campaign see John T. Kuehn, "Suvorov's Folly, Tactics and the Second Coalition of 1799," in the *Consortium on the Revolutionary Era, 1750 – 1850, Selected Papers 2006*, High Point University Press, N.C., 2007, 156-171.

45. Herman, 365.

46. Ibid., 366; Pocock, 232-233.

47. Herman, 366-367; Pocock, 236-240.

48. Pocock, 249-251, 281-286; Herman, 367-368, 370.

49. Herman, 372-373.

50. Sun Tzu (Sunzi), *The Art of War*, trans. S.B. Griffiths (Oxford: Oxford

University Press,1963), 77. "To Subdue the enemy without fighting is the acme of skill."

51. Vincent J. Esposito and John R. Elting, *A Military History and Atlas of the Napoleonic Wars* (New York: Praeger, 1966), map 45 and facing page text. See also Knight, 469-469. Latouche's strategy of playing cat and mouse with a "fleet in being" was slowly wearing Nelson's ships out.

52. Ibid.

53. Knight, 480.

54. Keegan, 27-30. Hore, 169. Keegan is among those who portray Calder in a poor light and argue that events surrounding Villeneuve's retreat were not strategically decisive. He makes no mention of the fact that Napoleon abandoned his invasion attempt and subsequently dispatched a replacement to relieve Villeneuve. Hore's judgment is fairer calling Calder's action "one of the decisive events of the whole war."

55. Herman, 386, relays that the French and Spanish certainly already felt defeated, see also Knight, 501-507 who does not state this explicitly but implies it.

56. Pocock, 322: Knight, 515-518.

57. Ibid., 327-328.

58. Knight, 519.

59. Ibid., 520.

60. See Ibid., 374, for an account of Nelson being "in the highest of spirits" immediately prior to his bloody victory at Copenhagen in 1801. John Keegan addresses Alexander's lust for battle in *Mask of Command* (New York: The Viking Press, 1987), 13, 87-91.

61. Cited in Herman, 395.

Chapter 5

John J. Pershing

"The Very Model of A Modern Major General?"

by Richard S. Faulkner, Ph.D.

When the news of the impending Armistice reached him at his headquarters at Chaumont at 6 a.m. on 11 November 1918, General John J. Pershing had every reason to reflect upon his seventeen-month tenure as the commander of the American Expeditionary Forces (AEF) in France. He commanded the largest American army yet assembled and oversaw the efforts of doughboys scattered across France from the battlefields of the Meuse-Argonne to the ports of Brest and St. Nazaire. Perhaps Pershing also considered the massive changes in warfare and generalship that had occurred over his thirty-two years in uniform. When Pershing entered active service as a cavalry officer in 1886, his world was one of horses, single-shot carbines and the occasional Gatling Gun or mountain howitzer. In those days, the army's strength hovered around 28,000 men. On 11 November 1918, Pershing 's world was one of rapid firing artillery, tanks, machine guns, aircraft, and the industrial- strength logistics and administration of an army of two million men in the AEF alone.

When one thinks of the famous commanders in history, the image that often comes to mind is the "great man on horseback": the general leading his army to battlefield victory by his charisma and battlefield presence, valor and skill. However, in the late 19th and early 20th century, the dramatic increase in the size of armies and the growing complexity of moving, supplying and leading them fundamentally changed the role and expectations of senior-level command in war. The era's arch military-technocrat, Alfred von Schlieffen, argued—

The modern commander-in-chief is no Napoleon who stands with his brilliant suite upon a hill...The commander is further to the rear in a house with roomy offices, where telegraph and wireless, telephone and signaling instruments are at hand, while a fleet of automobiles and motorcycles, ready for the longest trips, wait for orders. Here in the comfortable chair before a large table, the modern Alexander overlooks the entire battlefield on a map. From here he telephones inspiring words, and here he receives the reports from army and corps commanders and from balloons and dirigibles which observe the enemy's movements and detect his positions.[1]

In this new age, the "great captains" of war now acted less like Napoleon at Austerlitz and more like Andrew Carnegie, John D. Rockefeller and

Figure 5. General John J. Pershing, General Headquarters, Chaumont, France, 19 October 1918.
Photo by 2d. Lt. L.J. Rode

the "great captains" of industry. In fact, the American military reformer General J. Franklin Bell went as far to note in 1906—

Though differing in many important respects, there is a certain parallelism between the management of armies and the management of large business enterprises. The management of an army, and each of its units, should, as far as practicable, resemble that of any large, highly organized business undertaking. We need to study common sense business methods, which have demonstrated their soundness beyond cavil.[2]

Although foreshadowed by Ulysses Grant's experiences in 1864-1865, John J. Pershing was the first American general to exemplify the "great managerial commander" of the modern age.

Before diving into the subject, it is important to reiterate exactly what is meant by the term "great commander." A "great commander" is that leader who best understands and exploits the realities of warfare as practiced at his time. This understanding places the commander in a position to craft and execute operations that achieve the strategic endstate of the war with the most efficient use of resources at his disposal relative to the enemy and the military conditions of his moment in history. The "great commander" has the ability to overcome or capitalize on the social, political and economic circumstances upon which his army is built and, ultimately, on his skill at using that army to defeat the enemy at the strategic level of war. Using this definition, Pershing falls somewhat short in some areas of "greatness" while clearly excelling in others.

John Joseph Pershing was born in Laclede, Missouri, on 13 September 1860. Upon graduating from the North Missouri Normal School, he embarked upon a brief career as a teacher in a rural one room schoolhouse. In 1882, Pershing, growing weary of the staid life of a schoolmaster and hoping to expand his opportunities and horizons, accepted an appointment to the United States Military Academy. Although a rather mediocre scholar, his leadership abilities and military skills won Pershing the coveted position of cadet first captain in his senior year at the academy.[3] He graduated 30th in a class of 77 cadets in 1886 and was commissioned in the cavalry.

During his time at West Point, Pershing became acquainted with Robert Bullard, Payton March and other officers who would later serve with him, or influence his actions as the commander of the American Expeditionary Forces (AEF). At West Point Pershing also developed his lifelong views of military discipline and the role of the commander. Pershing's approach to obedience and order was best reflected in his directive, "General Principles Governing the Training of Units of the American Expeditionary Forces." In it he directed—

All officers and soldiers should realize that at no time in our history had discipline been so important; therefore discipline of the highest order must be exacted at all times. The standards of the American Army will be those of West Point. The rigid attention, upright bearing, attention to detail, uncomplaining obedience to instructions required of the cadets will be required of every officer and soldier of our Armies in France. Failure to attain such discipline will be treated as a lack of capacity on the part of the commander to create in the subordinate that intensity of purpose and willing acceptance of hardship which are necessary to success in battle.[4]

While this unbending vision of discipline was well-suited to cadets and hard-bitten regulars, it was perhaps not the best way of dealing with the citizen soldiers who filled the ranks of the AEF. This ensured that whereas Pershing was a respected (and feared) commander, he never exhibited the warmth and "common touch" that would inspire or endear him to the average doughboy.

Upon graduating from West Point, Pershing arrived in the American West just in time to fight the remaining Apache bands in Arizona and to participate in the last great Indian campaign: the Ghost Dance War of 1890. Following this stint on the closing frontier, the War Department assigned Pershing to the University of Nebraska as the school's chief military instructor. During this four year assignment, he also completed a law degree.[5]

The outbreak of the Spanish American War found Pershing serving as a tactical officer at West Point. His strict enforcement of the academy's regulations, and the subsequent unpopularity that flowed from this, led his cadets to give him the irreverent nickname "Black Jack" for his previous service with the African American 10th Cavalry.[6] After wrangling a release from his duties at West Point, Pershing returned to the 10th Cavalry and accompanied it to Cuba in June 1898. Although he was acting as the regimental quartermaster, Pershing often found himself close to the action during the attacks on Kettle and San Juan Hills. The 10th Cavalry's commander, Colonel Theodore Baldwin, later remarked that Pershing was "the coolest and bravest man I ever saw under fire in my life."[7]

While Pershing's service in Cuba had earned him the respect of many within the army, it was not until the War Department posted him to Mindanao in 1899 that Pershing was marked as a rising star outside the insular military community. In his operations against the Moro warriors Black Jack executed a balanced policy of "benevolent assimilation" and economic development coupled with a willingness to rapidly and ruthlessly suppress any challenge to American rule or local stability. Robert Bullard, who served with Pershing in Mindanao and later became one of Black Jack's most trusted subordinates in the AEF, recalled that

Pershing was one of the few American officers who made an effort to understand Moro culture and by "associating with them and studying them won their confidence and admiration."[8]

The success of Pershing's "carrot and stick" policy during his first tour in Mindanao and his later service as the military governor of Moro Province from 1909 to 1913 not only garnered the praise of his superiors, but more importantly, drew the attention of Capital Hill and the White House. In 1906, his performance in the Philippines led Theodore Roosevelt to promote the talented cavalryman from captain to brigadier general over the heads of 862 officers that ranked Pershing in seniority.[9] Of course it probably helped that when Pershing married Francis Helen Warren in 1905, he also gained the support of her father, Senator Francis E. Warren, a member of the Senate Military Affairs Committee.

Following his successful stint as the governor of Moro Province, Pershing took command of the 8th Brigade then stationed at the Presidio of San Francisco. He had scarcely settled into his new surroundings when in April 1914 he and his brigade were ordered to the Mexican border due to the tensions caused by the brief detention of American sailors in Tampico, which led to the subsequent American occupation of Vera Cruz and the general instability unleashed by the Mexican Revolution. Upon arrival in the southwestern borderland, Pershing's command expanded to include all American troops posted from Sierra Blanca, Texas, to Columbus, New Mexico.[10] Pershing's satisfaction at commanding nearly a division of soldiers was quickly marred by the death of his wife and three daughters due to an early morning fire at their quarters at the Presidio of San Francisco on 27 August 1915. [11]

In 1916, events on the Mexican border gave Pershing ample opportunity to escape his deep grief over the loss of most of his family. After years of meddling with Mexico's internal affairs, Woodrow Wilson grudgingly recognized Venustiano Carranza as the legitimate president of Mexico. To hasten the return of stability in Mexico, Wilson allowed Carranza's forces to move by train through US territory to reinforce their garrison at Agua Prieta. This move allowed the Carrancistas to inflict a stinging defeat upon Pancho Villa's army and deal a decisive blow against one of the last remaining challenges to Carranza's government. Not surprisingly, Villa was angered by the part that the US played in his defeat and began a series of attacks against American citizens and interests in Northern Mexico. His campaign of revenge culminated on the night of 8-9 March 1916 with a raid on the border town of Columbus, New Mexico. The raid killed eighteen Americans and approximately seventy-five to one hundred fifty of Villa's raiders.[12]

Retribution for Villa's attack on United States came swiftly and provided Pershing another opportunity to show his mettle. On 10 March 1916, the commander of the Southern District, General Frederick Funston, was directed by Secretary of War Newton Baker to—

...promptly organize an adequate military force of troops under the command of Brigadier General Pershing and will direct him to proceed promptly across the border in pursuit of the Mexican band which attacked the town of Columbus and the troops there on the morning of the 9th instant. These troops will be withdrawn to American territory as soon as the de facto government in Mexico is able to relieve them of this work. In any event the work of these troops will be regarded as finished as soon as Villa band or bands are known to be broken up.[13]

Pershing had been given command of the punitive expedition over the senior ranking, but mercurial, Funston because Secretary Baker believed that Pershing had a strong reputation for being "absolutely loyal to the policy of the civil authorities under whom he was serving."[14] This would not be the last time that Pershing's political reliability would serve him in good stead. The domestic and international ramifications of any incursion into Mexico and the risk of an all out war between the United States and the Carranza government dictated that the commander of the expedition be ever mindful of the political minefield in which he operated.

Pershing faced a host of challenges in his pursuit of Villa. The mountainous and arid terrain of Northern Mexico complicated his efforts to locate Villa's dispersed band and played havoc with the Americans' supply efforts. Pershing also had to contend with the anti-American hostility of the local population and the mounting resistance of Carrancista forces resentful of Washington's apparent disregard of Mexican sovereignty.

Black Jack was also beset by "mission creep" as the Wilson administration changed the goal of the punitive expedition from chastising Villa to pressuring Carranza to institute political reforms and safeguard American interests south of the border.[15] By 29 April 1916, Pershing was able to report that while his command had failed to capture Villa, by the expedition's "arduous and persistent pursuit," the attackers of Columbus "have been broken into smaller bands and scattered to different sections of the State of Chihuahua and elsewhere."[16] However, this military success had not halted the growing "cold war" between Pershing's forces and the Carrancistas. After an ugly skirmish between the 13th US Cavalry and Carrancista forces at Parral on 12 April, Pershing reminded his soldiers—

...that this expedition is operating within the limits of a friendly nation whose peaceful inhabitants should be treated with every consideration. It is also desirable to maintain the most cordial relations, and cooperate as far as feasible, with the forces of the de facto government.[17]

Although political considerations placed Pershing in a very difficult military situation, his dutiful support of policies which he personally believed wrong made a positive impression on Wilson and Baker. In February 1917, the defeat of Villa and the growing tensions with Germany finally led the Wilson administration to recall Pershing's command from Mexico.

Pershing's next task was not long in coming. Soon after the United States declared war on Germany in April 1917, Wilson determined that if he was to have any say in shaping the war's ultimate peace negotiations, the United States had to send a substantial army to France. The army general staff estimated that if the nation were to send an expeditionary force to Europe that had any hope of influencing the outcome of the war, the nation would have to expand the army from 18,000 officers and 200,000 soldiers (that was both regulars and national guardsmen) to a force of 200,000 officers and between two to four million men.[18] One of the pressing questions for Wilson and the War Department was who would lead the legions?

One of the major requirements for being a great commander in modern warfare is possessing a clear understanding of the political nature of war. Like it or not, senior commanders are political creatures who must have a sound comprehension of the social and political realities that drive their nations. John J. Pershing clearly understood this requirement and held the greatest political skill required of American generals: knowing when to keep his mouth shut. This skill was of vital importance in 1917.

Although Pershing's military record demonstrated his professional skills and talents, in the winter and spring of 1917, he was only one of a handful of capable officers who were in the running to command the AEF. General Tasker Bliss had a well earned reputation as one of the Army's leading intellectual lights and had served as the Assistant Chief of Staff of the Army since 1915.Major General J. Franklin Bell had gained a solid reputation as a battlefield commander during the Philippine Insurrection and had been instrumental in the professionalization of the army and supporting the reforms of Secretary of War Elihu Root. Then there was Major General Leonard Wood. Wood had won the Medal of Honor during the Geronimo Campaign of 1886. He led the cavalry brigade that attacked on San Juan Hill during the Cuban expedition of 1898, and had served with distinction in the Philippines. Wood also served as the Chief of Staff of the Army from 1910 to 1914.

Of these contenders, however, Bell was too old and infirm for an active command. Bliss was seven years older than Pershing and lacked recent combat experience. That left only Leonard Wood as a serious contender to Pershing's promotion. Pershing, however, did have some things going for him. His recent experience commanding the punitive expedition had demonstrated his ability to control complex operations. More importantly he displayed a knack for negotiating the political minefield that the expedition and the preparedness movement had created. On the other hand, from 1914 to 1916 Leonard Wood, and his close confidant Theodore Roosevelt, publically railed against the Wilson administration's failure to prepare the nation for war. While Wood's indiscreet comments drew a stern rebuke from Wilson, Pershing was the quiet and dutiful soldier who voiced any concerns he had about military matters through the proper channels. Pershing never hid the truth or manipulated facts for political effect, but he understood the strictures of the civilian control of the military and worked the system to correct the problems that he encountered.

In the end, Pershing's political reliability paid off in several important ways. Not only did he win command of the AEF, but Wilson and Secretary of War Newton Baker also granted him more leeway in building and fighting his army than perhaps any commander in American history. The guidance that Pershing received from his political masters prior to departing for France was clear in its intent and broad in the latitude that it gave the AEF's commander.

On 26 May 1917, Secretary Baker gave Pershing the following guidance:

In military operations against the Imperial German Government, you are directed to cooperate with the forces of other countries employed against that enemy; but in so doing the underlying idea must be kept in view that the forces of the United States are a separate and distinct component of the combined forces, the identity of which must be preserved. This fundamental rule is subject to such minor exceptions in particular circumstances as your judgment may approve. The decision as to when your command, or any of its parts, is ready for action is confided to you, and you will exercise full discretion in determining the manner of cooperation. But, until the forces of the United States are in your judgment sufficiently strong to warrant operations as an independent command, it is understood that you will cooperate as a component of whatever army you may be assigned to by the French government.[19]

With Wilson's backing, Pershing had the power he needed to fight off French and British attempts to place American soldiers under Allied command or to use them as mere replacements in their armies' depleted ranks. It also provided Pershing the ability to strong-arm the Allies on issues of shipping US troops overseas, aiding in the training of American forces, and establishing an independent American Army. When going up against such skilled political infighters as French Premier George Clemenceau and British Prime Minister David Lloyd-George, Pershing needed all the political muscle that Wilson and Baker could give.

When later confronted with Allied demands for amalgamating American troops with their own, Pershing generally had the authority to be as accommodating or unbending as the situation demanded. This skill was tested in the spring and summer of 1918 when a series of German offensives created a crisis on the Western Front. These attacks intensified calls from French and British leaders for Pershing to relinquish his control of American forces.

In a tense meeting at Versailles on 1 June 1918, Allied leaders insisted that the military situation obligated Pershing to ship only American infantrymen to France and to place them under Allied command upon their arrival. Pershing refused to be bullied. He rightly believed that such an action would indefinitely postpone the creation of an independent American Army. When British Prime Minister David Lloyd-George threatened to go over Pershing's head and refer the Allies' demands directly to President Wilson, Pershing replied, "Refer it to the president and be damned. I know what the president will do. He will simply refer it back to me for recommendation and I will make to him the same recommendation as I have made here today."[20] Pershing, the savvy political soldier, understood Wilson's intent and that for the United States to have a say in the peace, an American Army, under American command, would have to fight and bleed its way to the conference table.

To further assess Pershing's generalship, we must first understand his army and the nature of the war that he faced. The American army that entered World War I in 1917 was not prepared to wage a war against a modern battle-hardened and skillful enemy. While three years of attritional total war had forced the armies of Europe to evolve their weapons, doctrine and command structures, 1917 found the American army mired in the tactical paradigms of July 1914. The American Army lacked the weapons, manpower and "know how" to fight on the Western Front. Although the Punitive Expedition in Mexico was the largest force that the nation had fielded since the Philippine War, in reality, neither Pershing nor any other serving American officer had any experience commanding units larger than a brigade. In fact, one of Pershing's massive wartime divisions contained more soldiers than the entire Regular Army had on its rolls in 1898.

Although the United States pulled off a minor miracle in raising 4 million in 19 months, and shipping nearly two million of these soldiers to Europe before the Armistice, this prodigious feat was only made possible by cutting a number of corners. The vast majority of the AEF's junior line officers were products of three-month-long Officer Training Camps. These camps gave their so called "90 Day Wonders" only a thin veneer of military knowledge. To compound this leadership problem, the shortage of experienced NCOs meant that the draftees that reported to a training camp on Monday all-too-often often became the sergeants for the recruits arriving on Wednesday. Stateside training throughout 1917 was also hindered by problems that ranged from building the cantonments, to shortages of equipment, a lack of qualified instructors, and a general uncertainty over what exactly should be taught.[21]

The Army itself contributed to the training problem. Ever-changing War Department polices led to constant transfers of large groups of soldiers from one unit to another. The plight of the 82d Division was a case in point. In August 1917, the War Department activated the division and began to man it with draftees from Alabama, Georgia, and Tennessee. Less than two months later, with the division approaching full strength and already well into its training, the Army reversed itself and ordered most of the unit's enlisted men to be transferred to other divisions. These transfers left the 82d with a cadre of only 783 men. In October and November, the division was brought back up to strength with draftees from New England and the Mid-Atlantic states. These new soldiers brought with them other training problems, as a large number of the new men were recent immigrants unable to speak or read English. The division's manpower challenges did not end there. In an effort to pool soldiers with certain industrial skills, in late November 1917, Washington again ordered the 82d to transfer over 3,000 specialists from its ranks. The division's number of trained men was further reduced by the forced discharge of over 1,400 men the War Department considered to be enemy aliens and potential security risks.[22]

The 82d was far from being alone in this dilemma. The 86th Division was hit particularly hard by the War Department's willy-nilly transfers. Between January and April 1918, over 100,000 men passed through the division's ranks. This meant that some 80,000 soldiers came and went through a unit that was to have a deployed strength of only 28,000 men. With the arrival of each new levy of troops, officers faced the unenviable task of restarting or revising their training plans. Given this turmoil it is amazing that the unit leaders achieved anything in the way of training.[23]

In late 1917 and early 1918 it even seemed that nature was conspiring against the nation's efforts to field the AEF. The winter of 1917-18 was particularly harsh. Record snowfalls, and the mud that they left behind, ground training to a halt in camps as far south as Camp Seiver, South Carolina and Camp Gordon, Georgia. On 28 February 1918, the 83d Division's Intelligence Officer reported that the "unduly severe winter" at Camp Sherman, Ohio had so retarded the progress of the division's training that they were still working on the 18th week of the War Department's training plan when they were supposed to be working on the program for week 23. He also noted that, "trench work, of necessity, has been cut down to almost nil up until the present time."[24] The situation was even worse for the 4th Division at Camp Greene, North Carolina. The rain and snow in the winter of 1918 turned the post's red clay soil into such a viscous mess that "the troops simply could not work out of doors" for weeks at a time. Between 10 December 1917 and 4 March 1918, one officer recorded that the division's units experienced only 16 days where any meaningful outdoor training was even possible.[25] Adding to the misery of weather-induced inactivity, and further hindering training, were deadly outbreaks of Spanish influenza, measles, and other diseases. Disease hindered or halted unit training as whole companies were quarantined for weeks at a time to prevent the spread of the sickness. In all, the army lost 8,743,102 days of work and training from enlisted men laid low by the epidemics.[26]

It is also important to understand the nature of the war that Pershing faced on the Western Front. World War I was one of the greatest upheavals in history. It dwarfed previous wars in its scope, scale, and lethality. Massive armies equipped with an array of deadly weapons, such as rapid firing artillery, high explosive shells, bolt action magazine rifles and machine guns, were maintained at the front by modern state bureaucracies with the unprecedented ability to mobilize the human, material and financial resources of their nations. As these contending armies were generally mirror images of each other in their size, weaponry, doctrine and organization, none could gain an asymmetric advantage to the degree necessary to win a decisive battlefield victory. To make matters worse, the lethality of the new battlefield and the horrendous casualties of 1914 forced the armies to dig in just to survive. The establishment of a nearly unbroken system of trenches from the North Sea to the Swiss border only exacerbated the indecisiveness of combat operations by shifting the advantage to the defender.

Pershing is often accused of being slow to comprehend the vast changes to warfare that had been sparked by the World War.[27] There is much truth in this assertion. Pershing himself reinforced this perception with the "General Principles Governing the Training of Units of the American Expeditionary Forces," issued in October 1917. These principles served as the guide for instructing most of the American divisions that arrived in 1917 and 1918. It stated

The general principles governing combat remain unchanged in their essence. This war has developed special features which involve special phases of training, but the fundamental ideas enunciated in our Drill Regulations, Small Arms Firing Manual, Field Service Regulations, and other service manuals remain the guide for both officers and soldiers.[28]

The instructions also made clear that—

The rifle and the bayonet are the principal weapons of the infantry soldier. He will be trained in a high degree of skill as a marksman both on the target range and in field firing. An aggressive spirit must be developed until the soldier feels himself, as a bayonet fighter; invincible in battle.[29]

Despite obvious evidence to the contrary, nothing shook Pershing's fundamental belief in that the stalemate in France was an aberration that could be overcome by the American Army's superior drive, morale and marksmanship. Once free from the trenches and into "open warfare," the Americans' greater skill and ability at maneuver would allow them to corner and destroy the inferior German army.[30]

This being said, Pershing should be judged as much by his actions as by his words. Much of his insistence on "open warfare" was an attempt to fend off British and French efforts to amalgamate American soldiers into their armies by claiming American exceptionalism. More importantly, while Pershing proclaimed the superiority of "independent infantry," the organizational structure of his army shows that the AEF had embraced the centrality of firepower from the platoon to the corps level. Reflecting the lessons of the Allied and German armies, the AEF's units possessed a lavish and, for the American Army, an unprecedented array of artillery, machine guns and other highly lethal weapons systems.

The Great War also forever changed the parameters and expectations of senior army command. As previously noted, the day of the army commander as the great man on horseback, able to inspire his army by his presence on the battlefield and direct operations by on-the-spot inspiration, was over. Although there is some truth in the accusation that the commanders of the Great War were "chateau generals" callously out of touch with the human cost of their plans, this charge does not do justice to many of the war's senior leaders. Although weapon technology had leapfrogged forward in the decades prior to the war, there was no such technological breakthrough in the area of command and control. The one great advance in this realm, instant voice communication through the use of field phones, was unreliable in combat and tended to fix commanders to their headquarters. Thus, for better or worse, Schlieffen's prediction that the "modern Alexander" would fight the war "in the comfortable chair" overlooking the "entire battlefield on a map" was true.

There were, of course, some underperformers when it came to high command, but as a whole, the armies of the Great War were not "Lions led by donkeys" as some historian have inferred. Keep in mind that when commanders, such as Pershing, came face to face with the Great War's realities, they encountered a tactical and operational dilemma that nothing in their professional education, training or experience had prepared them to meet. The war's constant drain on the home fronts also meant that senior commanders were under great pressure from their political leaders to find quick solutions to the war's intractable challenges.

Realities on the battlefield and the inability of senior commanders to rapidly communicate their orders pushed the responsibility for combat decision-making down to regimental, battalion, and company officers. Although senior commanders still influenced operational planning and execution, their job shifted increasingly to managing the vast human and material resources required to wage modern war. At the highest levels, senior commanders also had to become power brokers in the byzantine intrigues of coalition warfare. .

In modern mass warfare, senior leaders were now as much great managers as they were great commanders. Upon his arrival in France, Pershing faced the daunting task of building the infrastructure needed to supply, move, equip, and ensure the health of an overseas army that was estimated by the War Department to reach a strength of four million soldiers. By the Armistice, Pershing had overseen the construction and operation of a vast logistical empire whose 231 hospitals and convalescence camps could accommodate over 276,000 patients, whose bakeries could produce nearly three million pounds of bread daily, and whose refrigeration plants could make 500 tons of ice per day and store 6,500 tons of meat. In addition to reconditioning 2,000 locomotives and 56,000 rail cars that the AEF obtained from the Allies, the Americans also constructed 1,500 locomotives and 18,000 rail cars that had been shipped in parts to France from the United States.[31]

Given the challenges that confronted him in standing up the AEF, one of the more important attributes that Pershing brought to his command was his keen eye for talent. Since 1914 the scope and scale of the war had made clear that no one individual had the knowledge, talent or span of control to master all the tasks required to move, supply, and fight million man armies. No longer could staffs follow the Napoleonic model of taking the great man's thoughts and simply turning them into orders. Pershing had a knack for finding individuals who had the intelligence, drive, toughness, and ability to handle the daunting task of building the AEF- men who often brought skill sets to the table that he did not possess.

An example of Pershing's ability to select the right man for the right job was the case of Charles Dawes. Dawes was a successful politician and businessman without an iota of military experience. Although Dawes had been Pershing's friend since Black Jack's time at the University of Nebraska, it was the businessman's organizational skills and ability to solve complex problems that led him to invite Dawes to join his staff. Dawes quickly worked his way into the job of being the AEF's Chief European Purchasing Officer. In this role, he was instrumental in establishing the army's supply and transportation infrastructure in France.[32] In fact, James Harbord, the AEF Chief of Staff and later Commander of the Services of Supply, was adamant that Dawes' "usefulness to the American Expeditionary Forces can hardly be overstated."[33] Dawes never shed his civilian sensibilities and Pershing, a notorious stickler for protocol and appearance termed Dawes "the most unmilitary human that ever lived."[34] But, Pershing overlooked Dawes' indiscretions because this civilian-in-uniform always delivered on his promises.

Pershing also possessed that rare trait of respecting those subordinates who dared speak truth to power when he was hasty or wrong in his decisions. For example Captain George Marshall and Major General Hunter Liggett both questioned Pershing's judgment and not only lived to tell the tale, but actually prospered due to their courage and abilities. On 3 October 1917, Pershing observed a tactical demonstration by units of General William Silbert's 1st Division. Pershing, who already believed that Silbert was unfit for command, berated him for the sloppiness of the exercise and the inability of the division staff to organize and improve the unit's training. Pershing's angry reproach infuriated George Marshall, one of Silbert's divisional staff officers. As Pershing stomped off to his car, Marshall tried to explain the division's situation and the practical reasons for the unit's poor showing. When Pershing angrily turned away, Marshall grabbed the general's arms and heatedly, but logically, made his unit's case.

All those witnessed the altercation believed that the young officer would soon be on a slow boat to America. Instead, Marshall's moral courage and skills as a staff officer soon landed him a key spot on Pershing's staff.[35] Marshall later noted of Pershing, "He could listen to more opposition to his apparent view and show less personal feeling than anyone I have ever seen." Marshall maintained that Pershing's willingness to listen to the council of others "was one of his greatest strengths" as a commander.[36]

Pershing's willingness to overlook reasoned dissent when the man or the argument merited was also evident in the case of Major General Hunter Liggett. From the moment that he took command of the AEF, Pershing made it clear that he would not tolerate any officer who was too old or unfit to endure the stress of combat. To appease Pershing, Secretary Baker required generals preparing to deploy their units to France to take a month-long tour of the AEF. Although these tours were intended to give the officers a greater appreciation for what they faced on the Western Front, it also gave Pershing time to evaluate their abilities and physical condition. If a general was not to Pershing's liking, he usually was excluded from returning to the AEF. When Liggett arrived in France for his tour, he was 61 years old and quite fat. When Pershing questioned his physical abilities, Liggett proceeded to run up a nearby hill to demonstrate his stamina. When Pershing criticized the large general's corpulence, Liggett simply and forcefully replied that the most important fact about his physique was that his fat stopped squarely at his neck, and in no way extended to his head. Impressed by Liggett's earnestness and proven intellect, Pershing accepted him into the AEF's fold. This proved to be a wise decision, for Liggett became one of the AEF's most reliable commanders. During the war he rose to command the 1st Corps and eventually the AEF's First Army.[37]

Balancing Pershing's well developed eye for talent was a predisposition to not suffer fools lightly. He was exacting in his demands for efficiency and discipline and strictly weighed the ability of his subordinates to achieve results on and off the battlefield. Major General Robert Bullard, one of the AEF's senior officers who consistently met the Iron Commander's rigorous standards, had worked closely enough to Pershing to understand the measure of the man. Bullard noted that when Pershing arrived at the front, he was often "good-humored" and "agreeable." However, Bullard recalled, "underneath [Pershing's] easy manner was inexorable ruin to the commander who did not have things right. He shows the least personal feeling of all the commanders that I have ever known, and never spares the incompetent."[38] John J. Pershing was a hard man who never allowed past friendships or attachments to influence his decisions. When asked about his feelings in removing an old friend, General Omar Bundy, from command of the 2d Division, Pershing simply said, "I don't care. Men's lives are involved."[39]

In March 1918 Pershing directed the establishment of a permanent Officer Reclassification and Efficiency Board in the town of Blois. This board was to judge officers who were viewed as being incompetent, unfit, or ill suited for their duties, and to determine if they were to be cashiered, demoted or reassigned to another branch or unit. The slang term for a magnificent failure or breakdown, "to go blooey," entered American English from the name of the town and its reputation for ruining budding military careers.[40] Although the majority of the officers sent to the reclassification center were lieutenants and captains, senior officers who failed to live up to Pershing's standards also found themselves quickly packed off to Blois. In one 30 day period during the Meuse Argonne Offensive, Pershing relieved one corps commander, Major General George Cameron, and three division commanders: Major Generals Beaumont Buck, John MacMahon and Clarence Edwards. A cold ruthlessness in the quest for military efficiency and effectiveness is certainly a characteristic of a great commander; however, such moves can sometimes have unintended consequences.

Although the times and stakes justified Pershing's callousness in summarily sacking those who he perceived as incompetent leaders, his reputation as a headhunter created a climate of fear within the AEF . The dread of being "blooyed" motivated many commanders to micromanage their subordinates and limit any actions that might reflect badly on their commands. As an officer in the Inspector General section later noted, "Officers commenced to exhibit a degree of fear and apprehension lest some unavoidable event, something which they could not control, might operate to ruin their careers."[41] Ironically, some commanders went as far as to prevent their more talented junior leaders from attending needed technical schools because of "the danger to themselves of being relieved of command for some error made by the less efficient officers."[42] Thus, the fear that Pershing inspired in some of his subordinates somewhat hindered the AEF's efforts to create an efficient and effective cadre of officers. More importantly, the terror of being relieved led some commanders to push attacks and endure mounting casualties long after the real possibility of success had passed.

In addition to the climate that Pershing established within the AEF, his status as a great captain must ultimately rest upon an assessment of his performance as a battlefield commander. Although Pershing was a savvy political operator with a talent for organization and picking the right men for tough jobs, his record as a commander was rather mixed. It can be difficult to assess his performance because it was so indelibly tied to the unexpected events that swirled around him in the second half of 1918. It must be understood that from the moment Pershing landed in France, he viewed the AEF as an army that would not come into its own until the spring of 1919. Pershing believed that the AEF would not be trained and ready until that time, and by then the decline of the French and British armies would make the American army the key to an eventual allied victory.[43] Unfortunately, as is so often the case in war, the enemy had not read Pershing's plan and failed to play the part that Black Jack intended for him. The German offensives of 1918 threw all of the American plans into chaos. Rather than the progressive and rigorous training plan that Pershing had mandated for his arriving divisions, all American units arriving in France from the spring of 1918 onward found their training compressed, rushed, or incomplete.

Some American units found themselves thrown into hastily planned and ill-supported operations. In attacks in the Aisne-Marne region in June, July and August 1918, inexperience, unskilled leadership and poor tactics led American divisions to impale themselves on German defenses. Although these operations also inflicted heavy casualties on the enemy, the attacks highlighted the fact that the Americans still needed much more schooling in modern warfare. While the Americans in these operations were under French command, Pershing tried to gain as much from these experiences as possible. He directed his staff to capture the "lessons learned" from these battles in hope of improving the overall performance of the AEF.[44] Unfortunately, the rapid pace of events generally prevented the Americans from profiting from the mistakes of others.

Pershing's true testing as a commander came with the establishment of the American First Army, with its own sector of the front, on 10 August 1918. Pershing understood the grave shortcomings that plagued his army, but he was determined to demonstrate that the Americans could hold their own in modern war. If part of the definition of a great commander is his ability to craft and execute operations that achieve the strategic ends of the war with the most efficient use of resources at his disposal, then Pershing's record was again mixed.

Pershing's desire to prove the American's mettle at times led him to be somewhat short-sighted in his operational thinking. This was evident in his plans for the St Mihiel Offensive in mid-September 1918. Pershing's staff had devoted much time and effort to ensuring that the Americans' debut as a separate army would be a sterling success. Unfortunately, Marshal Ferdinand Foch, the Supreme Commander of the Allied Armies, wanted the Americans to focus their efforts on an attack in the Meuse Argonne sector. To Foch, the Argonne Offensive was an important part of an orchestrated attack by all the Allied armies to sap the remaining German manpower reserves and place the enemy in an unwinnable attritional dilemma. While Foch remained dubious over the need for the St Mihiel operation, he bowed to Pershing's wishes with the caveat that as soon as the attack was over the Americans would shift their focus and resources to the Meuse Argonne and launch an attack in that sector by 26 September.[45]

To ensure the success of St Mihiel, Pershing committed his best minds, resources, and, most importantly, his best divisions to the battle. The planning and effort paid off. The offensive caught the Germans withdrawing from the St Mihiel salient and cost the enemy 5,000 casualties, 13,000 prisoners and 466 captured guns. The battle cost the Americans 2,000 dead and 6,000 wounded. The victory was a great boon to American morale, but was not, perhaps, a strong enough test of the AEF's command and control, fire support and logistics systems. Nor was the battle a reliable test of the AEF's doctrine. For most of the new divisions, their participation in the St Mihiel Offensive was not long or intense enough for them to gain the degree of experience required to season their officers and soldiers for the operations that lay before them in the Meuse-Argonne. Of the harsh shock his unit experienced in the Argonne drive, one 5th Division officer later stated, "the men still remembered the victorious rush at St Mihiel and dashed forward impetuously. But it was a different enemy here, one who was sticking till the last and fighting for every foot of ground."[46]

When the St Mihiel Offensive came to a close, the AEF faced a daunting challenge. The American Army had to move over 300,000 men, and all of their equipment, 40 miles to the northeast, take over a new sector of the front and launch a massive attack, with all the detailed preparations that that entailed, within ten days. To complicate matters, Pershing's decisions to use his best divisions at St Mihiel, meant that the nine divisions that would lead off the attack in the Meuse Argonne were inexperienced and under-trained. Furthermore, the planning for St Mihiel had so preoccupied the AEF staff, that it had made little effort to improve the Argonne's limited transportation and supply infrastructure. While undertaken for many good reasons, Pershing's decision to execute the St Mihiel Offensive later caused the AEF many problems in the Meuse Argonne.[47]

As soon as the Americans began the Argonne drive on 26 September 1918, they encountered a formidable landscape of rolling hills, thick forests and commanding heights. The area also boasted few roads. This was ideal defensive terrain for a skillful and determined enemy. Between 26 September and 1 October, the initial attacks by inexperienced American divisions quickly degenerated into a grinding attritional struggle. Most notably, the failure of the green 79th Division to capture the heights of Montfaucon on the first day of the battle stalled the American push and thus gave the Germans invaluable time to strengthen their defenses and bring up reinforcements. To make matters worse, by 1 October, the supply routes behind the front lines were nearly impassible due to massive traffic jams. Frontline units were being starved of replacements, food, water and medical care.

Faced with mounting casualties and with little to show for them, Pershing began a frantic effort to regain the momentum of the attack by replacing his battered green divisions with his more experienced units. Unfortunately, these measures did little to reverse the situation at the front. Attacks between 4 and 16 October again gained little terrain and came at the cost of an ever greater toll in American lives. High casualties, supply problems, and lack of progress brought the AEF and its commander to a crisis point. By mid-October, Hunter Liggett estimated that over 100,000 Americans soldiers had absented themselves from their units and were wandering the army's rear areas.[48] After visiting the front and witnessing the confusion behind the American lines, George Clemenceau even began back-channel efforts to have Pershing relieved from command.[49]

Pershing himself was far from oblivious to the condition of his army and the criticism of his leadership growing in the Allied ranks. On 12 October, he made one of his greatest and most morally courageous decisions. He divided his massive army into two separate armies. He placed the reduced First Army under the command of Hunter Liggett and the newly created Second Army under the charge of Robert Bullard. Pershing had rightly concluded that this original army was too large and unwieldy to be commanded by him alone. This reorganization removed Pershing from the direct operational command of American forces and allowed him to focus on overseeing the AEF's big picture and big problems in France. This decision was a hard one for a proud man like Pershing, but perhaps one of the more important traits of a commander is the ability to realize his limitations and to delegate tasks to talented subordinates. Pershing's organizational change and two weeks of scaled back American attacks, helped the AEF to regain its balance in the Meuse Argonne. When the Americans resumed major attacks on 1 November, the AEF's efforts were still rather ham-fisted, but it was at least better positioned to use its manpower and resource advantages to grind down the remnants of the German forces it faced. Although the AEF was an inelegant tool, in its commander's hand it accomplished Wilson's political endstate by making a major contribution to the allies' victory in 1918.

The return of peace did not end Pershing's service to the Republic. In fact what he did after the war may have had more far reaching importance than his time as the commander of the AEF. One of his first post-war acts was to establish a series of investigating boards to capture the American Army's hard won lessons from the war. The Lewis and Superior Boards brought together officers from all over the AEF and served as a point of departure for later army reforms and doctrinal development in the 1920s and 1930s. As Army Chief of Staff from 1921 to 1924, Pershing strove to make the army see beyond mere tactics and weapons when it came to its thinking about warfare. He expanded the army's school system and reemphasized the importance of professional education in the careers of army officers. One of these new schools, the Army Industrial War College, laid down the intellectual foundations that sought to solve one of the more embarrassing questions of the Great War—why had the world's largest industrial power been forced to beg ships and modern weapons from its allies? The work of the Industrial War College ultimately helped to make the US the Arsenal of Democracy in World War II.

Pershing's long-term influence was also seen in the personal relationships he built and in the professionalism that he engendered in others. He continued to mentor and mold the young officers that had come to his notice during the Great War—men such as George Marshall and George Patton. Pershing, in fact, was one of the last people that Patton visited before leaving for North Africa in 1942. He also aided Dwight Eisenhower, a man who had spent the Great War training tankers at Camp Colt, Pennsylvania. Pershing helped shape Eisenhower's future career and attitudes by sending him to France to study the AEF's battlefields and by having the young officer participate in the writing of the army's first studies of World War I. These Pershing acolytes readily acknowledged the Iron Commander's influence in the way they fought the Second Great War. In a cable to Pershing sent soon after the German surrender in 1945, Eisenhower wrote, "As the commander of the second American expeditionary force, I should like to acknowledge to you, the leader of our first, our obligation for the part that you have played in the recent victory…The sons of the men that you led in battle in 1918 have much for which to thank you."[50]

So, in the end, does Pershing merit the title of "great commander?"

Did he properly use the human and material resources at his disposal? Were the AEF's accomplishments proportional to the losses it suffered? Marshal Ferdinand Foch may offer some insight into these questions. Foch is reported to have once remarked that it took 15,000 casualties to train a major general. While this statement sounds callous and cynical to modern ears, in the context of World War I, Foch's observation was a sad but accurate statement of reality. Given the state of the American army and the situation in 1918, perhaps it took 48,000 dead to train Pershing as an army commander. Although Pershing never showed any great brilliance as an operational commander, he did show a steady growth in his understanding of what it took to fight and defeat a modern foe under the conditions of the Western Front. Foch had also noted, "There is no studying on the battlefield. It is simply a case of doing what is possible, to make use of what one knows and, in order to make a little possible, one must know much."[51] Like Ulysses Grant before him, Pershing accepted casualties because he could, and his enemy could not. In the end, it is not certain that Pershing was a great commander to rank among Caesar, Napoleon, or even Eisenhower. However, it is far from certain that any other American officer could have done much better if he were placed in Pershing's shoes. Perhaps for World War I, with the army he had, with the situation he faced, and with the enemy he fought, Pershing, while not a "great commander," was simply "Great War Good Enough."

Notes

1.   Quoted in, Robert Heinl, *Dictionary of Military and Naval Quotations* (Annapolis: Naval Institute Press, 1966), 132.

2.   J. Franklin Bell, "Reflections and Suggestions: An Address by General J. Franklin Bell" 17 March 1906, Combined Arms Research Library, Special Collections, Ft. Leavenworth, KS, 5-6.

3.   Frank Vandiver, *Black Jack: The Life and Times of John J. Pershing*, Vol. 1 (College Station: Texas A&M Press, 1977), 13-19, 36-43.

4.   "General Principles Governing the Training of Units of the American Expeditionary Forces" included in, AEF GHQ, "Program of Training for the 1st Division, A.E.F.," 06 October 1917, in, *World War Records, First Division*, Vol. XX, *Training First Division* (Washington D.C.: Army War College, 1930), not paginated.

5.   Donald Smythe, *Pershing: General of the Armies* (Bloomington: University of Indiana Press, 1986), 1-2.

6.   Vandiver, 168-172.

7.   Donald Smythe, *Guerrilla Warrior: The Early Life of John J. Pershing* (New York: Charles Scribner's Sons, 1973), 52.

8.   Robert Bullard, *Personalities and Reminiscences of the War* (New York: Doubleday, Page & Company, 1925), 44; also see James Arnold, *The Moro War* (New York: Bloomsbury Press, 2011), 40-58, 217-227.

9.   Henry B. Davis, *Generals in Khaki* (Raleigh: Pentland Press, 1998), 297.

10. Smythe, 205-6.

11. Smythe, 208-212, Vandiver, 592-4.

12. Andrew Birtle, *US Army Counterinsurgency and Contingency Operations Doctrine* (Washington D.C., Center of Military History, 1998), 200-1; Eileen Welsome, *The General and the Jaguar: Pershing's Hunt for Pancho Villa* (New York: Little, Brown and Company, 2006), 132-5.

13. Report of Major General John J. Pershing of the Punitive Expedition, 10 October 1916, Combined Arms Research Library Archives, Fort Leavenworth, KS, 3.

14. Quoted in Smythe, *Guerrilla Warrior*, 220-1.

15. Report of Major General John J. Pershing of the Punitive Expedition , 10-11; Birtle, 202-8.

16. Report of Major General John J. Pershing of the Punitive Expedition, 24-5.

17. Ibid., 25.

18. United States Department of War, *War Department Annual Report* (Washington D.C.: Government Printing Office, 1916), 242; Leonard Ayres, *The War With Germany: A Statistical Summary* (Washington, D.C.: US Government Printing Office, 1919), 16-21.

19. John J. Pershing, *My Experiences in the World War*, Vol. I (New York: Frederick A. Stokes Company, 1931), 38-9.

20. Quoted in David F. Trask, *The AEF and Coalition Warfare, 1917-1918* (Lawrence: University Press of Kansas, 1993), 74-5.

21. For a more detailed discussion of the challenges the United States faced in building its wartime cadre of officers and NCOs and the systemic problems of America's mobilization for the Great War, see Richard S. Faulkner, *The School of Hard Knocks: Combat Leadership in the American Expeditionary Forces*, College Station, Texas A&M Press, 2012.

22. G. Edward Buxton, ed. *Official History of the 82nd Division American Expeditionary Forces* (Indianapolis: Bobbs-Merrill Co., 1919), 1-6; U. S. Department of War, *Order of Battle of the United States Land Forces in the World War: American Expeditionary Forces*, Vol. 2, *Divisions*. (Washington D.C. Government Printing Office, 1931), 349. (Hereafter cited as *Order of Battle*)

23. *Order of Battle,* Vol. 2, 383.

24. Report from The Acting Intelligence Officer, 83rd Division to Chief, Military Intelligence Section, Subject: "General Information," dated 28 February 1918, NARA, RG 165 Records of the General Staff, Entry 377, Correspondence Related to Morale at Army Installations, Box 14, Camp Sherman file.

25. Christian A. Bach and Henry N. Hall, *The Fourth Division: Its Services and Achievements in the World War* (New York: Country Life Press, 1920), 23-4.

26. Edward M. Coffman, *The War to End All Wars* (Madison: University of Wisconsin Press, 1968), 81-84; Carol R. Byerly, *The Fever of War: The Influenza Epidemic in the U. S. Army during World War I* (New York: New York University Press, 2005), 8-9.

27. For example, see, Mark Grotelueschen, *The AEF Way of War: The American Army in Combat in World War I* (New York: Cambridge University Press, 2007), 25-36.

28. AEF GHQ, "Program of Training for the 1st Division, A.E.F.," 06 October 1917, in, *World War Records, First Division*, Vol. XX, *Training First Division* (Washington D.C.: Army War College, 1930), not paginated.

29. *Ibid.*

30. Pershing, *My Experience*, Vol I, 150-4 and Vol II, 237-8.

31. James Harbord, *The American Army in France, 1917-1919* (Boston: Little Brown and Company, 1936), 491-500; US Army Center of Military History, *American Armies and Battlefields in Europe* (Washington DC: Government Printing Office, 1992), 439-440.

32.   Harbord,   42;   Cooke, 10-11.

33.   Harboard, 126-7.

34.   Quoted in Smythe, *Pershing: General of the Armies*, 43.

35.   George Marshall, *The Papers of George Catlett Marshall*, Vol 1, *The Soldierly Sprit,* ed. Larry Bland and Sharon Ritenour (Baltimore: Johns Hopkins University Press, 1981), 112-113.

36.   Forrest Pogue, *George Marshall*, Vol. I, *Education of a General: 1880-1839* (New York: Viking Press, 1963), 153; Smythe, *Pershing: General of the Armies*, 55.

37.   Coffman, 249-250.

38.   Robert L. Bullard, *Personalities and Reminiscences of the War* (New York: Doubleday, Page and Company, 1925), 26-7.

39.   Quoted in Smythe, *Pershing: General of the Armies*, 153.

40.   For a deeper examination of the operation of the Blois Officer Reclassification Center, see Faulkner, *The School of Hard Knocks.*

41.   Col. M.G. Spinks, "Major Problems of the Inspector General, AEF, and Their Solution," lecture given to the Army War College, 9 October 1933, US-AMHI File AWC 401-A-5, 9.

42.   US Army Center of Military History, *US Army in the World War,* Vol. 14, *Reports* (Washington D.C. Government Printing Office, 1988),   401.

43.   Smythe, *Pershing: General of the Armies*, 146-17; Trask, *The AEF and Coalition Warmaking*, 78-9.

44.   For example, see AEF GHQ, *Notes on Recent Operations, No. 1*, issued 7 August 1918, and *Notes on Recent Operations No. 2* issued on 8 September 1918.

45.   Edward Lengel, *To Conquer Hell: The Meuse Argonne, 1918* (New York: Henry Holt and Company, 2008), 49-53.

46.   The Society of the Fifth Division, *The Official History of the Fifth Division* (Washington D.C.: Privately published, 1919), 154.

47.   George Marshall, *Memories of My Service in the World War 1917-1918* (New York: Houghton Mifflin Company, 1976), 149-158., Lengel, 69-74.

48.   Hunter Liggett, *AEF: Ten Years Ago in France* (New York: Dodd, Meade and Company, 1927), 207.

49.   David Trask, *The AEF and Coalition Warmaking, 1917-1918* (Lawrence: University Press of Kansas. 1993), 145.

50.   Smythe, *Pershing: General of the Armies*, 305-6.

51.   Quoted in US Army Infantry School, *Infantry in Battle* (Washington D.C.: Infantry Journal, 1939), 137.

Chapter 6
Rommel: Beyond the Desert Fox
by Mark M. Hull, Ph.D., J.D., FRHistS

Perhaps unique among his contemporaries, the reputation of German Field Marshal Erwin Rommel is stronger now than it was when he was alive – and he certainly achieved star status during his lifetime, among both Germans and his Allied opponents. His campaigns are still studied; his leadership style used as a model for command, and his participation in the plot to kill Hitler is still admired. His name conjures colorful images of the desert, where Rommel's hard-pressed *Deutsches Afrikakorps* fought with decency and no small measure of success. Among so many distinctions, the single greatest one might be that Rommel emerged from the ruins of the Third Reich with his reputation intact. For subsequent generations of Germans who were tainted by their country's Nazi crimes, Rommel's legacy became an important agent of social and military salvation. Hollywood in the 1950s did not often create movies which glorified the German soldiers who worked for Hitler; they made an exception for Erwin Rommel. However, nothing about Rommel is what it first seems.

This is the essence of the problem: to separate the truth about Rommel from its protective myth, and to separate the authentic Rommel from the Rommel that both Germans and Allies needed him to be. The true Rommel had flaws. He was disliked by most of his contemporaries, had a powerful ego and need for recognition, was out of his depth at anything beyond the operational level of war, and almost certainly was never an active member of the anti-Hitler conspiracy that so proudly listed him among its ranks. Essentially apolitical, Rommel nevertheless cultivated a privileged relationship with Hitler and enjoyed all the public and private benefits of that relationship until the war began to turn against Germany. His strategic sense was often questionable and seemingly deserted him during the Normandy invasion. However, the two seemingly contradictory portraits of Rommel are both true - and this is exactly what requires examination and synthesis. He emerges from that process as a less-than-Olympian figure, but one who still deserves his place on the list of great commanders of World War II. Rommel was neither perfect as a person nor as a general, but was almost always a talented commander who could be relied upon for an aggressive spirit and ingenuity, no matter what the odds against him – and when it counted most, he was invariably a decent man.

Since the end of the Napoleonic Wars, the ethos of the German military was guided by two powerful forces, the Great General Staff of Prussia

Figure 6. Field Marshall Erwin Rommel, 1942; photo provided by the German Federal Archives.

and the nobility who filled the ranks of the officer corps in the several (and, until 1871, independent) German states. Erwin Johannes Eugen Rommel, born on 15 November 1891 in Heidenheim, in the Kingdom of Württemberg, did not belong to either group. His father, also named Erwin, was the headmaster at the secondary school in Aalen. The son preferred athletic activities to scholarly pursuits, but had an interest in mathematics sufficient for him to consider a career in engineering. His father thought otherwise and Erwin was instead enrolled as an officer cadet in the 124th Württemberg Infantry.

Rommel learned his trade well and even early on, displayed physical toughness and determination, qualities that he retained for his entire career. In 1911, he met Lucia (called "Lucie") Marie Mollin during his course at the officer cadet school in Danzig, and the two soon became involved. However, upon returning home (Rommel was commissioned as a lieutenant in January 1912), his attention shifted away from Lucie and toward a young woman in Weingarten, Walburga Stemmer. Stemmer became pregnant and they had a child, Gertrude, in 1913. Despite initial plans to marry, they never did. Rommel later returned to Lucie, whom he married in 1916. Until the birth of Erwin and Lucie's son Manfred in 1928, Stemmer held on to the hope that Rommel would return to her; she committed suicide soon thereafter.[1]

Rommel had little time to worry about the complications of his domestic situation; when World War I began on 1 August 1914, he was a platoon leader with the 6th Württemberg Infantry and he soon had the opportunity to learn whether his skills were up to the task. Initially assigned to an artillery battery within the regiment, he returned to standard infantry duties and won the Iron Cross (1st and 2d class) for courage under fire, was wounded in an attempt to capture French soldiers – while holding an empty rifle – and moved with his unit twice from France to Romania and then back to the Western front. Wounded several more times, he established a reputation for daring, persistence, and a singular disregard for his own safety. When his unit was transferred to the Italian front in late 1917, he finally had the opportunity to showcase his quality: during a multi-day operation in November near Longarone, an attack led by Lieutenant Rommel (now a company commander), fought its way through several echelons of Italian defenses and captured more than 8,000 prisoners. It was a stunning achievement and earned Rommel the medal he had long coveted, the *Pour le Mérite*, Imperial Germany's highest award for bravery.[2]

Promoted to captain, Rommel continued to serve until the final collapse of Germany's military. Toward the end, he briefly held a staff appointment – a posting that did not please the young officer who was temperamentally more suited to the sound of gunfire. His vague distain toward essential General Staff tasks (and by extension, the professional, often pedigreed General Staff officers who normally performed them) was a recurring theme in his career, a tolerable attitude for a captain but problematic for a general. Germany's defeat in 1918 created many problems for her millions of soldiers. Following the Versailles Treaty, the German military was stripped of most heavy weapons and aircraft, and limited to a miniscule 100,000 men. Given his drive, enthusiasm, and repeated bravery in combat, it was unsurprising that Rommel was included among the 4,000 officers selected to form the core of a new army, the *Reichswehr*. He held both command and instructor assignments (he was evidently a popular instructor) in Stuttgart and Dresden before being assigned to battalion command in Goslar, Saxony. There, in 1934, Rommel's path took an auspicious turn when his unit was reviewed by the new Chancellor of Germany, Adolf Hitler. It was their first meeting.

Rommel was soon thereafter assigned as an infantry instructor at the *Kriegschule* (essentially an advanced educational course for professional Reichswehr officers) at Potsdam. It was a plum job and confirmed Rommel as being on an accelerated career track. He enhanced this further in 1937 when he published *Infanterie Greift An* (*Infantry Attacks*), the narrative version of his WWI experiences as used in his classroom lectures. Hitler certainly read it, and liked what he read. Rommel was very much the soldier's soldier – a perspective that Hitler appreciated, contrasted with social and intellectual inferiority the Führer often felt when around other Army officers, particularly those with a General Staff background. Now a star on the rise, Rommel twice briefly commanded Hitler's headquarters detachment during the Czechoslovakia occupation in 1939, and was recalled again in August 1939 – as preparations for the Polish campaign continued, well in advance of the "Gleiwitz Incident," a staged German attack on one of their own radio stations, intended to convince the German people, and the world, that Poland was the aggressor. For the full month of campaigning, Rommel was at Hitler's side, responsible for the multiple tasks, demonstrating his ability and reliability to the Führer, and witnessing first-hand a new style of warfare which was beyond his WWI or postwar experience: mobile, combined arms maneuver, subsequently referred to as "Blitzkrieg."

Hitler's patronage meant that Rommel had his choice of assignments after Poland, though the favoritism demonstrated on his behalf by the Führer began to alienate Rommel's fellow officers. Rommel asked for and was given command of the 7th Panzer Division and would bring his background in sharp, rapid infantry attacks to the most modern tool of war, the tank. He had a hidden talent for it. Despite optimistic German predictions that the western Allies would again negotiate a solution rather than face the Wehrmacht themselves, the Germans prepared to turn on the Low Countries and France in the spring of 1940. "Case Yellow" was a surprise armored thrust through the Ardennes – spearheaded by seven panzer divisions, including Rommel's 7th Panzer – that caught the Allies in the process of responding to an earlier attack through Holland and Belgium. Rommel's part in the campaign came near disaster when 7th Panzer attempted to cross the Meuse River at Dinant on 12 May. After suffering severe casualties among the engineers and assault companies, and thanks to excellent close air support from the Luftwaffe, Rommel was eventually able to cross his division and exert relentless pressure on the retreating French and British forces. His command style – leading from the front – was a legacy from his WWI experience and had both advantages and disadvantages. It meant that he was able to be at the point of attack with his advance units and make critical on-the-spot decisions, but it also meant that he was often out of contact with his own operations section and higher headquarters and thus less able to exercise broader control of his subordinate units. Rommel said, "In this war, the commander's place is here, right out front! I don't believe in armchair strategy. Let's leave that to the gentlemen of the General Staff."[3] He tended to disregard supply issues and pushed his tanks and supporting infantry dangerously close to their logistical limits. This was less of a critical factor in the restricted operational space of France, but became a nightmare when he later applied the same principles in the endless North African desert.

As 7th Panzer advanced, Rommel's continually innovative tactics paid off although he moved at a faster pace than his own flank units could maintain. Fortunately for the *Wehrmacht*, he was also moving faster than the Allied units could hope to respond. He left columns of broken French and British vehicles in his wake as he sliced through Cerfontaine, Avesnes, Cambrai, and Arras, escaping from one enemy trap after another.[4] By 10 June, his advance units reached the coast near Dieppe. Rommel again made the newsreels – he was by now a national hero thanks to heavy attention from the Propaganda Ministry – when he accepted a mass enemy surrender at Saint-Valéry on the 12th. Rommel's tactical brilliance more than justified Hitler's patronage and helped create an asymmetrical situation among the world's armies between those that could leverage the shock and speed of modern combined arms warfare (so far, only the Germans) and the many that could not. For his part in the *Wehrmacht's* success, Rommel was awarded the Knight's Cross, the first German division commander to receive it during the French campaign. His stunning performance and "just so" image was not only a gift to the German public relations machine but it also placed Rommel in a position to take advantage of the opportunity next offered to him – Africa.

When forecasting the likely operational reach of German forces, the OKW, *Oberkommando der Wehrmacht* – Armed Forces High Command, never envisioned sending troops to the desert. Italian defeat in Libya changed all that. By early 1941, what started as Mussolini's ambitious attempt to attack British forces in Egypt, seize the Suez Canal, and secure the Mediterranean basin had become a disaster. The British had instead driven the Italians across the coast of Libya, taken Tobruk, and threatened Tripoli. If Tripoli fell, it would extinguish the Axis presence in Africa and allow the British the freedom to attack southern Europe (specifically Italy) at the time and place of their choosing. Rather than watch these dominoes collapse, Hitler determined to save the Italian position by sending a minimal German contingent whose initial purpose was to act as last-ditch safety net.[5] One German division (5th Light) was assigned, and when this was thought insufficient, the 15th Panzer Division was added to the menu. The two divisions combined into a corps – the *Afrikakorps* – required a corps commander with guile and initiative who could make something of a dismal tactical and operational situation. That was Erwin Rommel.

The Germans' arrival was timely. The British commander in Africa, Major General Archibald Wavell, had sent a portion of his forces to help bolster the defense of Greece (Italy invaded Greece in October 1940, with Germany coming to the Italian's rescue in April 1941). The first elements of Rommel's lead formation – the 5th Light Division – arrived in February 1941, equipped with 150 tanks (some of them the Mark III and Mark IV models, with 50mm and 75mm main guns, respectively) and perhaps the most effective anti-tank weapon of World War II, the 88mm antiaircraft (FLAK) gun. The *Afrikakorps* joined five weary Italian divisions of various strengths, all of which were at the end of their endurance after more than a year of difficult fighting, bitter retreat, and a profound shortage of essential supplies.[6] In the proceeding few months, the British had advanced 500 miles across the open desert, taken over 100,000 Italian prisoners, and destroyed 400 tanks. The Axis position was indeed perilous. Rommel began considering the options.

Against Italian advice, he determined to hold the British forces where they were – some 250 miles east of Tripoli – regardless of the momentary weakness of the just-arriving *Afrikakorps* (5th Light would not reach full strength until April and 15th Panzer would not arrive until May). His plan was to put up a sufficient show of force in order to cause the British to halt and regroup which he did by sending Italian and German elements to hold the line at El Agheila and Sirte, having his troops make "tanks" out of wood, canvas, and car engines to fool Allied reconnaissance, and by staging a welcome-to-Africa parade for German troops – which featured panzers circling around for multiple passes, creating the impression for onlookers (and British spies) that his force was many times the size it actually was.[7] Unknown to Rommel, the British advance had reached its limit. The experienced British 7th Armoured Division ("The Desert Rats") had been returned to Egypt for refitting, replaced by the green 2d Armoured Division, of which half its force had been stripped for the mission to Greece. The highly effective British commander Major General Richard O'Connor, was promoted to command troops in Egypt and replaced by Lieutenant General Philip Neame. Allied tanks, too, were suffering from the sprint across the desert.[8] British intelligence forecast that the Germans would be incapable of operations until amassing a sufficient force, perhaps by May. The German High Command agreed; it had other operational priorities (Greece and, secretly, Russia) which in turn meant that Rommel was forbidden to launch an offensive with the few units he had. Rommel had no intention of obeying.

He ordered an attack on El Agheila on 24 March with the available troops from the 5th Light, the Italian Ariete Division, and buoyed by dummy tanks whose job was to create dust clouds and the impression of columns of moving vehicles. The British defenders withdrew 30 miles to the east; on 30 March, Rommel attacked these British positions at Mersa Brega. Despite clear instructions from both the German High Command and the Italian *Commando Supremo*, Rommel was prepared to roll the dice and attempt to seize the entire British position in Cyrenacia. Despite outrunning its logistics tether – forcing the 5th Light to suspend all operations until it could be resupplied by truck (there was no rail line serving the coastal road) – the *Afrikakorps* continued to snap at the heels of the swiftly retreating British army. Bengazhi fell on April 4th amid much fanfare from the German propaganda apparatus.[9] British General Neame, having now completely lost control of the battle and unwilling to visit the front, was superseded by General O'Connor. In headlong retreat with the rest of the British forces trying to escape Derna, O'Connor and Neame took the wrong road in the darkness and accidentally drove straight into the German advance. They spent three years in captivity.

Mechili fell on 8 April to German and Italian forces which followed an axis of advance parallel to the coastal road. Rommel had re-conquered Cyrenacia. Writing later of this whirlwind offensive, he noted:

A commander's drive and energy often count for more than his intellectual powers – a fact that is not generally understood by academic soldiers, although for the practical man it is self-evident. Later in the campaign, when I had a chance to establish closer relations with the troops, they were capable at all times of achieving what I demanded of them.[10]

Distaining the refinement or training of the General Staff, Rommel remained the man of action, but he was still subject to the physical realities of war. The all-important port city of Tobruk remained in enemy hands. As long the British held it, they prevented Rommel – whose supplies now had to travel hundreds of miles, one way, by truck from Benghazi – from any further significant advance toward Egypt. Even with only a portion of its eventual strength present, the *Afrikakorps* required 1500 tons of food and water each day, straining the German logistical system to its breaking point.[11]

Inspired by his unexpected successes, Rommel started making plans which dwarfed the original goal of the campaign. He never fully appreciated why these plans would necessarily go unrealized. By the time that German forces reached El Alamein in 1942, a substantial portion of their supplies had to be transported a distance of 1400 miles from Tripoli. Even factoring in the addition of Tobruk's potential port capacity (which was significantly less than that of Tripoli or Benghazi), the High Command calculated that just one division would require 350 tons of supplies per day – which worked out to thirty-nine columns of thirty-two trucks each day, travelling a minimum distance of 300 miles – a total of 5,000 trucks. This was in addition to the organic transportation assets of the division. Transport of supplies alone consumed 50 percent of the fuel the trucks carried.[12] There were not enough vehicles in the *Wehrmacht* inventory to satisfy the minimum needs of Rommel's multi-division force.[13] After the campaign was concluded, he still seemed unable to acknowledge the connection between supply and demand:

The reason for giving up the pursuit is almost always the quartermaster's growing difficulty in spanning the lengthened supply routes with his available transport. As the commander usually pays great attention to his quartermaster and allows the latter's estimate of the supply possibilities to determine his strategic plan, it has become the habit for the quartermaster staffs to complain at every difficulty, instead of getting on with the job and using their powers of improvisation, which indeed are frequently nil.[14]

Although the full impact of the logistical shortfall still lay ahead of him, in the summer of 1941 the conquest of Tobruk was the immediate task. Rommel hoped the momentum of the Axis advance would carry him through. British defenders occupied a 30-mile perimeter, with 220 miles of tank ditches, barbed wire, mines, and reinforced concrete defensive belts.

Tobruk's port also afforded the British ample supplies from the Mediterranean so long as the Royal Navy maintained superiority and the Luftwaffe was unable to bring the full weight of its tactical bombing to bear. Rommel optimistically expected the garrison to collapse but learned otherwise when the first of several attacks in April failed to break through anything more than the outer defenses; Rommel blamed his subordinate commanders, General Johannes Streich and Oberst Dr. Herbert Olbrich.[15]

The siege of Tobruk concerned Berlin, too. General Friedrich Paulus (who infamously discovered the tenacity of Russian defenders at Stalingrad in 1942-3) came to observe and report back to General Franz Halder, Army Chief of Staff. Halder was furious at Rommel's disobedience and believed that the *Afrikakorps* commander was "stark raving mad," but still recognized that the Hitler-Rommel bond was not to be taken lightly. Based upon Paulus' report, Army Commander in Chief Walter Brauchitsch ordered the Tobruk attack halted. This was done just in time, as the British – far from being ready to surrender Africa – launched Operation Battleaxe on 15 June. In a series of hard-fought engagements at Halfaya Pass and Fort Capuzzo, the more nimble German defenders blunted the British offensive and nearly decapitated the entire force. Churchill relieved General Wavell as Commander in Chief Middle East, replacing him with Lieutenant General Claude Auchinleck. This became a familiar pattern: while Rommel stayed, a rotating series of British commanders arrived, failed, and went. Auchinleck, in turn, named Lieutenant General Sir Alan Cunningham as commander of the Western Desert Force, expanded and renamed the Eighth Army.

Eighth Army, with fresh troops and equipment, was again put to the job of destroying the *Afrikakorps*, which itself was renamed as *Panzergruppe Afrika*.[16] The new British offensive, dubbed "Operation Crusader" brought a mass of firepower in the form of XXX Corps. Seven hundred British tanks faced off against 400 German and Italian armored vehicles, of which only 250 were modern. Rommel was meanwhile planning to resume his own attack on Tobruk, having at last received permission from OKW. Crusader launched on 18 November and despite being initially slow in responding to the unexpected attack, Rommel counterattacked at selected points in overwhelming force – the fighting was fiercest at Sidi Rezegh – and destroyed significant portions of the XXX Corps armored spearheads.

Coincident with the start of Crusader, British commandos attacked the German headquarters detachment at Beda Littoria on the night of 17/18 November intending to assassinate Rommel. Unknown to the attackers, he had ceased using the small, spare headquarters building there three months earlier and had moved closer to the fighting, now several hundred miles up the coast. As can so easily happen in special operations missions, a cascade of events went wrong. In addition to simply being at the wrong location, the men involved in this raid, code-named Operation Flipper, were unaware that Rommel was not even in Africa – he had gone to Rome two weeks prior. In the ensuing assault, the mission commander, Major Geoffrey Keyes, was killed along with four German occupants of Rommel's old headquarters building. A few commandos eventually made it back to Allied lines, but the remainder were killed or captured. Rommel ordered that Major Keyes be buried with honor, in a plot next to the graves of the slain Germans.[17]

Although Rommel won the first part of Crusader, numbers (and his determination to continue operations at Tobruk) weighed against his force. After inflicting severe damage on the British despite the imbalanced force ratio (Eighth Army by now had four tanks to each German tank), Rommel retreated to the prepared defensive line at Gazala. Cunningham was relieved and replaced by Major General Neil Ritchie. Ritchie launched a renewed attack on Gazala in mid-December, forcing *Panzergruppe Afrika* back along the coast road to El Agheila, covering the same ground it had seized earlier that year. However, this turn of events was typical of the see-saw war in Africa; the British offensive again reached the limit of its effectiveness and Rommel, reinforced with new panzers from home, counterattacked in early 1942, re-entering Benghazi on 28 January and resuming the Gazala position in early February. Like his predecessors, Ritchie's job was in jeopardy but Auchinleck left him in command. Rommel next attempted to penetrate the series of British positions, called "boxes" which lay between the extreme southern end of the British line and the coast. He ran into trouble almost immediately and only Ritchie's inexplicable inaction saved the German force – now re-designated *Panzerarmee Afrika* – from defeat. Instead, the Germans finally broke the Free French strongpoint at Bir Hakeim and rolled up the remaining Eighth Army positions. British losses were devastating; their Gazala positions crumbled and Rommel again resumed his single-minded pursuit of the main objective: Tobruk.

The British defenses at Tobruk were significantly weaker than they had been seven months earlier. British units had been repositioned to support the Gazala line and the fixed obstacles had been partially dismantled in connection with Operation Crusader. Following sustained Luftwaffe attacks, German forces broke through the hastily reassembled cordon of protective landmines. Tobruk surrendered on 21 June 1942, and 35,000 Allied soldiers marched into captivity. The Germans captured enough supplies to fuel the drive to Alexandria. Hitler promoted Erwin Rommel to the rank of Field Marshal; it was the apogee of his career.

On the other hand, Claude Auchinleck's career was at an end. He relieved Ritchie, took personal command of the Eighth Army, and retreated to a highly defensible position at a place called El Alamein. Although a mere 60 miles from Alexandria, it offered the last, best hope of stopping Rommel's advance. Auchinleck, though, had run out of time. He was relieved of command in August, replaced by General Sir Harold Alexander. To take Ritchie's vacant post with 8th Army, Churchill selected Lieutenant General Bernard Montgomery. In addition to priority of supplies and reinforcements (over 1,000 tanks arrived between August and October) Montgomery enjoyed the advantage of ULTRA intercepts – decrypts of German command-level messages sent via the Enigma machine. The allowed the British access to the entirety of German offensive plans; unit strengths and positions; supply situation; and even the enemy's assessment of the British defenses (quite erroneous, as it turned out). Rommel attempted several breakthroughs, only to run into unexpected minefields or unsuspected British defenses. Elaborate maneuver was out of the question, the coast marked the northern boundary of operations, as did the impassable Qatarra Depression to the south. Initial attempts to push through El Alamein failed and the Germans had little choice but to then wait for further reinforcements before attempting a final attack to Alexandria.

Montgomery, assisted by Ultra and a particularly effective air reconnaissance force, understood the Axis situation, defensive positions, and supply difficulties almost at well as his opponent. In the weeks leading up to the second battle at El Alamein, the British received personnel and equipment resupply, including new American M4 Sherman tanks, which all but guaranteed victory in the upcoming engagement. Contrasted with the dismal strength of *Panzerarmee Afrika* (it had 500 operational tanks, counting both antiquated Italian models and more modern German ones), the Eighth Army could field over a thousand, backed by close to a thousand artillery pieces. In addition, Montgomery, in his customarily thorough style, insisted that the assault troops, who would be first to pierce the dense German minefields, were trained to a fine edge. The British attack was scheduled for 23 October.

Rommel was away. Suffering from a host of physical ailments, the Desert Fox was recuperating in Austria, having left General Georg Stumme in command of the Axis forces. When the overwhelming British barrage started on the night of the 23 October, German positions up and down the line were pounded in a manner and intensity not seen since WWI. Some positions ceased to exist, communications were severed, and none of the defenders knew if the British main attack was occurring in his sector. General Stumme suffered a heart attack while attempting to visit his forward positions and was abandoned in the desert by his oblivious driver. At the moment when they most needed Rommel's clear leadership, the various German and Italian units were essentially on their own.

Rommel returned on the 25 October and assumed control of the defensive battle. Although the Germans inflicted savage punishment on Eighth Army at many points – and as usual the 88mm FLAK was stunningly effective – the relentless math of attrition insured resolution of the battle in Montgomery's favor; the Axis could not afford to replace its losses. Montgomery was several times under pressure from his subordinate commanders to suspend the offensive but he instead continued the attacks. Rommel ordered his battered army to withdraw on 2 November. He kept this fact hidden from the OKW for several critical hours, only incidentally mentioning that "the infantry units are already being withdrawn" in the text of a much longer, bleak situation report to the high command. Once Berlin realized the truth, Rommel's action drew an immediate response from the OKW and Hitler:

With me the entire German nation is watching your heroic defensive battle in Egypt, with well-placed confidence in your leadership and in the courage of your German and Italian troops. In your situation there can be no thought but to persevere, to yield not one yard, and to hurl every gun and every fighting man available into the battle. Considerable air reinforcements are being transferred over the coming days...Superior they may be, but the enemy are surely also at the end of their strength...to your troops therefore you can only offer one path – the path that leads to victory or death. Sgd: Adolf Hitler.[18]

At this moment, if at no other time before, Rommel began to question Hitler's orders, although he was not yet prepared to disobey them.[19] Though 15th Panzer was reduced to ten tanks and 21st Panzer to fourteen, the *Panzerarmee* commander ordered his units to hold. After consulting with Luftwaffe commander, Generalfeldmarschall Albert Kesselring on the 4 November, Rommel wired Hitler, asking for permission to save what was left of his army.[20] When the front collapsed later that same day, he again ordered the retreat without waiting for a response from Berlin. Hitler approved the retreat that evening.[21] Rommel's action, even delayed, was certainly the correct one.

The Germans put up a stubborn retreat toward more defensible lines, sowing mines in their wake and engaging in local counterattacks whenever the British pursuit overextended itself. Allied air superiority meant that Axis convoys were hit on a regular basis. Rommel's operational situation became even more acute when, on 8 November, American and British forces landed in Morocco, trapping German forces between them. Hitler disapproved Rommel's request of evacuation from Africa, something that was quite impossible from strategic, morale, and a practical perspectives. A subsequent meeting with the Führer did little to alter either Rommel's determination to retreat or Hitler's waning confidence in him.[22]

By the time *Panzerarmee Afrika* arrived at the Tunisian border, the distance between the two halves of the Allied force was a mere two hundred miles. Rommel, staying ahead of Montgomery, halted his force at the Mareth Line, a series of French-built fortifications which ran from the Mediterranean to the Matmata Hills near the Libyan-Tunisian border. It was a position all-but-impossible to take by frontal assault. With the Americans steadily approaching from the west, and the absolute necessity of keeping the enemy forces apart, Rommel recovered enough of his fighting spirit to plan and conduct a limited offensive against the US II Corps: Kasserine Pass.[23] On 14 February 1943, the Germans launched armored forces (accompanied by every available tactical air support aircraft) through a series of passes, and crushed the American and British units in their path. Although the attacks continued until 23 February, when Rommel – overcome with fatigue and caution, much to the dismay of Kesselring (now commanding all forces in the Mediterranean theater) – abruptly returned his forces whence they came, and refocused his attention on the British facing him at the Mareth Line.

Rommel had been designated as commander of *Heersgruppe Afrika* (Army Group Africa), but it was an empty, meaningless title. Actual command belonged with his subordinate leaders, General Hans-Jürgen von Arnim (Fifth Panzer Army) and General Giovanni Messe (First Italian Army).[24] The Desert Fox's days were numbered and everyone knew it. Sadly for his reputation, Rommel did not end his African campaign at Kasserine. Starting on 6 March, he launched the ill-conceived Operation Capri at Medenine. It was designed as a spoiling attack, to preemptively break up the British offensive that was coming against Mareth. German forces ran headlong into prepared British anti-tank and artillery positions, losing over fifty tanks in the process and making no appreciable gain. Although Enigma intercepts forewarned Montgomery of Rommel's attack, the coordination of German forces was so poor that it likely stood little chance of success no matter the circumstances. The attack ended that same evening. On 9 March, three days afterward, Field Marshal Erwin Rommel left Africa forever.[25]

Heersgruppe Afrika survived until 12 May, under the command of von Arnim, when approximately 230,000 German and Italian troops surrendered.[26] Perhaps 40,000 Axis soldiers were killed, wounded or missing in the last phase of the campaign, significantly fewer casualties than those suffered by the Allied forces against them.[27] With the conquest of Africa, the Americans and British were free to choose their next point of attack on Fortress Europe – Sicily, Italy, Greece, or even Southern France.

Officially, Rommel remained a shining star in Germany's war machine. Privately, he was in the limbo reserved for German officers who had failed at their task and now waited for the phone call that meant a new, almost certainly less glorious assignment. After recovery time in Wiener Neustadt, Rommel was first sent to Greece (in response to an Allied diversionary operation that suggested the next point of invasion would be there; it was Sicily instead), and then in August to command Army Group B in Northern Italy, but this soon brought him into personal and professional conflict with the ambitious Kesselring, the Mediterranean theater commander. This particular pond was too small for two large fish. OKW ordered Rommel to transfer Army Group B command headquarters to France, where he was now charged with preventing the successful Allied invasion of northern France.

Rommel immediately started a comprehensive tour of his new area, visiting every forward unit and position up and down the Atlantic coast. What he saw shocked him. Lacking precise information on where the Allies would strike – though the intelligence services were [wrongly] confident that it would be Pas de Calais – German resources were stretched along more than a thousand miles of coastline. Moreover, defending the coast of France was not among Germany's top military priorities, given the fact that the tide had turned against German forces on the eastern front. The coastal defense units were composed of less-combat-ready personnel and were under strength. With the change of command, and Hitler's growing realization that the invasion of France must come soon, physical and personnel priorities likewise changed.

As one might expect in the National Socialist system, personalities and in-fighting had unfortunate effects on military operations. Rommel disliked both Generalfeldmarschall Gerd von Rundstedt, overall German commander in the West, and Rundstedt's senior panzer commander, General der Panzertruppe Geyr von Schweppenburg. The feeling was mutual. There were several contentious issues, but the most significant concerned the operational control of the panzer force reserve, which included the powerful 1st SS Panzer Division "Leibstandarte SS Adolf Hitler, " and Panzer Lehr Division.[28] Von Rundstedt and von Schweppenburg believed that until the exact location of the Allied landing was established, it would be foolish to position Germany's most powerful forces too far forward; if they were wrongly supporting the defense of the Pas de Calais and that landing was a feint, then Allied airpower would prevent the Germans from repositioning their forces to oppose the actual landing site. Using the same assumptions, Rommel argued for the opposite solution: because of Allied air superiority in the upcoming invasion, it was essential that he be given operational of the panzer divisions and that these divisions be staged as far forward as possible, to counter the landing immediately and destroy the Allies before they could establish a foothold on the continent. Listening to both arguments, Hitler decided on a middle course, a portion of the panzers would constitute an OKW reserve and be released to the theater commander only when the site of the main Allied landing was evident.[29]

When the invasion came on 6 June 1944, Rommel was on leave at his home in Herrlingen, hundreds of miles from Normandy. Because it was still uncertain that the Normandy beaches were the main effort, OKW refused to release the panzers until later that afternoon, well after the time they should have most effectively intervened. Rommel arrived back at his headquarters late at night on 6 June. He immediately took control of the battle but the critical opportunity had passed. Rommel continued to expect a second invasion – probably at Pas de Calais – for weeks to come.[30]

The Normandy battle went badly for Rommel, although his forces stubbornly held the British to a draw near Caen for longer than expected. On June 29, at a conference with Hitler at the Berghof, Rommel briefly attempted to inject his view that the battle was lost and that the political conclusions (i.e. negotiation was necessary with the western Allies) were self-evident.[31] Hitler dismissed him from the conference but Rommel retained his command.

At the height of the Normandy battle, fate removed Rommel from further participation. On 17 July his staff car was strafed by a British fighter-bomber and the Field Marshal was seriously wounded. Three days later, while Rommel drifted in and out of consciousness, Oberst Claus von Stauffenberg set off a bomb at Hitler's headquarters in Rastenburg, East Prussia. A wide-ranging investigation by the Gestapo and SD (*Sicherheitsdienst* – SS Security Service) followed. It uncovered a diverse group of conspirators, many revealed in the brief interval between the bomb explosion and the collapse of the "Valkyrie" plot later that same day. To Hitler's dismay, many senior Wehrmacht officers were among those involved, and as the interrogations continued, Rommel's name emerged.

The circumstances were suspicious and suggestive; several plotters were directly connected to Rommel. Chief of Staff of Army Group B, Generalmajor Hans Speidel, was a member of the conspiracy and Rommel's name was mentioned in connection with the plotters only after Speidel's arrest and interrogation. Unlike so many others, Speidel did not hang from piano wire at Plötzensee Prison, suggesting the strong possibility that he and another conspirator, Oberstleutnant Caesar von Hofacker, offered up Rommel to save themselves. Ultimately, Speidel benefited both from his association with the Feldmarschall and his membership in the 20 July plot. His survival meant that he became the *de facto* manager of Rommel's legacy and was named commander of NATO ground forces in 1957.[32] Hofacker was executed.

When the Gestapo investigation uncovered Rommel's name, interrogation statements and the investigative report were forwarded to Hitler and the OKW. Rommel – perhaps because of his previous special relationship with the Führer, perhaps because of his esteem among the German people, was given a choice not available to others named in the plot: a public trial for treason; or suicide, which would be disguised as death from his wounds.[33] In the latter case, his family would be spared. When Generalmajors Ernst Maisel and Wilhelm Burgdorf arrived at Rommel's home on 14 October 1944, they brought the dossier of evidence, a cyanide capsule, and two options. Rommel explained the situation to Lucie – that General der Infanterie Carl-Heinrich von Stülpnagel, Speidel, and Oberstleutnant Caesar von Hofacker had implicated him – and that he had already made his decision.[34] He left the house with the two generals from Berlin. A subsequent phone call informed Lucie that her husband had died of a heart attack. Hitler kept his word; Rommel was given a state funeral in Ulm, complete with guard of honor, and von Rundstedt was dispatched to deliver the eulogy.

Despite the circumstances of this death, Rommel's participation in the anti-Hitler conspiracy is problematic, and rests on weak evidence.[35] Although Rommel had become disillusioned with Hitler and the High Command in the weeks after Normandy – and following his own inability to contain the Allied landings – there is an absence of evidence to show active participation in the plot, let alone joining in Stauffenberg's decision to kill Hitler. He certainly mentioned to several people that a realistic appraisal of the overall situation was necessary – that is, that Hitler should work toward a negotiated peace before the war was lost. As time passed and the certainty of Germany's defeat became clearer, Rommel became less cautious in expressing this view. This does not equate with Rommel being a member of the 20 July assassination attempt or any of the other collateral plots, both within and outside the *Wehrmacht*, to overthrow the Nazi regime. The evidence suggests that Rommel became vaguely aware of plots but neither joined them nor informed his superiors of them. That alone was treason, albeit of a passive kind.

In the sensitive political atmosphere of postwar Germany, military heroes from the recent world war were few and far between. Except for the 20 July conspirators, other legitimately talented senior *Wehrmacht* officers – Manstein, Guderian, Kesselring, etc. – were unsuitable role models. The taint of Nazism, or at least their lack of active resistance to Hitler, was sufficient to make them pariahs. Rommel did not fit into that paradigm; thanks to his able performance in Africa, Desmond Young's highly readable biography and Speidel's somewhat self-serving recollections, both published in 1950, the 1953 publication of *The Rommel Papers,* and the fact that Rommel had been forced to commit suicide because of suspicion of his involvement in the assassination conspiracy, put the Desert Fox in a different category – an acceptable hero, essentially. This applied not only to the German public but likewise to the victorious Allied nations that defeated Rommel. They, too, needed a talented and gallant opponent to maximize the degree of their own success and it was evident that Erwin Rommel was truly both of these – talented and gallant. The problem, though, for both the postwar Allies and the postwar Germans was that for Rommel to be an acceptable hero, it was essential that he be separated from the immoral deeds of his Nazi masters. Hollywood helped: when *The Desert Fox: The Story of Rommel* was released by 20th Century Fox in 1951 (it premiered in Germany in 1952), it was generally well-received.[36] The film depicts Rommel (played by British actor James Mason) as an active member of the 20 July conspiracy, even trying to recruit von Rundstedt – a conversation that never happened. Strict historical accuracy is seldom the goal of filmmakers and it is perpetually the case that images shown on film have a magical way of seeping into the public consciousness; the movie narrative often becomes more of an indelible truth than the facts ever could be.

Rommel was portrayed on the big screen several times afterward, always in a sympathetic light: *The Longest Day* (1962), *Patton* (1970), and *Raid on Rommel* (1971).[37] Treatments on the small screen have become increasingly more critical, with the Rommel family objecting (in advance) to a soon-to-be released televised film that is highly critical.[38] A ZDF documentary production in 2007, "Rommel's War" was likewise negative, although the research attempting to show that Rommel was a war criminal by association ("he paved the way for the machinery of destruction with his victories") is patently absurd.[39] The facts show otherwise.[40]

A fair summary of Erwin Rommel's life and career is no easy task. To be sure, he had limitations; von Rundstedt once referred to him as "just a good division commander," implying that Rommel's competency ceiling was at that level. For many reasons, that estimation is both unfair and inaccurate. Rommel was a superb division commander, perhaps the best that Germany produced, and it is impossible to judge his handling of corps and army-level formations in North Africa by the ultimate result alone. Greatness is not merely a function of outcome – the fact that Rommel was beaten in Africa in 1943 does not diminish his abilities and achievements. For two years, he challenged the generally more numerous, better-equipped British and Commonwealth forces in what is perhaps the harshest climate on earth.

He was an intelligent, crafty, and highly adaptive commander. In the midst of a war characterized by brutality and crime, he came as close as humanly possible to fighting a war with honor and decency – although he willingly served a dictator who valued neither quality. Rommel's role as anti-Hitler conspirator does not withstand scrutiny but neither does it detract from the other evidence in his favor: when it was apparent in 1944 that continued military resistance would only lead to meaningless loss of life, he gradually moved to a position where he could no longer support Hitler's leadership. There is, of course, a wide chasm between what Rommel did and what we might today like for him to have done. He was politically naïve, especially during the period when Hitler's strategic decisions appeared to be correct, and it was fundamentally against his nature as a man and as an officer to be a revolutionary. However, Rommel finally arrived at a point where this imperative was no longer true, but never quite to the point of leading an insurrection or participating in a plot to kill the chief of state.

The best barometer of his command, and his life, might be that from his earliest successes in WWI through his command in Africa, to the final days in Normandy, Rommel earned the loyalty of his troops, even in defeat. They believed, with some justification, that he could do anything. Unlike the case with veterans of some other German wartime military organizations, *Afrikakorps* soldiers rightfully enjoyed the postwar respect of both their country and their former opponents. There is no question but that this is due to the quality of their commander; it was due to Erwin Rommel.

Notes

1. The Stemmer episode was a closely-held family secret until the Rommel to Stemmer letters were revealed by Gertrude's son. Even Rommel's son only knew his half-sister as "cousin Gertrude." John Bierman and Colin Smith, *The Battle of Alamein: Turning Point, World War II* (Viking, New York, 2002), p. 55-6.

2. Rommel complained loudly and often about two previous occasions, one of them at Mount Mataiur, when his actions should have won the *Pour le Mérite* promised to the first officer to take the enemy position. David Irving, *The Trail of the Fox*, pp. 14-5.

3. Irving, p. 45.

4. Rommel made sure that there was no repeat of the incident in Italy in WWI where he felt proper credit was denied him. He prepared a summary dispatch of his unit's activities and sent it directly to Hitler. When Hitler summoned his senior commanders on June 2 to discuss the next phase of the campaign, Rommel was the only division commander invited to meet with him (Irving, p. 48).

5. Führer Directive 22, of 11 January 1941 for the conduct of operations in the Mediterranean area specified the limited operational goal: "Tripolitania must be *held*" [italics added]. It was not, at least by Hitler and the OKW, envisioned as a major secondary theater of war.

6. Bierman and Smith, p. 67.

7. Richard Collier, *The War in the Desert* (Time-Life, NY, 1977), p. 61 and Erwin Rommel, *The Rommel Papers* (Da Capo, NY, 1982), p. 103.

8. Rommel, p. 104.

9. *Die Deutsche Wochenshau*, Nr. 554, 6 April 1941. The newsreel footage was accompanied by a new marching song written for the *Afrikakorps*: "Panzer rollen in Afrika vor"

10. Rommel, p. 119.

11. Collier, p. 67.

12. Jay Hatton, Logistics and the Desert Fox, http://www.almc.army.mil/alog/issues/JanFeb01/MS610.htm. Despite, at times, heavy losses from Royal Navy and Royal Air Force attacks, the Italian Navy managed to deliver 72,000 tons of supplies per month from July to October 1941, slightly more than Rommel's required minimum.

13. Historian Wolf Heckmann wittily observed "The code name for the commitment of German troops in Africa was Sunflower. Unconsciously, someone had hit upon the perfect symbol: a huge and showy flower at the end of a long and rather fragile stem." *Rommel's War in Africa* (Konecky & Konecky, NY, 1981), p. 24.

14. Rommel, p. 96.

15. Rommel, p. 125. It would be fair to say that the feeling was mutual; Streich did not care for Rommel, who had him reassigned to the OKW reserve, effective 1 June 1941. Complaints about Rommel's command style were many (Irving, p. 102-3).

16. Rommel created a new division, 90th Light, and redesignated the existing 5th Light Division as the 21st Panzer Division. Now with two panzer divisional formations (21st and 15th), plus the addition of two Italian corps, meant that the "Afrikakorps" label was insufficient.

17. Bierman and Smith, pp. 94-5 and Rommel, p. 156. Keyes was posthumously awarded the Victoria Cross. His brother sold the medal – Britain's highest award for courage under fire - at auction in 1995. In October 1942, Hitler issued the infamous "Commando Order," which stipulated that such commandos were to be "killed to the last man." Rommel refused to pass along this order to his troops. Heckmann, p. 232.

18. Rommel, p. 321, and more accurate translation at Irving, p. 211.

19. Ralf Georg Reuth, *Rommel: End of a Legend*, p. 56.

20. Rommel, p. 324. The situation was more acute than in terms of tanks alone; the climate and conditions took their toll. In August 1942 alone, 30,000 Germans and Italians were evacuated from the theater, most sick rather than wounded (Heckmann, p. 322, n. 2).

21. Irving, p. 215.

22. Irving 225-7.

23. The offensive was aimed at multiple points along the Western Dorsal mountains, Fraser, pp. 402-6.

24. Von Arnim had been named commander of Fifth Panzer Army, the force sent to Tunisia after the Allied landings during Operation Torch.

25. Writing to Mussolini after Rommel's departure from Africa, Hitler said, "Whatever posterity may judge of Field Marshal Rommel, to his troops and particularly to the German soldiers he was beloved in every command he held. He was always dreaded as an opponent by his enemies, and he still is." Irving, p. 260.

26. For unclear reasons, neither government sources nor scholars agree on a precise number. Estimates range from 200,000 to 300,000.

27. Collier, p. 195.

28. Along with the 17th SS Panzer Grenadier Division and 12th SS Panzer Division "Hitler Jugend," these units constituted the 1st SS Panzerkorps.

29. Fraser, p. 467. The "If only Hitler has listened to Rommel" argument has no foundation. Normandy was only one of several possible sites and neither Hitler nor Rommel correctly identified it as the exclusive Allied objective. British intelligence, using a multiple-axis approach (double agents, radio messages, dummy vehicles, notional units, etc) successfully convinced the German intelligence ser-

vices that the true target was at the Pas de Calais.

30. Fraser, p. 492. This is due to the British deception plan. FUSAG (First United States Army Group), an imaginary formation complete with phony unit patches, was central to the fake Allied order of battle that the Germans expected to be part of the main invasion.

31. Rommel expressed the idea to several people that he felt he could use his influence to broker a deal between Germany and Britain/United States, a preposterous notion at that stage in the war – although it was also an idea shared by the various anti-Hitler resistance groups.

32. Irving, 398-9. Speidel also acted as a conspirator in other ways. He – by his own admission – withheld two German panzer divisions from the Normandy battlefield, thus denying German forces the reinforcements they desperately needed. When, in the 1950s, this conduct could be seen as politically counterproductive to a general quickly rising in NATO ranks, Speidel quietly omitted the incident it in subsequent editions of his book (Irving, 348-9).

33. Two other Field Marshals were not so lucky. Field Marshal Gunther Kluge committed suicide and Field Marshal Erich von Witzleben was executed after being subjected to many indignities at his trial before the notorious People's Court.

34. Fraser, p. 551.

35. Indeed, Lucy Rommel stated that her husband was never a member of the 20 July plot – although it would have been advantageous for her to say the exact opposite (Fraser, pp. 532-3).

36. Lucie Rommel was listed as a consultant on both *The Desert Fox* and *The Longest Day*, although it is unclear in what way she could have contributed to the latter. There were some notable exceptions to the positive reaction for *The Desert Fox*. In a 28 October 1951 review, an outraged (and shrill) correspondent Bosley Crowther wrote "if postwar discoveries had apprised us that Rommel had really done some great and heroic service in the cause of democracy then there might be some moral justification for a soft-hearted film about him."

37. Rommel is also periodically mentioned in the American television series "Rat Patrol," which aired from 1966-1968. The series was historical in no way whatsoever.

38. http://www.sueddeutsche.de/medien/swr-film-ueber-erwin-rommel-koenigs drama-und-kriminalfilm-1.1145848

39. Richard Evans uses the same logic but is more careful than the false analogy set up by the ZDF documentary. See*The Third Reich at War* (Penguin Press, NY, 2009), p. 150: "Rommel was widely regarded as a hero not only in Germany but even in Britain. Yet his victories opened up new opportunities for the Nazis and their allies to implement their doctrines of racial superiority on defenceless minorities." Neither ZDF nor Evans produced any evidence that Rom-

mel had actual or even constructive knowledge of any war crimes in his area of operations.

40. Rommel refused to carry out the order to execute captured members of the Jewish Brigade (Bruce Watson, *Exit Rommel: The Tunisian Campaign*, 1942-43, Stackpole Books, 2006, p. 139).

Chapter 7
Curtis E. LeMay
by John M. Curatola, Ph.D.

In a discussion of great commanders, one may ask, "Why is Curtis LeMay on this list?" He did not establish an empire, change political boundaries, or rule a kingdom, nor did he shape legal, social, or economic landscapes. LeMay's contributions to history may not have been of the same magnitude as Genghis Khan or Napoleon. However, as the introduction of this book points out, "the truly great commander is generally considered to be one who attains the unexpected, who stands above his contemporaries through his skill on the battlefield, or through the sheer magnitude of his accomplishments." With these criteria in mind, LeMay certainly merits inclusion. During his time in the US Army Air Corps, Army Air Forces, Air Force, his accomplishments not only met, but exceeded the requirements suggested in the introduction. Through a review of his life and military achievements, he stands to be counted as one of the truly great commanders in history.

LeMay's enduring reputation as the "ultimate Cold Warrior," a pragmatic, brutally honest, and brave leader, is often contrasted with accusations levied against him as being a war-criminal, murderer, and even madman. In 1945, during the execution of the Japanese firebombing raids, *Time* Magazine referred to him a "level-headed devoted airman."[1] However by the time of his retirement in 1965 political satirist "Izzy" Stone referred to LeMay as a "cave man in a jet bomber."[2] Such contrast in his reputation makes LeMay a unique figure, but this dichotomy matches the man himself. LeMay was a figure of extremes who saw issues in black and white, with little room for grey. His daughter Janie noted that her father had "a strong sense of right and wrong."[3] Even LeMay intimated at this contrast, when referring to his penchant for smoking by stating "[I] don't like doing anything half-heartedly, even if it's a wicked and self-destructive avocation like smoking cigars."[4]

LeMay served as general officer for twenty-two years and as a four-star general for thirteen. Despite this exceptional record of service at the highest levels of the U.S. military, LeMay came from the humble of beginnings. Born November 15, 1906 in Columbus Ohio, LeMay was the oldest of six children to Erving and Arizona LeMay. One of his earliest memories is sighting an airplane around the age of five and trying to chase it down and catch it. While he failed to grab hold of the airplane, the episode of trying to catch something elusive was a vision that stayed with LeMay his entire

Figure 7. General Curtis LeMay.

life.[5] LeMay's father, Erving, was a menial laborer who worked various jobs to support his large family. In Erving's effort to remain employed, the family uprooted numerous times and, as Curtis remembered, "we moved like nomads."[6] Curtis thought his father was a dreamer and not a very practical man. Being the oldest, Curtis assumed responsibilities at a young age and was looked upon by some of his siblings as the figure of authority in the LeMay household.[7] LeMay recalls a winter episode when there was not enough food for dinner, so he took it upon himself to go fishing in order to feed the family while his father sat unconcerned by the furnace.[8] His humble origins and assumed responsibilities for his siblings engrained a work ethic and a sense of duty that never left him.

Young LeMay showed an early interest in mechanics and electronics. During his high school years he built his own radio and worked various jobs to support his interests. He was not a sociable student in high school and, as he put it, "the girls stuff cost money-sodas, sandwiches and all-and I thought my personal cash would be better expended in some other direction-something really valuable, say like a [radio] crystal set."[9] Graduating from high school in 1924 he attended The Ohio State University with an interest in becoming a civil engineer. While he had enough money to pay for his freshman year, he needed a job to cover the tuition for the following three years. He took a job as a steel caster working nights while attending classes in the day. The steel casting job paid thirty-five dollars a week, an ample sum of money in the 1920s. His salary allowed him to pay his tuition while he lived at home and also helped pay family expenses. Working nine hours a day, six days a week took at toll on LeMay and his grades. His late nights and lack of sleep resulted in his failing a class on "Railroad Curves" twice in a row.[10]

While attending Ohio State, he joined the Reserve Officer Training Corps (ROTC) in hopes of attaining a commission, with the additional goal of becoming an aviator. At the end of his junior year he opted to take a commission in the National Guard, applied to become a "flying cadet," and decided to forgo his senior year. LeMay still needed fifteen hours to complete his engineering degree, but the desire to become an aviator was too great, and in September 1928 he was approved to enlist as a flying cadet. A month later he boarded a train and headed to March Field, near Riverside, California to begin his flight training.[11] After completing the training at March, LeMay transferred to Kelly Field near San Antonio, Texas and eventually was placed into the pursuit (fighter) aviation track. On October 12, 1929, LeMay, along with forty-seven other members of his class, received his wings and a commission as a second lieutenant.[12]

LeMay's initial assignment sent him to Selfridge Field, Michigan. While stationed there he convinced his commanding officer to have him assigned temporarily to Norton Field near Columbus, Ohio. In this arrangement, LeMay was able to attend classes at Ohio State in Columbus in the morning and conduct his duties at Norton in the afternoon and evenings. As a result he completed the remaining fifteen hours of study and received his engineering degree. It was at this time that a fellow officer arranged for a couples blind date with two coeds from the University of Michigan. Upon the men's entrance into the foyer of the women's dormitory for their first date, one of the two women, Helen Maitland, spied the officers from a distance. Not knowing either man, she told her roommate "I'll take the fat one (LeMay)."[13] After this inauspicious beginning, the two began a courtship that result in marriage in June 1934.

The inauguration of Franklin Delano Roosevelt in 1933 brought about two brief, yet unique assignments for LeMay. The first was a posting in the spring of 1933 to serve as second-in-command of a Civilian Conservation Corps (CCC) camp near Brethren, Michigan. The CCC was one of Roosevelt's initiatives to employ young men to cultivate national parks, forest, and assist in other infrastructure improvements as a means to address widespread unemployment during the depression. LeMay loathed the assignment as it was, to him, merely glorified babysitting. Fortunately for LeMay, by late summer he received orders relieving him of CCC duty and sending him to navigation school at Langley Field, Virginia. The education at Langley served him well in the upcoming years and helped establish his early professional reputation.

In February 1934 Roosevelt cancelled government air mail contracts with civilian carriers and directed the Army Air Corps to assume the mission. Despite the claims of the Air Corps chief, Major General Benjamin Foulois, military aviators were neither trained nor equipped to conduct these air delivery operations in a safe and competent manner.[14] After navigation school LeMay was assigned as part of the air mail effort. While originally sent to Atlanta, he eventually flew an assigned mail route which stretched from Richmond, Virginia to Greensboro, North Carolina.[15] Though he suffered no accidents during this assignment he was forced down by weather on at least one occasion. On June 1, civilian contracts were renewed, but the entire episode was a disaster for the Air Corps as it lost twelve pilots, sixty-five aircraft, and suffered humiliation in the eyes of the American public.[16]

Following his service in the air mail debacle, Curtis and Helen were married on June 9, 1934 and subsequently stationed at Schofield Barracks, Wheeler Field, Hawaii. Because of his training at Langley, upon arrival in Hawaii LeMay was assigned to establish a navigation school on Oahu.[17] In 1935 LeMay was promoted to First Lieutenant and in the following year transferred to Langley Field, Virginia. However, the move from Hawaii was not just a geographical change; it was a professional one as well. Since the beginning of this flying career, he had been a pursuit pilot flying aircraft such as the P-12 and P-26. With the transfer to Langley, LeMay also transferred from pursuit aviation to bombardment and began flying the very latest aircraft available, Boeing's B-17 "Flying Fortress."

The B-17 was a major leap in aviation design and technology. The Chief of the Army Air Corps, General H. H. 'Hap' Arnold, compared the B-17s importance to that of the first military aircraft built by the Wright brothers.[18] As a result of its four engines, graceful lines, and superior performance, LeMay, as he put it, "fell in love with the [B]17 at first sight."[19] The plane was not just a technological development, but signaled the advent of a new primary function for the Army Air Corps--strategic bombing. Upon arrival at Langley, LeMay was again initially assigned to establish a navigation school. However, this time LeMay avoided the duty and was instead assigned as the operations officer of the Second Bomb Group under the command of Lieutenant Colonel Robert Olds. Olds was an exacting boss and had a great influence on LeMay's professional development.

In addition to his transfer to bombers, LeMay established a superb reputation as a navigator. In exercises in August 1937 he was assigned as the lead navigator of a group of B-17s directed to locate the USS Utah off the coast of California. However, in two instances the Navy gave LeMay erroneous coordinates that were one degree off, equating to a sixty mile error. In the first instance the B-17s never sighted the naval vessels. However, in the second instance LeMay was aware of the navigation error, and despite the Navy's oversight, he successful plotted a course to the USS Utah. In February 1938 he was again assigned as a lead navigator, this time for a good-will flight to Argentina. With no reliable aerial maps available, LeMay used charts out of National Geographic to navigate the Miami-Lima-Buenos Aries route, transiting over the Andes Mountains. For this achievement the mission was awarded the MacKay Trophy for the most outstanding military aerial feat of the year. In May 1938 he again proved his aerial navigation skills by intercepting the Italian luxury liner Rex with the entire episode broadcast by NBC Radio and covered by New York Times reporter Hanson Baldwin. Despite having his charts soaked by a leak in the navigator's window, and in exceptionally turbulent weather, LeMay successfully pinpointed the exact time and location of the interception.[20]

In May 1940 he was promoted to Captain with subsequent promotions to Major and Lieutenant Colonel in the next two years. By the time the United States become involved in World War II, LeMay was the Commanding Officer of the 305th Bomb Group at Wendover, Utah. In preparing his unit for aerial combat, LeMay established a rigorous training schedule. This emphasis on training continued when the unit arrived as part of the Combined Bombing Offensive (CBO) in the European Theater.

It would be a hallmark of LeMay's command philosophy throughout his career. During this assignment, his demanding training regimen and exacting standards earned him the nickname "Iron Ass" from his subordinates.[21] While never said to his face, he was aware of the moniker, and even smirked when he heard of it.[22] Adding to this reputation, just before the unit departed for Europe, LeMay came down with Bell's Palsy (an ailment affecting facial nerves). The palsy caused the right side of this face to become numb with an accompanying loss of control of the facial muscles. Though he recovered much of the feeling in his face, his upper lip remained immobile and did not smile along with the rest of his mouth, thus leaving him with something of a permanent scowl.[23] This only added to the "Iron Ass" reputation and the legend that LeMay never smiled.

As American crews arrived in Europe in 1942, the doctrine of daylight precision bombing was still just a theory. Could strategic bombing force the capitulation of Nazi Germany? With that end in mind, could the United States Army Air Forces (USAAF) hit a target while being shot at by enemy fighters and anti-aircraft defenses? Could the bomber really survive such an environment? LeMay was on the forefront of this grand aerial experiment and his ideas and practices would make a significant difference in the execution of the Combined Bomber Offensive—a campaign that involved British bombers attacking German-occupied Europe by night, while the Americans conducted high altitude precision bombing by day.

The 305th arrived in England in October 1942 and was eventually based at Chelveston as part of the USAAF's 8th Air Force. LeMay continued to execute a busy training schedule with his command, placing special emphasis on formation flying. He surmised that the only way to hit a target from high altitude was for the bomber formation to fly a straight and steady bomb run with no evasive action. A steady bomb run would provide the bombardier a stable platform for an accurate bomb drop. Up to that time, USAAF bomber crews initiated evasive action when attacked, and as a result their bombing accuracy was less than expected. On 23 November, eight days after his thirty-sixth birthday, LeMay executed his fist combat mission over Nazi-occupied Europe with an attack on German U-boat pens at St Nazaire, France.[24] Committed to being as accurate as possible with his bombs, LeMay instructed his crews that despite enemy fire, they were not to conduct any evasive action during the bomb run. When one airman protested the idea saying that it could not be done, LeMay set the example by replying, "Yes it can…and you'll see me do it first because I will be in the lead plane."[25]

LeMay led the Group steady on the bomb run for seven minutes while placing twice as many bombs on the target as any other group.[26] The 305th lost two B-17s to enemy fighters, but none to anti-aircraft fire, though LeMay's aircraft did take shrapnel in both wings.[27] By not conducting evasive action and holding at a steady airspeed and altitude, the 305th under LeMay set a precedent for future bombing operations. Within a few weeks the entire 8th Air Force adopted LeMay's non-evasive action tactic as standard procedure.

This was not the only initiative of LeMay's that would be adopted by the entire 8th Air Force. While the B-17 bristled with as many as ten machine guns for self-protection, LeMay surmised that the bomber formations prescribed by doctrine did not maximize available defensive firepower. As a result, in December 1942 LeMay discarded the widely accepted, and loosely defined, "box formation" used throughout the USAAF and developed instead the "Javelin Down" formation. This formation not only maximized defensive firepower, but allowed for better flexibility and was easier to control.[28] While numerous variations on the LeMay formation came about, his basic defensive formation also became a standard practice of the 8th Air Force.[29]

In addition to these initiatives, LeMay also instituted a "lead crew school." In this effort he teamed up the most proficient bombardiers and navigators, and had each team study a particular enemy target.[30] When LeMay's group flew a mission against one of these targets, he placed the lead crew specializing in that target at the spearhead for the formation, with the other bombers dropping their payloads when the lead crew dropped. This same practice survived the war and later became standard procedure in Strategic Air Command.[31]

While LeMay was the catalyst for many tactics, techniques, and procedures during the Combined Bomber Offensive, what stands out most is his leadership ability during this difficult time. As LeMay was taking the 305th Bomb Group into combat, and subsequently leading divisions, he flew in some of the first American missions against the German Luftwaffe. Effective German flak and fighter defenses resulted in exceedingly high casualties for the 8th Air Force during 1943-1944. Loss rates from individual missions could average around two to three percent of the attacking force, meaning, statistically, that crews would not survive their required compliment of twenty-five missions. Of the crews that arrived in mid to late 1942, 73 percent would not finish their 25-mission requirement.[32] Within the first 10 months of operation, US airmen counted as killed or missing rose as high as 57 percent with another 16 percent seriously wounded or psychologically incapacitated.[33] During the first six months of 1943 when the USAAF started hitting targets in Germany proper, bomber loss rates climbed above six percent lost with another 35 percent damaged.[34] When asked about flying such dangerous missions as the commanding officer LeMay replied: "How can any commanding officer send his people out into combat when he knows nothing about it? So I started out leading all missions personally. Not only did I feel that I ought to lead the people fighting under me, but I had to find things out... you have to get in there and fight to find out what it is all about."[35]

An example of the dangerous environment in which LeMay operated was the infamous Schweinfurt-Regensburg raid of 17 August 1943. In this mission LeMay led the 4th Bomb Wing with over 100 B-17s on a strike to the Messerschmitt aircraft factory at Regensburg, Germany. The mission was unique in that instead of heading home to England after the raid, the Wing was to turn south and land in North Africa to refuel. In addition to the 4th Bomb Wing, the 1st Bomb Wing was to take off simultaneously and raid the ball bearing factories at Schweinfurt, thus hopefully splitting the German fighter defense force. LeMay's 4th Bomb Wing's 146 aircraft took off on time and subsequently proceeded to its target while the 1st Wing remained grounded by fog.[36] This delay on the part of the 1st Bomb Wing allowed Luftwaffe fighters to focus their efforts solely on LeMay's bombers. With LeMay in the lead aircraft, the 4th Bomb Wing lost eighteen percent of the force with 240 men killed, captured, or missing.[37] LeMay's command returned to England after a brief stay in Africa with only eighty-two flyable aircraft.[38]

Prior to the Schweinfurt-Regensburg raid, in spring 1943 LeMay had been promoted to Commander of a provisional bomb wing and left for his new headquarters at Thurleigh. This assignment was short lived as in June he was again promoted and placed in charge of the 3rd Air Division.[39] In September 1943 his rank was finally reflective of his new responsibilities as he was promoted to Brigadier General. In his role as a division commander LeMay had been serving in the capacity of a general officer while still only a colonel. Upon his promotion, LeMay's only response was a sardonic "it's about time."[40] By November 1943, LeMay was ordered back to the United States to participate in "Bond Drives" to help sell the war effort to the American public. While public speaking was certainly not LeMay's strength, the trip home allowed him to visit Helen and spend some time with his daughter Janie who was born in 1939.

Returning to England, LeMay remained commander the 3rd Air Division and was promoted to Major General in March 1944. Three months later, shortly after the invasion of Normandy, he returned to the United States to assume new responsibilities. In his memoirs, LeMay fondly recalls his time in the European theater—"that [tour] somehow was the concentration of my career as an airman. I was close to the people with whom I worked, and I could fly along with them and share their perils. We felt the intimacy of proven human devotion while doing our job together..."[41] While his tour with the 8th Air Force was most memorable, LeMay's subsequent assignment in the Pacific would prove to be one that would make him a household name.

While LeMay was flying combat missions over Europe, the USAAF was developing a new bomber that would carry larger bomb loads over longer distances than the existing B-17 and B-24 fleet. The "Very Long Range" (VLR) bomber looked to carry almost twice as much payload and with a range of over 1000 miles further than existing bombers.[42] This innovative and technologically advanced design eventually became known as the B-29 "Superfortress." The B-29 was a high priority for General Henry H. ("Hap") Arnold, chef of the USAAF. He allocated a significant portion of the nation's aviation resources to this single program. The B-29 alone constituted the biggest single expenditure of the US during the war. The program's 3 billion dollar price tag exceeded the 2 billion spent on the Manhattan Project that developed the atomic bomb.[43]

However, as with any radically new technology, the B-29 was initially fraught with a number of engineering and design problems. Especially troublesome were the bomber's newly designed R-3350 engines that had a tendency to overheat, catch fire, and bring the whole aircraft down. Engines were not the only issues. The bomber suffered from landing gear problems, a propeller feather system that often failed, poorly designed cowl flaps, as well as a host of other malfunctions. Indicative of the larger design issues was that each B-29 coming off the assembly line in early 1944 needed 54 major modifications before it could be deployed.[44] When first fielded, B-29 performance was much lower than expected and crews were concerned more with the performance of the airplane, particularly its ability to take off and clear the runway, than they were with the enemy's defenses. LeMay knew about the design challenges of the B-29 and remarked, "If you ever saw a buggy airplane this was it...B-29 had as many bugs as the entomological department of the Smithsonian Institution. Fast as they got the bugs licked, new ones crawled out from under the cowling."[45]

Despite the design challenges, and with Arnold eager to strike at Japan, the first deployment of B-29s went to the Asian mainland as part of Operation "Matterhorn." However, the initial results of XX Bomber Command flying B-29s out of the China-Burma-India (CBI) Theater were disappointing. Having spent so much time and effort on the Superfortress, and with his professional reputation on the line, Arnold was determined to get the plane's problems rectified. LeMay's accomplishments in Europe gave him a reputation within the USAAF as a dynamic and results-oriented commander. In August 1944 Arnold ordered LeMay to Asia to take charge of Matterhorn and assume the leadership of the XX Bomber Command.

The issues facing XX Bomber Command were not just the troublesome nature of the B-29, but the logistical challenges of moving fuel, bombs, and other supplies over the Himalayas to the bomber base at Chengtu, China. Some of the worst flying weather in the world surrounded the Himalayan Mountains, and crews were in constant peril of crashing or disappearing while flying over "the hump." Upon assumption of command at his headquarters at Kharagpur India, LeMay received permission to fly at least one combat mission in order to his assess this new combat environment.[46] (The Air Staff in Washington forbade LeMay from flying any more combat due to his rank.) After the mission he determined that Japanese air defenses were not as formidable as the German, but LeMay also recognized that his crews need more training and practice to fully exploit the capabilities of the B-29.[47] While Arnold was impatient for results, LeMay took the more prudent course of "standing down" the entire XX Bomber Command to conduct training for both air and ground personnel.

LeMay's assumption of command came at the expense of his predecessor, Brigadier General Kenneth Wolfe, whom Arnold had removed. In September, a trusted subordinate of Arnold, Lieutenant General Carl "Tooey" Spaatz, paid a visit to LeMay's command. In a report to Arnold after his visit, Spaatz wrote, "With all due respect to Wolfe, he did his best, and he did a grand job, but LeMay's operations make Wolfe seem very amateurish."[48] Despite all the efforts to maximize the use of the B-29 during Operation Matterhorn, the best XX Bomber Command could muster was about four missions a month. The main constraint was the fuel supply available at Chengtu. LeMay called the entire logistical situation "utterly impossible."[49] Despite LeMay's hard work, the logistical limitations of Matterhorn proved too formidable, and by January 1945 the B-29s were withdrawn from China.

However, LeMay was quickly transferred to XXI Bomber Command in the Guam-Saipan area to take over from yet another commander fired by Arnold, Brigadier General Haywood Hansell. Hansell was one of the original framers of the USAAF's daylight precision bombing theory. He was a veteran of the Combined Bomber Offensive in Europe, and tried to employ the same doctrine in Japan with the B-29 as he had in Europe with the B-17. However, much as had been the case with Matterhorn, Hansell's XXIst Bomber Command was not producing the results Arnold expected. Winds at high altitudes, mechanical problems, and towering weather fronts precluded efficient precision bombing. Arnold directed LeMay's transfer from China to Guam in an attempt to get the most out of the B-29.[50] After a few weeks studying the unique nature of the Japanese weather patterns, target characteristics, and considering the design problems of the B-29, LeMay took a more pragmatic approach to bombing operations than Hansell had.

Despite USAAF commitment to high altitude precision bombing, LeMay turned doctrine on its head and single-handedly changed the nature of the bombing campaign against Japan. On the night of March 9, 1945 LeMay launched over 330 B-29s against the Japanese capital of Tokyo.[51] On his own initiative and without approval from Arnold, LeMay had the bombers stripped of most of their defensive armament and loaded them with incendiary bombs instead of high explosives. Furthermore, he had the bombers fly at lower altitudes, staggering the airplanes from five thousand to fifteen thousand feet. This change in altitude increased the range of the planes, allowed greater payloads, reduced the stress on the problematic R-3350 engines, and avoided the jet stream and its exceedingly high headwinds. Regarding this new approach to strategic bombing, after the war LeMay remembered that is was, "a combination of several people's ideas, but the low altitude part…was my own thinking."[52] Once the bombers took off, he felt "anxiety I'd not wish to experience again."[53] "I was nervous about it, I made the decision. I had weighed the odds. I knew the odds were in my favor. But still it was something new. I could have lost a lot of people, [and] appear to be an idiot."[54]

Around 2:00 AM Guam time, the mission commander radioed in the initial results: "Bombing the primary target visually. Large fires observed. Flak moderate. Fighter opposition nil."[55] Follow-on reports echoed the initial one. LeMay was relieved. The raid devastated the Japanese capital. LeMay's bombers dropped 1,665 tons of incendiaries and burned sixteen square miles of the urban landscape. [56] The incendiaries created firestorms the wreaked havoc upon the largely wood and paper structures of the city. As many as 83,000 people were killed in the raid, with another 40,000 injured.[57] Furthermore, over 270,000 structures were destroyed with crewmen reporting the glow from the conflagration was visible as much as 150 miles away.[58] LeMay's gambled paid off.

Upon hearing the news of the Tokyo raid, Arnold sent a laudatory message to LeMay: "Congratulations. This mission shows your crews have the guts for anything."[59] The Tokyo mission set a precedent. Days after the 9 March attack, similar raids were conducted against Nagoya, Osaka, and Kobe. LeMay's command was so busy dropping bombs that at one period in March it ran out of incendiaries.[60] Further incendiary raids continued against Japan's urban areas until the nation's eventual surrender. After the war, the US Strategic Bombing Survey determined that LeMay's command targeted 106 square miles of urban areas in the five largest Japanese cities, of which it destroyed 102 square miles.[61] For all B-29 missions, up to 180 square miles in 66 major cities were destroyed, including 600 factories, 25 aircraft manufacturers, 18 oil production centers, and 6 major arsenals.[62]

LeMay understood the moral implications of the firebombing effort, but measured them against the larger imperative of ending the war. LeMay observed, "We knew we were going to kill a lot of women and kids when we burned a town. [It] had to be done."[63] Regarding the morality of the firebombing campaign he later observed, "Killing Japanese didn't bother me very much at the time. It was getting the war over that bothered me. So I wasn't worried particularly about how many people we killed in getting the job done. I suppose if I had lost the war I would have been tried as a war criminal...every soldier thinks something of the moral aspects of what he is doing. But all war is immoral and if you let that bother you, you're not a good soldier."[64] Present at the surrender ceremonies on the deck of the USS Missouri, in September 1945, LeMay arranged for 462 B-29s to participate in a victory flyover during the proceedings. At the ceremony and with the war over, LeMay simply recalled that he felt "pretty tired."[65]

Following the war LeMay was assigned as the head of USAAF Research and Development, a job he generally disliked. Working in the Pentagon and having to participate in the Washington D.C. social scene was certainly not field command, where LeMay excelled. With the introduction of jet engines and rocket propulsion, aviation technology was advancing by leaps and bounds. LeMay understood the importance of the work, but loathed the political side of military procurement. Fortunately the assignment lasted only two years. On October 1, 1947, two weeks after the establishment of the independent US Air Force (USAF), LeMay was promoted to Lieutenant General and assigned as Commander of US Air Forces in Europe (USAFE).

LeMay had been in his new command for a few months when in June 1948 the Soviet Union imposed the Berlin Blockade and shut off ground transportation to the British, American, and French zones of the city.

General Lucius Clay, US Military Governor in the American zone asked LeMay if it was feasible to supply the city with coal via airlift. This first request was the foundation for what became the Berlin Airlift. Initially referred to as "LeMay's Coal and Feed Company," it became obvious that the effort required more than the organic assets and people assigned to USAFE.[66] More crews and planes were sent to Europe and by the time the operation was over in 1949, the airlift had moved over 2.3 million tons of food and supplies to Berlin.[67] The airlift became so efficient that a plane could be 'turned' every five minutes.[68]

While LeMay initiated airlift operations for humanitarian purposes during summer of 1948, he also arranged for the forward deployment of B-29s to Europe as a strong military message to the Soviets. While most B-29s were not able to carry nuclear weapons, he believed that the mere presence of strategic bombers would serve a strong warning to the communists.[69] While others might call this move provocative and aggressive, he saw it as prudent deterrence. Despite the B-29 deployment, the Soviets continued with the blockade with LeMay eventually drawing up plans to forcibly open the city.[70] LeMay and Lieutenant General Arthur Trudeau, Commander of the American Constabulary Force, devised a coordinated air and ground attack that was, fortunately, never implemented.[71]

Ever the pragmatist, LeMay understood that the logistical requirements for sustaining the airlift required some unique solutions. Because of post-war military demobilization, the Air Force was short of trained mechanics to service the cargo aircraft involved. To address this deficiency, LeMay hired local Germans, who had previously served in the wartime Luftwaffe, to maintain the American aircraft. [72] Instead of working on German Messerschmitt and Focke-Wulf aircraft as during the war, these mechanics now serviced American Douglas and Boeing cargo planes. Additionally, the Berlin airlift required more runways and ramp space to handle the dramatic rise in air traffic. Even with a substantially large number of aircraft, the airlift effort could ill afford to move concrete and construction supplies to build the new airfield infrastructure. In addressing this situation, LeMay's command cut up buildings damaged in the war and used them as ballast for the new runways and parking aprons. Ironically, Berlin's new air facilities constructed during the airlift were built from the rubble of the old Nazi Third Reich.[73]

Following his tour in Europe, in 1948 LeMay was assigned to perhaps his most famous posting as the Commander of Strategic Air Command (SAC) at Offutt Air Force Base, Nebraska. When he assumed command on October 19, he inherited an organization that was lacking in airplanes, manpower, training, and planning. The previous commander had expended little energy in running the command, and internal manpower policies precluded effective aircrew training.[74] Despite the American reliance on atomic weapons for post-war national security, the entire nuclear delivery capability of the US consisted of only twenty-three specially designed "Silver Plate" B-29s flown by crews that were less than fully proficient.[75] In order to test his new command, in January 1949 LeMay directed a nighttime practice raid on Dayton, Ohio. Crews were given a picture of the city and directed to use their radar to "bomb" selected parts of the city from 30,000 feet. The entire operation was a fiasco as not one crew successfully carried out the mission as briefed. While many crews aborted their mission altogether, of the 303 bombing runs made on the city, almost two-thirds of the simulated bomb drops were more than 7,000 feet off target with the average error being over 10,000 feet.[76] LeMay called the practice raid "the darkest night in American aviation history."[77] The results from this mission were a far cry from what bomber crews had been able to do during the war, just a few years earlier. As one senior Air Force officer put it, during this time "SAC was far more symbol than reality."[78]

One of the first things LeMay did as Commander of SAC was to bring in the "right people." [79] These were officers he had come to know and trust during his wartime experience in both the Combined Bomber Offensive and the Pacific campaigns; men who, in his opinion, truly understood strategic bombing. Not satisfied with the overall quality of the SAC staff, he removed people who he thought were a detriment to the organization, with one fellow officer describing this 'cleaning house' process as "bloody."[80] Furthermore he instilled a sense of urgency and purpose within SAC and made no qualms about establishing a frame of mind that affirmed, "We are at war now."[81] Regarding the SAC mission and its combat posture, LeMay ordered the command "to be ready to go to war not next week, not tomorrow, but this afternoon."[82]

For LeMay, effective defense required an airborne "Sunday punch" capability that could knock out a potential adversary in a single massive strike. With the advent of atomic weapons, LeMay was convinced that conventional warfare was a thing of the past, and believed that the nuclear deterrent was the best bid for a lasting peace in the Cold War world. LeMay was convinced that the next war would be an atomic one, asserting that "all conventional forces do is delay the inevitable nuclear confrontation."[83] Not a proponent of gradualism, LeMay was convinced that a strong "air force in-being" with a substantial nuclear capability at the onset of war was the only way to ensure national survival. Under LeMay, SAC came to realize the full strength of the atomic air offensive and what it meant for American security and for the free world. The atomic nuclear shield of SAC built by LeMay became a cornerstone of the American defensive strategy throughout much of the Cold War. LeMay reported, "My goal was to build a force that was so professional, so strong, so powerful that we would not have to fight. In other words, we had to build a strong deterrent force."[84] LeMay wasn't alone in his sentiment. In a 1950 Gallup poll, seventy-seven percent of Americans thought we should use nuclear weapons in case of war.[85] Similarly, seventy percent felt that the United States should not preclude the "first use" of atomic weapons.[86]

Under LeMay, SAC grew four-fold from 46,000 airmen in January 1949 to over 200,000 by the end of his tenure as commander in 1957.[87] The size of the strategic bombing fleet also grew as the mission of SAC became more prominent in American National Security policies as outlined in national security documents NSC 68 and NSC 162/2. By 1955 SAC had over 2,800 aircraft and maintained a series of airbases throughout the globe that allowed LeMay's bombers to reach the Soviet Union.[88] Under LeMay's watch the command also grew significantly in capability as older aircraft were replaced by more technologically advanced bomber designs. While SAC had only a few "Silver Plate" nuclear capable B-29s after the war, in 1948 the Air Force began fielding the B-36 "Peacemaker" with its extended range and a larger bomb load. In the 1950s, LeMay oversaw SAC's initial transition to an all-jet bomber force with the introduction of the B-47 "Stratojet" to replace the old B-29/B-50s in the medium bombing fleet. During LeMay's leadership at SAC, the Air Force began designing an even more capable bomber, the B-52 "Stratofortress." Initially fielded in 1955, this design, amazingly, remains in the Air Force inventory to this day. LeMay's vision also extended beyond the development and employment of bomber aircraft. During his tenure at SAC, he instituted air-to-air refueling capabilities that significantly increased the range of the strategic bomber fleet.[89] In this effort he advocated the employment of the KC-97 "Stratofreighter" and the development of the venerable KC-135 "Stratotanker" refueling aircraft. Finally, in the last few years of his tour at SAC, LeMay embraced not only the introduction of the strategic missile fleet into SAC's arsenal, but thermonuclear weapon as well. Under his charge, SAC came to provide two of the three legs of America's nuclear triad—manned bombers and land-based ballistic missiles, with the Navy's submarine-launched ballistic missiles constituting the third.

While aircraft and weapons were the most tangible manifestations of America's military might during the 1950s, during this same period SAC also served as the center for nuclear war plan development. Having staffed SAC with what he referred to as the "right people," LeMay's command was one of the first organizations to establish war plans that exploited America's atomic capabilities. According to LeMay, "There wasn't anything that came out of Washington [D.C.]. As a matter of fact, I don't think we got anything out of Washington other than a little guidance on targets that should be hit. We did the plan right up till the time I left in 1957."[90] As for national policy regarding atomic weapons, LeMay asserted, "our job at SAC was not to promulgate national policy...our job was to produce...We put America in that situation of incipient power..."[91] He declared, "I never discussed the problem with President Truman or President Eisenhower...I stuck to my job at Offutt...I never discussed what we were going to do with the force we had or what we should do with it...Never discussed it with topside brass, military or civilian. All I did was to keep them abreast of the development of SAC."[92]

In October 1951 he was promoted to full general at the age of 44. However, LeMay's advocacy of strategic nuclear bombardment made him a controversial figure. His belief in the atomic air offensive seemed simplistic and draconian to his many critics. By asserting SAC's primacy in the realm of national security, LeMay placed himself in a position of great influence. However, the dependence on nuclear applications that LeMay advocated, created what critics viewed as short-sighted nation security strategies. Indicative of such criticism is Air Force historian Robert Futrell, who captured the essence of Air Force planning efforts during this era with the observation, "the emphasis of air planners [was] in making war fit the weapon-nuclear power-rather than making the weapon fit the war."[93]

Much as he had done when commanding the 305th Bomb Group, XX and XXI Bombing Commands during the war, LeMay continued to emphasize training and flying proficiency. Upon assuming command of SAC, the organization had an abysmal safety record. In 1948 SAC had an accident rate of some sixty-five mishaps per 100,000 hours of flight time.[94] However, after the enforcement of Standard Operating Procedures, holding commanders responsible for flight safety, and publishing various training manuals, by 1950 SAC's accident rate dropped to forty-three mishaps per 100,000 hours and in 1956 only nine accidents were reported.[95] Furthermore, to instill combat readiness, LeMay conducted "no notice" readiness inspections. He would schedule an inspection at one air base, then cancel the planned visit, and land at another command without warning. Upon arrival he would then instruct the unsuspecting wing commander to execute his war plan immediately.[96] Furthermore, LeMay required wing commanders to brief their assigned war plan and target sets personally to their superiors.[97] Installing a rigorous training program made the command one of the most proficient military organizations in the world. For Air Force personnel assigned to SAC, one quipped, "Training at SAC was harder than war. It might have been a relief to go to war."[98]

Indicative of the effective training regimen he implemented, in 1954 LeMay ordered another bombing exercise similar to the January 1948 debacle. The 1954 event included 150 bombers, with 133 aircraft successfully "hitting" their targets, with only 24 crews having to abort prior to "dropping" their ordnance because a number navigation systems failed through no fault of the aircrew.[99]

While SAC became and elite organization under LeMay, other elements of the Air Force, such as the fighter and attack communities, languished. These elements complained about being "SACumcized" as resources and budgets were largely allocated for the service's strategic mission. By the end of the 1950s SAC had grown to 538 B-52s, 1,292 B-47s, 19 B-58s, and over 1,000 aerial refueling tankers.[100] In addition the command had also deployed an intercontinental and intermediate range ballistic missile fleet.

Despite his reputation as a tough and unrelenting taskmaster, LeMay understood the need to ensure the welfare of his airmen and recognize superior performance. In the early 1950s, he instituted within SAC a spot promotion program for both officers and enlisted personnel that encouraged initiative and proficiency in the rank and file. [101] Furthermore, in looking out for his subordinates he instituted significant barracks and housing improvements for airmen and their families while advocating support organizations to deal with potential family issues caused by deployments and long work hours.[102] One subordinate of LeMay recalled that during the period of SAC's major expansion in the early 1950s, the commander spent up to two-thirds of this time working on improving living conditions and family housing.[103]

After nine years as the commander of SAC, on April 4, 1957 LeMay was appointed as the Vice Chief of Staff for the US Air Force with an assignment to Washington DC, where he served as the deputy to General Thomas D. White. The two men were cordial and worked well together, but were not close friends. The assignment was relatively trouble-free but posed an obstacle for LeMay as he was again thrust into an environment he loathed, the Washington social circuit. Furthermore, LeMay, who saw things in absolutes, had to learn the art of negotiation and comprise. However, just because he was appointed as Vice Chief did not mean he was the heir apparent to the Chief of Staff. In 1960 John F. Kennedy assumed the presidency, and LeMay's blunt style and lack of diplomatic skills stood in stark contrast to the new president. However, on May 22, 1961 Kennedy announced that LeMay would succeed White as Air Force Chief of Staff.

The formal ceremony installing LeMay as Chief was a harbinger of things to come. The ceremony took place with retiring General White in attendance, along with Senator Stuart Symington, and Vice President Lyon Johnson, but conspicuously absent was the Secretary of Defense Robert S. McNamara.[104] McNamara, who had come from the Ford Motor Company, subscribed to mathematical analysis and was not prone to make decisions on gut instinct.[105] When McNamara arrived as Secretary of Defense, he brought with him a group of young Ivy League intellectuals to help manage the national defense establishment. These young intellectuals became known as the "whiz kids" and were largely loathed by LeMay and other military professionals who viewed them with distrust and suspicion.[106] When McNamara's thirty-four year old head of Research and Development, Harold Brown, told LeMay which bomber the Air Force should buy, the Air Force Chief supposedly replied "Why that son-of-a-bitch was in junior high school while I was out bombing Japan."[107] Many uniformed military professionals hated the "whiz kids", and the feelings were mutual.

Ironically McNamara had worked as a lieutenant colonel in the Statistical Control Office of the 20th Air Force under for LeMay during the Japanese firebombing campaign. However, McNamara was now LeMay's superior as the Defense chief. The two agreed on very little during LeMay's tenure as Chief of Staff. The underlying problem for both men was a fundamental difference regarding American military posture. LeMay firmly believed that the only way to secure the nation was through overwhelming strength that would deter a potential adversary. McNamara looked more toward parity and rational thought as key elements in national security.[108] The two clashed over a number of defense related issues, including funding for the Air Force's new supersonic bomber, the XB-70 "Valkyrie," the procurement of new B-52s and B-58s, and the Tactical Fighter Experimental (TFX) program. Ever the analyst, McNamara saw many of the Air Force's programs as bloated, outdated expenditures that could be streamlined or cut entirely. Underpinning much of this disagreement was McNamara's belief that with the advent of Inter-Continental Ballistic Missiles (ICBMs), manned strategic bombers were becoming obsolete.

During the Cuban missile crisis of October 1962, LeMay fully endorsed an invasion of the island nation even at the risk of global nuclear war. LeMay was forceful in expressing his opinions with the President, but not insubordinate.[109] Fortunately, cooler heads prevailed, but in LeMay's mind, the episode was indicative of an overall dismissal of military advice by the civilian leadership. LeMay believed that "the Kennedy Administration came in and right from the start we [military leaders] got the back of the hand. Get out of our way. We think nothing of you and your opinions. We don't like you as people. We have no respect for you. Don't bother us."[110]   Given the animosity between LeMay and McNamara and the apparent tension between the Kennedy Administration and the military leaders at the Defense Department, it was a surprise to many in Washington when LeMay was given a one year extension as Air Force Chief of Staff near the end of this first tour. [111] Despite his frequent opposition to the civilians in the Kennedy Administration, his extension was based on LeMay's popularity in the Congress, the respect he garnered from his military service, and his reputation as a "cold warrior."

As America became involved in Vietnam, LeMay again found himself at odds with the civilian leadership in the Pentagon and in the White House. While McNamara and Kennedy embraced the idea of "Flexible Response" and gradualism with regard to military force, LeMay believed that it was important to go with a strong first response instead of a piece-meal, incremental approach. In his 1968 book, *American is in Danger*, published years after his retirement, he criticized the policy of Flexible Response by stating "This doctrine has a fine-sounding ring to it, but as practiced it is graduated and inflexible. It is graduated in that force is brought to bear against an enemy in increments which never seem enough to do the job, and "inflexible" because we fail to apply force at places and times of our choosing where we can profit by our strength and exploit enemy weakness...and unhappily we are again pursuing it in Vietnam."[112]   Much like his experience in the Cuban Missile Crisis, LeMay believed that the war in Vietnam was being run too much by the civilian leadership without sufficient input from the Joint Chiefs and other military commanders.[113]

While he did not advocate the use of atomic weapons in Vietnam, he did advocate expanding the bombing campaign in the north. For LeMay the best way to end the Vietnam conflict was to stop "pussyfooting" around and embrace large-scale bombing in North Vietnam by closing Haiphong

Harbor completely, eliminating all power generation plants and the country's industrial capacity, destroying the transportations system, and if necessary attacking the irrigation system to reduce agricultural output.[114] While McNamara argued that the enemy cannot "be bombed to the negotiating table," LeMay argued that he could see "no other sensible way of getting him there."[115] In December 1972 the US conducted "Operation Linebacker II," the unrestricted bombing of North Vietnam. The effect of this wholesale bombing effort did, in effect, bring the North Vietnamese back to the negotiations that resulted in the Paris Peace Accords. One could conclude that LeMay's vision of an effective bombing strategy eventually came to fruition despite McNamara's convictions to the contrary.

After the assassination of President Kennedy in November 1963, Lyndon Johnson assumed the presidency. The following spring, LeMay's one year extension as the Air Force Chief was due to expire. However, Johnson asked LeMay to stay on for yet another year-long extension. Observers speculated that this was a political maneuver to keep LeMay in the Air Force, thereby precluding him from running for elected office, possibly with Senator Barry Goldwater in the 1964 election. Such speculation aside, LeMay's last year in uniform proved to be anti-climactic. It was obvious that he was a "lame-duck" to the Johnson Administration as he was largely ignored. LeMay focused mostly on running the Air Force and conducting inspection tours.[116] He retired on February 1, 1965 and in a short speech he reminded his staff "stick to your guns and keep fighting for what you want."[117]

In assessing his term as the Air Force Chief, it could be argued that LeMay was largely a failure. He lost all his battles with McNamara over the XB-70, FTX, and missile/bomber ratios. Furthermore the Kennedy and Johnson Administrations ignored much of his advice regarding Cuba, Vietnam, and the policy of Flexible Response. His lack of political savvy and inability to compromise might explain some of these failures, but in the historical analysis, it appears that LeMay's opinions in many of these issues were simply erroneous.

After his retirement LeMay could easily have found employment with some large defense contractor, but he felt that the appearance of impropriety was too great.[118] Job offers were sparse, but he finally took a position with a small electronics firm. This was not the kind of employment befitting a man of LeMay's caliber and he quit after two years. In 1965 he published his memoirs, *Mission with LeMay,* and three years later published *America is in Danger.* While his autobiographical work met with some success, the book generated controversy. One sentence dealing with the Vietnam War read, "My solution to the problem would be to tell them frankly they've got to draw in their horns and stop their aggression or we are going to bomb them back to the stone age."[119] While LeMay never actually voiced that phrase, the fact that it was published in his book will forever connect it to him. In fact, this singular quote is perhaps the most widely-known aspect of LeMay's entire legacy. He later asserted that he had intended to delete that passage before publication, and that he merely failed to do so when proofreading the manuscript.

In 1968, after twice being approached by George Wallace's presidential campaign, LeMay agreed to be the running mate for the Alabama governor as part of the American Independent Party. While seemingly a bad fit for politics, LeMay agreed to run in hopes of splitting the Democratic Party vote and thus ending the policies of Johnson and McNamara by helping Republican candidate Richard Nixon gain the presidency. The Wallace-LeMay ticket garnered only 13.5 percent of the popular vote and gained a mere 46 electoral votes. Ill suited for the kind of nuanced talk required by politicians, LeMay's tour as a vice-presidential candidate fortunately lasted only a month, but was considered largely a failure.

After the 1968 election, he returned to being a private citizen, and with Helen, settled in Newport Beach, California. He read, hunted, and developed a close circle of friends during his last years. While he gave up flying after his retirement, he tinkered around is home and even served on the board of directors for the National Geographic Society and frequently flew to Washington. With himself seen as an icon of the Cold War, LeMay lived to see another icon destroyed when the Berlin Wall come down in November 1989. However, less than a year later, LeMay passed on October 1, 1990. He suffered a severe heart attack in the middle of the night and died a month short of his eighty-fifth birthday.[120]

Contemporary military strategists define war by three interconnected levels—the strategic, operational, and tactical. The strategic level of war deals with the larger political rationale for war and how it meets national goals and objectives. The operational level focuses on theater applications of war and governs campaigns or larger operations. Lastly the tactical level of war is associated with actual combat and the engagement of opposing forces. While many could argue that at the strategic level of war LeMay may have been ineffective as an Air Force Chief of Staff and had the wrong vision regarding the application of military power, the same cannot be said about the operational and tactical levels of war. At these two levels LeMay was an exceptional commander and clearly excelled. Starting with his command of the 305th Bomb Group in Europe and continuing through his operations with XXI Bomber Command in the Pacific, LeMay was unmistakably an innovative and effective leader of men at the tactical level of war. He trained his men thoroughly, not only to ensure success in the aerial battlefield, but also to help save their lives. At the operational level, when in command of SAC, LeMay's vision, drive, and leadership acumen clearly resulted in one of the finest military organizations ever assembled. He built SAC into one of the most proficient, professional, and lethal military forces human history has ever known.

For all his controversy and his arguably draconian ideas regarding national defense, LeMay stands as one of the great commanders in history. He was given very difficult tasks and missions during World War II, and through creativity and pragmatism, solved the very difficult problems he encountered. He led his men into combat, flew the most dangerous missions, and developed the most effective ways of employing his command. He laid the foundations for American defensive strategy for over forty years, while developing a capability that successfully employed an entirely new type of military power. Furthermore he served as an effective leader during a time of great social, political, technological, and military change. In returning to the definition of a great commander offered at the beginning of this book, LeMay was a commander who certainly attained the unexpected, clearly possessed exceptional skills in the aerial battlefield, and accomplished what few others could have.

Notes

1. "VLR Man," *Time* Magazine, Aug 13, 1945.

2. Karl Weber (Editor), *The Best of I.F. Stone* (New York, NY: Public Affairs Publishing, 2006), 326-338.

3. Warren Kozak, *LeMay: The Life and Wars of General Curtis LeMay* (Washington D.C.: Regnery Press, 2009), 360.

4. Curtis E. LeMay and Mackinlay Kantor, *Mission with LeMay: My Story*, (Garden City, NY; Doubleday Press, 1965), 60.

5. Ibid., 14.

6. Ibid.,15.

7. Thomas Coffey, *Iron Eagle: The Turbulent Life of General Curtis LeMay*,(New York, NY: Avon Books, 1986), 194.

8. LeMay and Kantor, 30.

9. LeMay and Kantor, 30.

10. Coffey, 198.

11. Kozak, 17; LeMay and Kantor, 45-47.

12. LeMay and Kantor, 67-68.

13. LeMay and Kantor, 79.

14. Ibid., 101; Coffey, 223.

15. LeMay and Kantor, 103; Coffey 223.

16. Coffey, 223.

17. Ibid., 228,

18. LeMay and Cantor, 130.

19. Ibid., 131.

20. LeMay and Kantor, 191; Coffey 239.

21. LeMay and Kantor, 217.; Coffey 21.

22. Coffey, 21.

23. LeMay and Kantor, 221-222; Kozak, 83-84.

24. Kozak, 107 and 109.

25. Coffey, 36; LeMay and Kantor, 241-242; Kozak 106.

26. Coffey, 37-38.

27. Ibid; LeMay and Kantor, 243.

28. Roger Freeman, *The Mighty Eighth War Manual* (New York, NY: Sterling Publishing Co, 2001), 40-42.

29. Ibid.

30. LeMay and Kantor, 256; Kozak, 121; Coffey, 50-51.

31. LeMay and Kantor, 258.

32. Donald Miller, *Masters of the Air* (New York, NY; Simon and Schuster, 2006), 143.

33. Ibid.

34. Coffey, 74.

35. Ibid., 94.

36. Martin Middlebrook, *The Schweinfurt-Regensburg Mission* (New York, NY: Scribners and Sons, 1983), 257.

37. Richard G. Davis, *Bombing the European Axis Powers: A Historical Digest of the Combined Bomber Offensive, 1939-1945* (Maxwell AFB, AL: Air University Press, 2006), 159; Middlebrook, 258.

38. LeMay and Kantor, 296; Middlebrook, 284.

39. LeMay and Kantor, 285; Kozak 130.

40. Coffey, 96; Kozak 148.

41. LeMay and Kantor, 310.

42. Headquarters Army Air Force, *Aircraft Commanders Manual for the B-29* (Reprint) (Dayton, OH: Otterbein Press, 1945), 5; Jacob Vander Meulen, *Building the B-29* (Washington D.C.: Smithsonian Institution Press, 1995), 16.

43. Vander Meulen, 21.

44. Curtis LeMay and Bill Yenne, *Superfortress* (New York, NY: Berkeley, 1989), 70.

45. LeMay and Kantor, 321 and 323.

46. LeMay and Kantor, 329; Coffey 112-113.

47. Coffey, 113-114; Kozak 186.

48. Coffey, 122.

49. LeMay and Kantor, 332; Coffey127; Alvin Coox, "Strategic Bombing in the Pacific" in *Case Studies in Strategic Bombardment,* ed. R. Cargill Hall (Washington, DC; Office of USAF History), 292.

50. LeMay and Kantor, 347.

51. Coox, 318.

52. Ibid., 316.

53. Ibid., 318.

54. Coffey, 162.

55. Richard Frank, *Downfall* (New York, NY: Random House, 1999),66.

56. Coox, 319; Coffey, 164.

57. Coox, 321; Coffey, 164.

58. Coox, 319, 321;LeMay and Kantor, 354.

59. LeMay and Cantor, 353; Coffey 165.

60. LeMay and Kantor, 368.

61. US Strategic Bombing Survey, *The Strategic Air Operation of the Very Heavy Bombardment in the War Against Japan Final Report (Twentieth Air Force)* (Washington, D.C.: US Government Printing Office, 1 September 1946),

62. Ibid., 6.

63. LeMay and Kantor, 384.

64. Richard Rhodes, *Dark Sun* (New York, NY: Simon and Schuster, 1995), 21-22; Stephan Budiansky, *Air Power* (New York, NY: Penguin Books, 2004), 338.

65. LeMay and Kantor, 390.

66. Ibid., 416.

67. Coffey, 267.

68. LeMay and Kantor, 417.

69. Coffey, 262.

70. Ibid., 263.

71. Ibid.

72. LeMay and Kantor, 417.

73. Ibid., 419-420.

74. Joseph Harahan, Richard Kohn, *Strategic Air Warfare: An Interview with Generals Curtis E. LeMay, Leon W. Johnson, David A. Burchinal, and Jack J. Catton* (Washington D.C.: Office of Air Force History, 1988), 74-75.

75. Walton S. Moody, *Building a Strategic Air Force* (Washington D.C.: US Government Printing Office, 1996), 125; Harry Borowski, *A Hollow Threat: Strategic Air Power and Containment Before Korea* (Westport, CT: Greenwood Press, 1982), 145-146.

76. Moody, 233.

77. Borowski, 167,

78. As quoted in Steven Reardon, "U.S. Strategic Bombardment Doctrine Since 1945" in *Case Studies in Strategic Bombardment* , Ed. R. Cargill Hall (Washington D.C.: U.S. Government Printing Office, 1998), 389.

79. Ibid., 402.

80. Harahan and Kohn, 82.

81. LeMay and Kantor, 436.

82. Budiansky, 361.

83. Mike Worden, *Rise of the Fighter Generals-The Problems of Air Force Leadership 1945-1982* (Maxwell AFB, AL: Air University Press), 149.

84. Harahan and Kohn, 84.

85. George H. Gallup, *The Gallup Poll, Public Opinion 1935-1971, Volume 2 1949-1953* (New York, NY: Random House, 1972), 929.

86. Ibid., 839.

87. Moody, 265; As quoted in Steven Reardon, "U.S. Strategic Bombardment Doctrine Since 1945," 403.

88. Coffey, 335; Kozak, 308.

89. Harahan and Kohn, 104-107.

90. Harahan and Kohn, 90.

91. LeMay and Kantor, 482.

92. Ibid.

93. Robert Futrell, "The Air Power Concept", 269, as referenced in Budiansky, 371.

94. Kozak, 291; Coffey 322.

95. Coffey 322; LeMay and Kantor, 439-440.

96. Harahan and Kohn, 98; LeMay and Kantor, 446.

97. Harahan and Kohn, 99.

98. Harahan and Kohn, 97.

99. Rosenberg and Moore, Document One, "Memorandum Op-36C/jm, Subj: Briefing given to the representatives of all services at SAC headquarters, Offutt Air Force Base Nebraska," 18 March 1954, pg

100. Office of the Historian, Headquarters, Strategic Air Command, *Development of Strategic Air Command* (Offutt AFB, NE; Office of the Historian, Strategic Air Command, 1976), pp 79-81.

101. Moody, 405; Coffey, 291-292.

102. Moody, 406-407; Coffey 292-293.

103. Coffey, 316.

104. Ibid, 358.

105. Coffey, 360-361.

106. Kozak, 331; Fred Kaplan, The Wizards of Armageddon (Stanford, CA:

Stanford University Press, 1983), 255.

107. Kaplan, 256.

108. Coffey, 372-373.

109. Kozak, 350.

110. Coffey, 369.

111. Coffey, 423; Kozak, 354.

112. Curtis E. LeMay and Dale O. Smith, *American is in Danger*, (New York, NY: Funk and Wagnalls, 1968), 25.

113. Coffey, 421.

114. LeMay and Smith, 262-263.

115. Ibid., 263.

116. Kozak, 358; Coffey 343-345.

117. Coffey, 436; Kozak, 359.

118. Kozak, 360.

119. LeMay and Kantor, 565.

120. Kozak, 385-386.

Bibliography

Alexander the Great

Arrian, *The Campaigns of Alexander (Anabasis de Alexandros),* London: Penguin Books, 1958.

Bamm, Peter, *Alexander The Great; Power As Destiny,* New York: McGraw-Hill Company, 1968.

Cartledge, Paul, *Alexander The Great; The Hunt For A New Past,* New York: Vintage Books, 2004.

Engles, Donald. *Alexander the Great and the Logistics of the Macedonian Army,* Berkely: University of California Press, 1978.

Fuller. J.F.C., *The Generalship Of Alexander The Great,* New Brunswick: Rutgers University Press, 1960.

Hanson, Victor Davis, *The Wars Of The Ancient Greeks,* London: Cassell, 1999.

Sekunda, Nick and John Warry, *Alexander The Great; His Armies and Campaigns,* London: Osprey, 1998.

Genghis Khan

Allsen, Thomas, *Culture and Conquest in Mongol Eurasia,* Cambridge, Massachusetts: Cambridge University Press, 2004.

May, Timothy, *The Mongol Art of War: Chinggis Khan and the Mongol Military System,* Yardley, Pennsylvania: Westholme Publishing, LLC, 2007.

Morgan, David, *The Mongols, 2d edition,* Malden, Massachusctts: Blackwell Publishing, 2007, 1st edition was published in 1986.

Ratchnevsky, Paul, *Genghis Khan: His Life and Legacy,* Malden, Massachusetts: Blackwell Publishing, 1991.

Saunders, J.J., *The History of the Mongol Conquests,* Philadelphia: University of Pennsylvania Press, 2001. Originally published in 1971.

Weatherford, Jack, *Genghis Khan and the Making of the Modern World,* New York: Crown Publishers, 2004.

Napoleon

Englund, Steven, *Napoleon: A Political Life.* New York: Scribner, 2004.

Chandler, David, *Campaigns of Napoleon: The Mind and Method of History's Greatest Soldier,* New York: MacMillan, 1966.

Elting, John, *Swords Around a Throne: Napoleon's Grande Armée,* New York: MacMillan, 1989.

Esdaile, Charles, *Fighting Napoleon: Guerrillas, Bandits, and Adventures in Spain, 1808-1814,* New Haven: Yale University Press, 2004.

Lieven, Dominic, *Russia Against Napoleon: The Battle for Europe, 1807 to 1814,* New York: Penguin Books, 2009.

Horatio Nelson

Corbett, Sir Julian, *Some Principles of Maritime Strategy,* with an introduction and notes by Eric J. Grove, Annapolis, MD: Naval Institute Press Reprint, 1988, originally published 1911.

Herman, Arthur, *To Rule the Waves: How the British Navy Shaped the Modern World,* New York: Harper Collins, 2004.

Hore, Captain Peter, *The Habit of Victory,* London: The National Maritime Museum, 2005.

Knight, Roger, *The Pursuit of Victory: The Life and Achievement of Horatio Nelson,* New York: Basic Books, 2005.

Pocock ,Tom, *Horatio Nelson,* New York: Alfred A. Knopf, 1988.

John J. Pershing

Coffman, Edward M, *The War to End All Wars,* Madison: University of Wisconsin Press, 1968.

Cooke, James, *Pershing and His Generals: Command and Staff in the AEF,* Westport: Praeger, 1997.

Lengel, Edward, *To Conquer Hell: The Meuse Argonne, 1918,* New York: Henry Holt and Company, 2008.

Smythe, Donald, *Pershing: General of the Armies,* Bloomington: University of Indiana Press, 1986.

Vandiver, Frank, *Black Jack: The Life and Times of John J. Pershing*, 2 volumes, College Station: Texas A&M Press, 1977.

Erwin Rommel

John Bierman and Colin Smith, *The Battle of Alamein: Turning Point, World War II* (Viking, NY, 2002).

David Fraser, *Knight's Cross: A Life of Field Marshal Erwin Rommel* (HarperCollins, NY, 1993).

Wolf Heckmann, *Rommel's War in Africa* (Konecky and Konecky, NY, 1981).

Ralf Georg Reuth, *Rommel: End of a Legend* (Haus,London, 2009).

Erwin Rommel, *The Rommel Papers* (Da Capo, NY, 1982).

Curtis LeMay:

Coffey, Thomas, *Iron Eagle: The Turbulent Life of General Curtis LeMay,* New York: Avon Books, 1986.

Harahan, Joseph and Richard Kohn, *Strategic Air Warfare: An Interview with Generals Curtis E. LeMay, Leon W. Johnson, David A. Burchinal, and Jack J. Catton,* Washington, DC: Office of Air Force History, 1988.

Leighton, Richard, *Strategy Money, and the New Look,* Washington D.C.: History Office of the Secretary of Defense, 2001.

LeMay, Curtis E. and Mackinlay Kantor, *Mission with LeMay: My Story,* Garden City, NY: Doubleday Press, 1965.

Sherry, Michael, *The Rise of American Airpower: The Creation of Armageddon,* New Haven: Yale University Press, 1987.

Contributors

Mr. Edward L. ("Bud") Bowie is a Supervisory Professor in the Department of Military History and inter-departmental teaching team leader at the US Army Command and General Staff College at Fort Leavenworth, Kansas. In 1980, he received a Regular Commission in the Field Artillery as a Distinguished Military Graduate from the ROTC program at Washington & Lee University. He holds a Baccalaureate degree in Anthropology, a Masters degree in Military History, and is a graduate of the US Army Command and General Staff College, the Joint Forces Staff College, and the Defense Language Institute. While on active duty, Mr. Bowie served as a senior advisor for strategic plans and policy to the Commander of NATO troops in Bosnia and as Chief of War Plans for Allied Land Forces Central Europe. He retired from active military service in August 2004. His areas of expertise include Operational Planning, Military Theory and Doctrine, and Military History.

Dr. Terry Beckenbaugh received his Ph.D. from the University of Arkansas-Fayetteville in 2001, where his research focused on American Civil War and Reconstruction, 19th Century US History and Military History. He earned his BA and MA in History from Shippensburg University of Pennsylvania in 1989 and 1993, respectively. He taught for four years at McNeese State University in Lake Charles, Louisiana, before moving to Washington, DC where he worked at the US Army Center for Military History (CMH). He is currently an assistant professor within the Department of Military History at the US Army Command and General Staff College.

Dr. Mark T. Gerges is an associate professor of military history at the US Army Command and General Staff College at Fort Leavenworth. A retired armor lieutenant colonel, he has taught at the United States Military Academy at West Point before obtaining his Ph.D. from the Institute on Napoleon and the French Revolution at Florida State University. He has published papers on British cavalry doctrine, the cavalry under the Duke of Wellington in the Peninsula War, and is working on a manuscript on the command and control of the mounted arm under Wellington.

Dr. John T. Kuehn is an Associate Professor of Military History at the US Army Command and General Staff College at Fort Leavenworth. He retired after 23 years as a naval aviator with the rank of commander in 2004. He was awarded his Ph.D. in History in 2007 by Kansas State University. He is also a distinguished graduate of the Naval Postgraduate School with a degree in Systems Engineering. He has published numerous. articles, reviews, editorials, and two books—*Agents of Innovation* (Naval Institute Press, 2008) and *Eyewitness Pacific Theater* (with Dennis Giangreco, 2008). He was recently awarded a Moncado Prize from the Society for Military History in 2011 for "The US Navy General Board and Naval Arms Limitation: 1922-1937." He is also an adjunct professor for the Naval War College Fleet Seminar Program and with the MA in Military History (MMH) and MA in History Programs at Norwich University, earning the MMH Faculty Member of the Year Award in 2010-2011.

Dr. Richard S. Faulkner served 23 years in the US Army as an armor officer. He received a BA in History for Kennesaw College in 1985, a masters degree in American history from the University of Georgia in 1996, and a Ph.D. in American history from Kansas State University in 2008. He taught American history at the United States Military Academy at West Point, New York, and has taught military history at the US Army Command and General Staff College, Fort Leavenworth, since 2002. His book, *The School of Hard Knocks: Combat Leadership in the American Expeditionary Forces* was published by Texas A&M Press in 2012.

Dr. Mark M. Hull is an Associate Professor with the Department of Military History at the US Army Command and General Staff College, specializing in German intelligence history and war crimes prosecution. Dr. Hull earned his Ph.D. from University College Cork (NUI) and is also an attorney. He was admitted as a Fellow of the Royal Historical Society in 2010 and is the author of the book, *Irish Secrets: German Espionage in Wartime Ireland* (Irish Academic Press, 2004), as well as numerous articles on intelligence history and law.

Dr John M. Curatola is an Assistant History Professor at the US Army Command and General Staff College. Prior to this position he was an active duty Marine Corps officer and retired in 2009 after 22 years of service, including deployments to Somalia in 1992 and Operation Iraqi Freedom in 2003. Dr. Curatola received a BA in Political Science from the University of Nebraska. He holds a master's degree from George Mason University in US History and a Master of Military Arts and Science from the Army Command and General Staff College in military history. He received his Ph.D. in US History from the University of Kansas.

About the Editors

Dr. Christopher R. Gabel holds a Ph.D. from Ohio State University. He serves on the faculty of the Command and General Staff College since 1983, where he teaches courses on general military history, military innovation, the Civil War, and World War II. His publications include *The US Army GHQ Maneuvers of 1941,* studies on the Army in the World War II period, railroad logistics in the Civil War, and a staff ride handbook for the Vicksburg campaign.

Dr. James H. Willbanks is the General of the Army George C. Marshall Chair of Military History and Director of the Department of Military History at the US Army Command and General Staff College. He has been on the faculty since 1992 after he retired from the Army as a Lieutenant Colonel with twenty-three years service as an Infantry officer in various assignments, to include a tour as an advisor with a South Vietnamese regiment during the 1972 North Vietnamese Easter Offensive. He holds a BA in History from Texas A&M University, and an MA and Ph.D. in History from the University of Kansas. He is the author of *Abandoning Vietnam* (University Press of Kansas, 2004), *The Battle of An Loc* (Indiana University Press, 2005), *The Tet Offensive: A Concise History* (Columbia University Press, 2006), *Vietnam War Almanac* (Facts on File, 2009), and the editor of *America's Heroes: Medal of Honor Recipients from the Civil War to Afghanistan* (ABC-CLIO, 2011) and *The Vietnam War*, a volume in *The International Library of Essays on Military History* (Ashgate Publishing of London, 2006).